SOCIAL SECURITY LAW AND PRACTICE

IN A NUTSHELL®

FRANK S. BLOCH
Professor of Law Emeritus
Vanderbilt Law School

JON C. DUBIN
Board of Governors Distinguished Service
Professor of Law
Rutgers University Law School,
Newark Campus

WEST
ACADEMIC
PUBLISHING

444 Cedar Street, Suite 700
St. Paul, MN 55101
1-877-888-1330

Printed in the United States of America

ISBN: 978-1-64708-686-2

PREFACE

This book is intended to provide a succinct exposition of Social Security law and practice, including administrative advocacy and federal court review, offering its readers—lawyers, law students, Social Security administrators and judges—a clear and concise explanation of the major cash benefit programs of Social Security Act. Its primary focus is on the Act's programs most relevant to Social Security practice: Old Age, Survivors, and Disability Insurance (OASDI), set out in Title II, and Supplemental Security Income (SSI), set out in Title XVI. Moreover, because the vast majority of contested Social Security cases—that is, those that involve the services of an attorney or qualified non-attorney representative—are claims for disability benefits, the Act's disability programs are covered in greatest detail. Other programs under the Act, such as basic welfare programs, Medicare and Medicaid, and unemployment compensation and unemployment insurance, are covered in other titles in the Nutshell series.[1]

In preparing this book, we have drawn on a number of our prior publications in this field, including Bloch & Dubin, CASES AND MATERIALS ON

---

1 See LAFRANCE, WELFARE LAW: STRUCTURE AND ENTITLEMENT IN A NUTSHELL (1979), Frolik & Kaplan, ELDER LAW IN A NUTSHELL (7th Ed. 2019), Hood, Hardy, & Simpson, WORKER'S COMPENSATION AND EMPLOYEE PROTECTIONS LAWS IN A NUTSHELL (6th ed. 2017).

SOCIAL SECURITY LAW AND PRACTICE (2016, Supp. 2021), Kubitschek & Dubin, SOCIAL SECURITY DISABILITY LAW AND PROCEDURE IN FEDERAL COURT (2021), and Bloch on Social Security (available exclusively on Westlaw), as well as decades of experience representing clients with our students in the clinical programs at our respective law schools. Our goal is to describe and explain in a single accessible volume what has been described as "the most intricate [Act] ever drafted by Congress"[2] and the "Mt. Everest of bureaucratic structures."[3] We were assisted in the effort by Megyn MacMullen, Rutgers Law School class of 2022, who provided consistently thorough and helpful research assistance.

—FSB
Nashville, Tennessee

—JCD
Newark, New Jersey

---

2 Weisbrod v. Sullivan, 875 F.2d 526, 528 (5th Cir.1989).

3 Paul R. Verkuil, *The Self Legitimating Bureaucracy*, 93 YALE L.J. 780, 781 (1983).

OUTLINE

TABLE OF CASES

References are to Pages

SOCIAL SECURITY LAW AND PRACTICE

IN A NUTSHELL®

CHAPTER 1
INTRODUCTION

This book is intended to provide a broad overview of Social Security law and practice. The central legislation is, of course, the Social Security Act; however, most cases handled by Social Security lawyers involve claims for benefits under one or both of two titles: Old Age, Survivors, and Disability Insurance (OASDI), set out in Title II of the Act, and Supplemental Security Income (SSI), set out in Title XVI. A typical Social Security practice is even more limited, as the vast majority of contested Social Security cases—that is, those that require the services of an attorney—involve claims for disability benefits. Accordingly, this book covers only OASDI and SSI, with a special focus on the disability provisions of those programs. It does not cover the other major Social Security Act programs: unemployment insurance, Medicare and Medicaid, and Temporary Assistance for Needy Families (TANF).

The purpose of this introductory chapter is to place current Social Security law and practice in its historical context. What follows is a brief description of social legislation in the United States leading up to the enactment of the Social Security Act and the events surrounding the passage of the Act in 1935, a listing of the major amendments to the Act since 1935, and a review of key Supreme Court decisions that have impacted the coverage and administration of OASDI and SSI.

The remaining chapters can be grouped into three parts: Chapters 2, 3, and 4 describe the central eligibility requirements for benefits under both programs; Chapters 5 and 6 delve more deeply into the requirements for disability benefits; and Chapters 7, 8, and 9 focus on the administration of the programs, including the roles of lawyers and other claimant representatives, administrators and administrative judges, and federal courts.

A. THE SOCIAL SECURITY ACT IN HISTORICAL CONTEXT

There is a rich history of social legislation in Europe that dates from long before the passage of the original Social Security Act in 1935. The European experience was widely known and was drawn upon to some extent by individual states before the federal government entered the field. Most notable among early federal legislation were various pension programs for veterans, the most significant being a series of benefit programs for veterans of the Civil War passed by Congress in stages from the end of the war through the early 1900s. By 1910, over 90% of surviving Civil War veterans were receiving federal disability or old-age pension benefits; however, that group made up less than 1% of the population. While some states and local communities initiated broader programs of social support for the "deserving poor" modeled after the Elizabethan Poor Laws, the vast majority of Americans were not covered by any public pension scheme.

It took the economic disaster of the Great Depression for President Franklin Delano Roosevelt to propose a comprehensive federal plan to combat income insecurity. He laid out a broad concept of social security for the country in a famous message to Congress in 1934, proclaiming that he was "looking for a sound means which I can recommend to provide at once security against several of the great disturbing factors in life—especially those which relate to unemployment and old age." Franklin D. Roosevelt, Message to Congress Reviewing the Broad Objectives and Accomplishments of the Administration (June 8, 1934). Following up on this message, President Roosevelt appointed a Committee on Economic Security that prepared and presented a report that became the basis of the Social Security Act of 1935.

The Committee recommended, and President Roosevelt sent to Congress, four elements of a national program for economic security: unemployment compensation; old-age benefits, including compulsory and voluntary annuities; federal aid to dependent children through grants to States; and limited federal aid to State and local public health agencies. President Roosevelt acknowledged that "I am not at this time recommending the adoption of so called 'health insurance,' although groups representing the medical profession are cooperating with the Federal Government in the further study of the subject and definite progress is being made." Franklin D. Roosevelt, Message to Congress on Social Security (January 17, 1935). As he noted upon signing the

Social Security Act into law on August 14, 1935: "We can never insure one hundred percent of the population against one hundred percent of the hazards and vicissitudes of life, but we have tried to frame a law which will give some measure of protection to the average citizen and to his family against the loss of a job and against poverty-ridden old age." Franklin D. Roosevelt, Presidential Statement upon Signing the Social Security Act (Aug. 14, 1935). As noted later in this chapter, the original Social Security Act included only the old age provision of the current Old Age, Survivors, and Disability Insurance program. Those benefits were, as they are today, a form of "social insurance" funded by a payroll tax assessed against both workers and their employers.

The new Social Security Act was challenged almost immediately on the grounds that the programs it created and the mechanisms established to fund them were beyond the power of Congress and a usurpation of the powers left to the states by the Tenth Amendment to the Constitution. In two cases decided on the same day, the Supreme Court upheld the constitutionality of the Act. *See* Charles C. Steward Machine Co. v. Davis, 301 U.S. 548 (1937) (unemployment insurance); Helvering v. Davis, 301 U.S. 619 (1937) (old age benefits).

B. MAJOR AMENDMENTS TO THE SOCIAL SECURITY ACT

Shortly after passing the original Social Security Act in 1935, Congress began to enact a series of amendments that have expanded significantly the scope of the Act's programs. In 1939, Congress amended the Act to expand its coverage to include certain dependents of recipients of old-age insurance benefits and survivors of insured workers who died—essentially their spouses and children. *See* Social Security Act Amendments of 1939, 53 Stat. 1360 (1939).

The extension of coverage to include disability began in 1950 when Congress created a new public assistance program for disabled adults, Aid to the Permanently and Totally Disabled (APTD). *See* Social Security Act Amendments of 1950, Pub. L. No. 81–734, 64 Stat. 477. Congress added social insurance disability coverage as well in 1956 by adding disability benefits to a newly re-titled Old Age, Survivors, and Disability Insurance program. *See* Social Security Act Amendments of 1956, Pub. L. No. 84–880, 70 Stat. 807. Initially, only persons age 50 or over could qualify for benefits; that limitation was dropped, however, a few years later. *See* Social Security Amendments of 1960, Pub. L. No. 86–778, 74 Stat. 918.

In 1958, Congress extended its earlier coverage for dependents of disabled and retired workers. Social insurance benefits became available to wage earners' wives and dependent husbands who had reached retirement age, their unmarried dependent children, including older children who had become disabled in childhood, and their wives who had an eligible child in their care. *See* Social Security Amendments of 1958, Pub. L. No. 85–840, 72 Stat 1013.

As noted earlier, medical benefits were explicitly excluded in the original Social Security Act. Congress remedied this by adding the Medicare and Medicaid programs to the Act as part of President Lyndon B. Johnson's Great Society legislation in 1965. *See* Social Security Amendments of 1965, Pub. L. No. 89–97, 79 Stat. 286. Medicare provides hospital benefits for Social Security beneficiaries over the age of 65 (and some disabled beneficiaries under the age of 65), as well as optional Supplemental Health Insurance benefits that cover physician services funded in part by additional premiums. Medicaid is a federal/state public assistance program jointly funded—and administered—by the states, which provides hospital and physician coverage for all recipients of federal/state public assistance benefits and, based on subsequent amendments, optional coverage for "medically indigent" individuals not eligible for welfare benefits.

In the early 1970s, Congress began to review the status of the Social Security Act's joint federal/state public assistance programs, including the original Aid to Dependent Children program (which by then had been retitled Aid to Families with Dependent Children, or AFDC) and the later-enacted Aid to the Permanently and Totally Disabled program (APTD), also known as Aid to the Aged, Blind, and Disabled (AABD). The result was the replacement of the various federal/state programs for the elderly, blind, and disabled with a fully federal public assistance program for the elderly, blind, and disabled called Supplemental Security income (SSI). The new program, which became effective on January 1, 1974, established a uniform national system of public assistance benefits for the elderly and disabled. (The larger and more controversial AFDC program remained a federal-state program.)

A few other legislative changes warrant mention. In 1996, Congress eliminated eligibility for both OASDI and SSI disability benefits based on drug or alcohol addiction, ended the long-standing Aid to Families with Dependent Children (AFDC) program by replacing it with a more limited Temporary Assistance for Needy Families (TANF) program, and significantly tightened the criteria for child's SSI disability benefits. *See* Contract with America Advancement Act, Pub. L. No. 104–121, 110 Stat. 847. In 2000 (pursuant to legislation passed in 1983) the age at which beneficiaries could receive full retirement benefits under the OASDI program began increasing gradually, from 65 to 67. *See* Social Security Amendments of 1983, Pub. L. No. 98–21, 97 Stat. 65.

C. CONSTITUTIONAL LIMITS ON DEFINING, ALLOCATING, AND ADMINISTRATING BENEFITS

As the scope of coverage has expanded and more categories of persons have become potentially eligible for Social Security benefits, persons arguably within a covered category but excluded under the provisions of the Act began challenging statutory classifications. Structuring the old age program as social insurance, as opposed to aid to dependent children, which was funded by general revenues, was a deliberate political choice. As President Roosevelt is reported to have recalled at a meeting on social security taxation in the summer of 1941, "We put those payroll contributions there so as to give the contributors a legal, moral, and political right to collect their pensions and their unemployment benefits. With those taxes in there, no damn politician can ever scrap my social security program." The decision to structure the program as social insurance would come to frame much future litigation over constitutional challenges to the Act.

Many years after the Supreme Court had upheld the overall constitutionality of the Social Security Act, the Court first addressed the nature of benefits awarded under the Act's social insurance programs. The question in Flemming v. Nestor, 363 U.S. 603 (1960) was what rights, if any, would be infringed if an insured worker's benefits were taken away. Noting that social insurance benefit payments are not tied directly to the amount of a worker's contributions but are calculated on the basis of a progressive formula using the amount of the worker's earnings, the Court declined to characterize them as accrued property rights. At the same time, the Court made it clear that "[t}his is not to say, however, that Congress may exercise its power to modify the statutory scheme free of all constitutional restraint. The interest of a covered employee under the Act is of sufficient substance to fall within the protection from arbitrary governmental action afforded by the Due Process Clause." 363 U.S. at 611.

Over the years, the Supreme Court has been called upon to balance congressional power and constitutional restraints in a number of important cases challenging specific provisions of the Act. For example, in Weinberger v. Wiesenfeld, 420 U.S. 636, 95 S. Ct. 1225 (1975) the question was whether providing benefits based on the earnings of a deceased husband and father to both the widow and the couple's minor children in her care—while providing benefits based on the earnings of a deceased wife and mother only to the minor children and not the widower—violated the due process clause of the Fifth Amendment to the Constitution. Noting that the purpose of those survivor benefits is to enable the surviving parent to remain at home to care for a child, the Court concluded that "the gender-based distinction of § 402(g) is entirely irrational." 420 U.S. at 651, 1225 S. Ct. at 1235. In Califano v. Goldfarb, 430 U.S. 199, 206–07, 97 S. Ct. 1021 (1977), the Court invalidated a requirement that widowers seeking survivors benefits on the earnings record of their spouse—but not widows—had to show that they had been receiving at least one-half support from their spouse when they died. Drawing in part on its decision in *Wiesenfeld*, the Court concluded that "the gender-based differentiation created by § 402(f)(1)(d) that results in the efforts of female workers required to pay social security taxes producing less protection for their spouses than is produced by the efforts of men is forbidden by the constitution." 430 U.S. at 206–07, 97 S. Ct. at 1027. On the other hand, in Califano v. Boles, 443 U.S. 282, 99 S. Ct. 2767 (1979) the Court upheld the denial of benefits to mothers of deceased wage earners' children who were not married to the wage earner, reasoning that "Congress could reasonably conclude that a woman who has never been married to the wage earner is far less likely to be dependent upon the wage earner at the time of his death." 443 U.S. at 289, 99 S. Ct. at 2772. *But see* 443 U.S. at 297, 99 S. Ct. at 2776 (Marshall, J., dissenting) (arguing that denial amounted to unconstitutional discrimination against "illegitimate" children).

In a landmark constitutional decision on the administration of public assistance programs, the Supreme Court held that due process guarantees beneficiaries of welfare benefits an "evidentiary hearing" prior to termination of those benefits. Goldberg v. Kelly, 397 U.S. 254, 90 S. Ct. 1011 (1970). While the ruling in that case clearly applies to terminations of SSI benefits and full hearings have always been applied to SSI terminations, the Court refused to apply it's reasoning to terminations of disability insurance benefits in Mathews v. Eldridge, 424 U.S. 319, 96 S. Ct. 893 (1976). This difference in due process rights was justified by the Court in part on the assumption that for beneficiaries of social insurance "other forms of government assistance will become available where the termination of disability benefits places a worker or his family below the subsistence level." 424 U.S. at 342, 96 S. Ct. at 906. Congress has since extended the payment of benefits pending appeal to OASDI cases as well, if the termination was based on medical grounds. 42 U.S.C. § 423(g); *see also* 20 C.F.R. § 404.1597a.

CHAPTER 2

OVERVIEW OF COVERAGE

The Social Security Act includes a number of separate programs set out in various titles, which together provide a broad, but limited, range of benefits. The two programs covered in this book are Old Age, Survivors, and Disability Insurance (OASDI), found in Title II of the Social Security Act, and Supplemental Security Income (SSI), found in Title XVI. Persons receiving benefits under these programs are also entitled, for the most part, to benefits under one of the Act's two medical assistance programs: Medicare, in the case of OASDI recipients, and Medicaid, in the case of SSI recipients. Access to these programs is extremely important to OASDI and SSI beneficiaries. However, they are governed by their own Titles of the Social Security Act (Title XVIII for Medicaid, 42 U.S.C. §§ 1395 et seq., and Title XIX for Medicare, 42 U.S.C. §§ 1399 et seq.), which have extensive separate rules and regulations. Accordingly, coverage of the various benefits Medicare and Medicaid provide OASDI and SSI recipients is beyond the scope of this book.

Eligibility for both OASDI and SSI is governed by two basic sets of criteria, but many details differ depending on whether the claim is for benefits under one program or the other. The first set of criteria relates to a claimant's financial circumstances. Because OASDI is a social insurance program available only to persons who are "insured" by having paid Social Security taxes while employed (including self-employed), financial eligibility is based on their employment record. SSI, on the other hand, is a public assistance program available only to persons with limited income and resources. Therefore, financial eligibility for SSI is based on financial need. The first two sections of this chapter describe these separate sets of financial requirements in some detail.

A second set of criteria relates to personal circumstances. In addition to the financial requirements mentioned above, a claimant for OASDI or SSI must fit within one of a limited set of categories in order to be eligible for benefits. Two key personal requirements in the Social Security Act are old age and disability. Persons who are elderly or disabled may be eligible for OASDI, SSI, or both. In addition, OASDI "survivors" benefits may be available under certain circumstances to dependents or survivors of persons insured under the program. That would be persons whose insured parent or spouse (or, in certain special situations, whose insured child) has died, has retired, or is disabled. The eligibility criteria for old age, disability, and survivors benefits are described briefly in the remaining sections of this chapter. Later chapters examine them in greater detail, especially those related to proof of disability.

The financial criteria discussed in this chapter relative to eligibility for benefits may also be relevant in determining the amount of benefits. For example, a wage earners' employment history plays an important role in calculating the amount of OASDI benefits to which they or their survivors and dependents are entitled. Similarly, the amount of a claimant's income (if any) is a key element in determining the amount of SSI benefits awarded. The rules for determining benefit amounts for both OASDI and SSI are discussed in Chapter 7.

A. EMPLOYMENT-BASED ELIGIBILITY (OASDI)

Social Security employment records are measured in terms of quarters of coverage (QCs). QCs are periods of three consecutive calendar months ending on March 31, June 30, September 30, or December 31. Individuals are credited with one QC for each quarter during which they had at least a minimum amount of earnings on which Social Security taxes were paid, including self-employment income. While employment covered by Social Security was limited early in the program, today the vast majority of wage earners pay into the system.

Initially, QCs were based on the wages earned for a particular quarter; however, beginning in 1978 wages are recorded on an annual basis. Therefore, for calendar years after 1977 individuals are credited with as many QCs that are covered by their total income in a given year—up to a maximum of four QCs per year. The amount of wages and self-employment income an individual must have for each QC depends on the year the wages were earned. For calendar year 1978, the amount per QC is $250 (for calendar years before 1978, the amount is $50, or $100 for persons self-employed.); for later years, the amount is published in the Federal Register. For example, the amount for earnings in calendar year 2004 is $900 per QC; for calendar year 2020, it is $1410. Therefore, someone who earned $3600 (or more) in calendar year 2004 would be credited with four QCs ($900 × 4 = $3600); on the other hand, someone who earned the same amount in calendar year 2020 would be credited with only two QCs. To be eligible for three QCs in 2020, one would have to had earned at least $4230 ($1410 × 3 = $4230); to be eligible for four QCs, one would have had to earn at least $5640 ($1410 × 4 = $5640).

1. "INSURED STATUS" REQUIREMENT

An individual must be "fully" insured in order to be eligible for OASDI benefits, although an individual's spouse or child may, under certain circumstances, be eligible for benefits if the individual was only "currently" insured. *See* 20 C.F.R. § 404.101. Whether an individual has the required insured status depends on the number of QCs in his or her Social Security employment record, which—as noted above—is based on when and how long they worked at a job where Social Security taxes were paid.

In most instances, a claimant needs 40 QCs to be fully insured. A person is considered fully insured as of the first day of the calendar year quarter in which he or she acquired the last-needed QC. The 40 QCs can be accumulated at any time. To be fully insured on the basis of less than 40 QCs, a claimant must have accumulated a minimum of 6 QCs—at least one of which must have been earned in each calendar year after the year in which the individual reached the age of 21 and continuing until the year the individual reached retirement age, became disabled, or, with respect to survivors benefits, died. 42 U.S.C. § 414(a); 20 C.F.R. § 404.110.

Individuals who die or become disabled before they can become fully insured may instead be classified as "currently" insured. Currently insured status does not entitle one to OASDI benefits; however, spouses and children of persons currently insured wage earners may be entitled to certain secondary benefits. To be currently insured, one must have earned a minimum of 6 QCs within a thirteen-quarter period immediately preceding death or eligibility for old age or disability insurance benefits. 42 U.S.C. § 414(b); 20 C.F.R. § 404.120(a). Excluded for the most part from the thirteen-quarter period are quarters without sufficient earnings to qualify as a QC, but that qualify nonetheless as a "period of disability." 20 C.F.R. § 404.120(b). Periods of disability are discussed later in this chapter.

Meeting the earnings requirement for a single QC can be critical in establishing eligibility for OASDI benefits in cases where one additional QC is needed to meet the insured status requirement. Moreover, the minimum earnings requirement for covered employment to qualify as a QC is applied strictly. Courts have rejected a *de minimis* rule in close cases, in part to avoid the cost and subjectivity inherent in making individualized determinations regarding a wage earner's insured status. *See, e.g.*, McGlocklin v. Chater, 948 F. Supp. 589, 592, 52 Soc. Sec. Rep. Serv. 527 (W.D. Va. 1996), aff'd, 129 F.3d 1259 (4th Cir.

1997) (claimant $1 short of QC amount; "While the doctrine of de minimis may be a valuable one in some areas of law, it is unavailable here. The Act and its regulations draw bright lines of eligibility which I am not authorized to forgive.")

2. "DISABILITY INSURED STATUS" FOR DISABILITY-BASED BENEFITS

In order to qualify for Disability Insurance Benefits, a claimant must—in addition to being "fully insured"—also achieve "disability insured status." For most claimants, this is done by meeting the requirements of what is known as the "20/40" rule. Thus, claimants qualify for "disability insured status" if they have at least 20 QCs in the 40-quarter period ending with the quarter during which their disability began. *See* 42 U.S.C. § 423(c)(1)(B)(i); 20 C.F.R. § 404.130(b). As a practical matter, this means that a claimant must have worked at covered employment for at least 5 years during the 10 years preceding the onset of disability.

The 20/40 rule operates to screen out persons who do not have a substantial and relatively recent attachment to the workforce. Depending on the regularity of a claimant's work history, the time between stopping work and becoming disabled can be limited to as little as one quarter. For example, if someone worked for 10 years but only every other quarter, coverage under the 20/40 rule would lapse after only two quarters of not working. The more quarters one works in a row (and for which one receives QC credit), the more quarters can pass in which one remains insured after stopping work. However, in no event can there be a lapse of more than 20 quarters, or five years, between stopping work at covered employment and becoming disabled. Applying a separate and additional 20/40 requirement for disability benefits to otherwise "fully insured" claimants has survived constitutional challenge. *See* Harvell v. Chater, 87 F.3d 371, 373, 51 Soc. Sec. Rep. Serv. 144 (9th Cir. 1996) (Congress limiting disability benefits to persons with reasonably recent covered employment, which indicates that they probably were dependent on their earnings, was not a "patently arbitrary classification, utterly lacking in rational justification.") (citing Flemming v. Nestor, 363 U.S. 603, 611, 80 S. Ct. 1367, 1373 (1960)).

A separate rule for achieving disability insured status applies to persons who become disabled before age 31. In such cases, claimants are insured for purposes of Disability Insurance Benefits so long as they have QCs for at least six quarters and for at least one-half of the quarters that passed between reaching the age of 21 and becoming disabled. 42 U.S.C. § 423(c)(1)(B)(ii); 20 C.F.R. § 404.130(c). Additionally, under certain circumstances claimants who had a period of disability before age 31 can qualify if they become disabled again before the 20/40 requirement could be met. *See* 42 U.S.C. § 423(c)(1)(B)(iii); 20 C.F.R. § 404.130(d).

Because the disability insured status period is limited, the date disability is alleged to have begun (referred to as the "onset date") can be a critical factor in determining eligibility. For claimants who worked off-and-on and then stop working before becoming disabled, a subsequently developed disability may not be covered because it began after their disability insured status expired. A contested onset date can be difficult to prove. ALJs may, but are not required to, call a medical expert on the question of onset date. *See* SSR 18–1p (2018) ("The decision to call on the services of an ME is always at the ALJ's discretion. Neither the claimant nor his or her representative can require an ALJ to call on the services of an ME to assist in inferring the date that the claimant first met the statutory definition of disability.")

The additional disability insured status requirement does not apply to persons who are statutorily blind. 42 U.S.C. § 423(c)(1)(B); 20 C.F.R. § 404.130(e). Thus, claimants who are disabled by blindness, as defined in the Act and regulations, need to show only that they are fully or currently insured in order to qualify for benefits.

3. CORRECTING AN EARNINGS RECORD

Earnings information that the Social Security Administration uses to determine an individual's QCs is based on employment records reported to the Internal Revenue Service when Social Security taxes are paid. These records are presumed to be correct, but not conclusive, within a time period of three years, three months, and 15 days after the end of the calendar year in which the earnings were received. 20 C.F.R. §§ 404.802, 803. The records are conclusive after that time limit, with ten exceptions. *See* 42

U.S.C. § 405(c)(5)(A)–(J); *see also* 20 C.F.R. § 404.822. Revising self-employment records can be very difficult. *See* Brando v. Chater, 972 F. Supp. 867, 870, 54 Soc. Sec. Rep. Serv. 148 (D.N.J. 1997) ("The stringent provisions on correction of earnings records for self-employed individuals were drafted intentionally by Congress to avoid claims based on earnings in periods many years past for which here could be no effective rebuttal."). The time limit can be extended, however, in extraordinary circumstances on equitable grounds. *See, e.g.*, Smith v. Shalala, 910 F. Supp. 152, 160, 49 Soc. Sec. Rep. Serv. 857 (D.N.J. 1995) ("equities favoring tolling" found to be "compelling" where wage earner's husband, who exercised economic control over her by physical and emotional abuse, forced her to sign the challenged returns; because she lacked control over the completion and filing of the original returns, "it is inappropriate for the Secretary to presume conclusively that her records of income for Smith, based upon the Original Returns, are correct.").

B. NEED-BASED ELIGIBILITY (SSI)

In contrast to the OASDI program, Supplemental Security Income (SSI) is a need-based public assistance program. As such, benefits are available only to persons with limited income and resources. Thus, an applicant's income, if any, is a major factor in deciding both eligibility for and the amount of SSI benefits. Resource limitations, on the other hand, apply only to determinations of eligibility. In other words, a claimant's income must be below a certain level in order to be financially eligible for benefits; if eligible, any income will also affect the amount of benefits awarded. A claimant's resources also cannot exceed the maximum limits; however, once eligible and so long as the amount of resources remains below the maximum amount allowed, the amount of resources that a claimant has is irrelevant in determining the amount of benefits received. Treatment of income for purposes of determining the amount of SSI benefits is covered in Chapter7.

1. INCOME REQUIREMENTS

Federal regulations define income as "anything you receive in cash or in kind that you can use to meet your needs for food and shelter"; in-kind income is distinguished from cash as "food or shelter, or something you can use to get one of these." 20 C.F.R. § 416.1102. Certain items are excluded from being counted as income because they cannot be used as food or shelter or cannot be used to obtain food or shelter. 20 C.F.R. § 416.1103. Examples of items that are not counted as income include certain types of medical care and services (such as those provided free of charge), certain types of social services, income tax refunds, and bills paid by someone else. 20 C.F.R. § 416.1103(a)–(j). Additionally, anything received from the sale or exchange of one's own property is considered a "resource" as opposed to income. 20 C.F.R. § 416.1201(a).

Income limits for SSI eligibility are set annually, based on the prior year amount plus a cost-of-living increase, based on the national rate of inflation. The amounts effective in 2021 are $794 per month for an individual and $1191 per month for an eligible couple (meaning a couple where both are eligible for and receiving assistance). Some states supplement the federal SSI benefit with additional payments which render the total SSI benefit levels higher in those states. *See* 20 C.F.R. §§ 416.110(f), 2001. Having an income that is low enough to make an individual eligible for SSI does not necessarily mean that the individual will receive "full" SSI benefits; as noted earlier and discussed further in Chapter 7, income that an SSI applicant/claimant has will be taken into account in determining the amount of benefits.

Income is counted differently depending on the source, and some income is not counted at all. (These rules for counting different types of income apply equally to eligibility and to the calculation of the amount of benefits.) There are two different kinds of income—earned and unearned—and the method for counting each differs. 20 C.F.R. §§ 416.1110, 1120.

Earned income includes wages and net earnings in cash or in-kind, including from self-employment. However, not all earned income is counted in determining benefit eligibility and amount. Earned income is most important with respect to SSI claims based on old age; while persons applying for or receiving disability benefits may still work to a limited extent, that happens rarely and any earnings are usually relatively insignificant.

Unearned income is all income that is not earned, whether in cash or in-kind, and includes most types of periodic payments such as annuities, pensions, Social Security benefits, veterans' benefits, workers' compensation payments, railroad retirement benefits, and unemployment insurance benefits. Unearned income also includes alimony and support payments, dividends, interest, and rents.

In-kind support and maintenance are covered in detail in the regulations. Of particular importance is the "one-third reduction rule," by which—instead of determining the actual dollar value of in-kind support—there is a flat reduction of the federal benefit rate by one-third if the beneficiary lives in another person's household and receives both food and shelter from that person.

The various rules on calculating earned income, unearned income, and in-kind support and maintenance are discussed further below.

a. Earned Income

Earned income consists of wages received for working as an employee, earnings from self-employment, federal tax refunds and advance payments by employers pursuant to the earned income credit provisions of the Internal Revenue Code, payments for services at sheltered workshops or work activities centers, and certain royalties and honoraria. 20 C.F.R. § 416.1110. Earned income can be in cash or in-kind; however, in-kind pay is not counted as earned income for domestic or agricultural workers.

Earned income is counted in different ways depending on the type of income that is at issue. *See generally* 20 C.F.R. § 416.1111. Wages are determined on a monthly basis and are counted when they are received, when they are credited to an individual's account, or when set aside for use, whichever is earliest. 20 C.F.R. § 416.1111(a). Net earnings from self-employment are counted on a taxable year basis, but the total amount is divided equally among the months of the taxable year to determine how much is received in each month. If an individual has net losses from self-employment, the losses are divided over the taxable year in the same way and are deducted from the individual's other earned income. 20 C.F.R. § 416.1111(b). In-kind earned income is calculated based on the current market value in the individual's locality. 20 C.F.R. § 416.1111(d). If an individual receives an item not fully paid for and is responsible for the unpaid balance, then only the paid-up value is considered as income. *Id.* For example, if an individual is paid with an automobile valued at $1500 but is responsible for $1000 in payments that are still due, only $500 is counted as income.

Although claimants and beneficiaries must disclose the source and amount of all their earned income, certain earned income is excluded when determining eligibility and benefit amount. However, earned income is never reduced below zero for these purposes and unused earned income exclusions are never applied to unearned income. 20 C.F.R. § 416.1112(a). The following types of earned income are excluded, and when a claimant has income of this type it is excluded in the following order: as authorized by other federal laws; refunds of federal income taxes and to earned income tax credit payments; up to $30 of earned income per month, if received irregularly or infrequently; up to certain monthly and yearly maximum amounts of earned income for children under the age of 22 and regularly attending school; any portion of the $20 monthly unearned income exclusion that has not been excluded from unearned income in the same month; $65 of earned income per month; earned income used to pay "impairment-related work expenses" if the individual is disabled but not blind and under age 65 or received Supplement Security Income as a disabled person for the month preceding age 65; one-half of any remaining earned income in a month; earned income used to pay expenses "reasonably attributable" to earning the income, if the individual is blind and under age 65 or received Supplemental Security Income as a blind person for the month preceding age 65; any earned income received and spent on an approved plan to achieve self-support, if the individual is blind or disabled and under age 65; and payments made to participants in certain AmeriCorps programs. 20 C.F.R. § 416.1112(b)–(c).

b. Unearned Income

Unearned income, which can also be received in cash or in-kind, is defined simply as all income that is not earned income. 20 C.F.R. § 416.1120. It include annuities, pensions, and other periodic payments; alimony and support payments; dividends, interest, and certain royalties; rents (minus expenses) incurred in the taxable year that are ordinary and "necessary for the production or collection of the rental income"; death benefits, including payments received as a result of the death of another person "except for the amount of such payments that [one] spend[s] on the deceased person's last illness and burial expenses"; prizes and awards; gifts and inheritances, except those used to pay the expenses of another person's last illness and burial; and in-kind support and maintenance, including food or shelter. 20 C.F.R. § 416.1121(a)–(h). In-kind support and maintenance is discussed in greater detail below.

Unearned income is counted each month, either when received or otherwise available for the person's use, whichever is earliest. 20 C.F.R. § 416.1123(a). Unearned in-kind income is calculated typically based on the current market value, less any balance due. 20 C.F.R. § 416.1123(c). However, calculation of in-kind support and maintenance is subject to special treatment, as is discussed further below.

In some situations, SSA will count unearned income at a higher amount than actually received. *See generally* 20 C.F.R. § 416.1123(b). For example, most benefit payments, such as Social Security, are counted in full even when reduced to recover a previous overpayment. SSA will also include more than an individual actually received if amounts were withheld from unearned income "because of a garnishment, or to pay a debt or other legal obligation, or to make any other payment such as payment of . . . Medicare premiums." 20 C.F.R. § 416.1123(b)(2). On the other hand, SSA will deduct certain expenses incurred relative to the payment. *See* 20 C.F.R. § 416.1123(b)(3). As discussed in detail further below, under certain circumstances SSA may "deem" someone else's income as available to a claimant and therefore is counted as well. 20 C.F.R. § 416.1123(b)(4).

As with earned income, SSA does not count all of a person's unearned income in determining benefit eligibility and amount, unearned income is never reduced below zero, and unused unearned income exclusions are not applied to earned income—except for the $20 general exclusion discussed below. 20 C.F.R. § 416.1124(a) Also as with earned income, there are types of unearned income that are excluded under other federal laws. 20 C.F.R. § 416.1124(b). Additional exclusions are applied, including: any public agency's refund of taxes on real property or food; need-based assistance that is wholly funded by a state; grants, scholarships, or fellowships used for paying tuition, fees, and educational expenses; food raised by the individual or the individual's spouse if consumed by his or her household; federal emergency assistance; up to $60 of unearned income per calendar quarter if received irregularly or infrequently; payments for providing foster care to an ineligible child placed in an individual's home; certain support and maintenance assistance; one-third of support payments made to or for a child applicant by an absent parent; the first $20 of any unearned income received in a month other than income based on need; and all unearned income spent on an approved plan for achieving self-support, if the individual is blind or disabled; the value of certain assistance paid with respect to a dwelling unit; the value of any commercial transportation ticket received as a gift for travel and not converted to cash;

and payments received from a State fund to aid victims of crime. 20 C.F.R. § 416.1124(c). Certain veterans' benefits are also treated differently for purposes of counting unearned income. 20 C.F.R. § 416.1123(e).

The most commonly used income exclusion in disability cases is the $20 per month of unearned income not based on need, which includes OASDI benefits. Thus, individuals who are eligible for both OASDI and SSI because the amount of Disability Insurance Benefits they receive is relatively small, can have $20 per month of the OASDI benefits excluded in determining SSI eligibility and payments.

Payments of retroactive monthly OASDI benefits are treated as unearned income, but the amount is calculated as if the retroactive benefits were received on a regular monthly basis. 42 U.S.C. § 1320a–6; 20 C.F.R. § 416.1123(d). The idea is to prevent potential windfalls to an individual who may qualify for both OASDI and SSI benefits. Thus, the retroactive benefits are reduced by an amount equal to the amount of SSI payments that would not have been paid if the benefits had been paid when regularly due, rather than retroactively. 20 C.F.R. § 416.1123(d)(1). As a result, a large retroactive payment of OASDI benefits will not necessarily preclude eligibility for SSI.

c. In-Kind Support and Maintenance

As noted above, both earned and unearned income can include items received in kind. 20 C.F.R.

§ 416.1130. Regulations define in-kind support and maintenance as "any food or shelter that is given to you or that you receive because someone else pays for it," with shelter defined further as including "room, rent, mortgage payments, real property taxes, heating fuel, gas, electricity, water, sewerage, and garbage collection services." 20 C.F.R. § 416.1130(b). In-kind support and maintenance received as unearned income is calculated in one of two ways: by the "one-third reduction rule" or the "presumed value rule," depending on whether the individual is living in the household of the person providing the support and maintenance and whether food or shelter are also provided. 20 C.F.R. §§ 416.1121(h), 1130–1147. Until the early 1990s, SSA treated any in-kind contributions of food and shelter as income, even if provided as a loan. That policy was challenged successfully in the courts and SSA no longer considers in-kind contributions loaned to claimants as income. *See* SSR 92–8p (1992).

The "one-third reduction rule" is used to count in-kind support provided for individuals and eligible couples that live in another person's household for a full calendar month and receive food and shelter from that person. Instead of determining the actual dollar value of the in-kind support, SSA uses a flat rate of one-third of the current SSI benefit amount. 20 C.F.R. § 416.1131. The one-third reduction rule applies in whole or not at all, so when it applies SSA will not count any other in-kind support or maintenance received.

The "presumed value rule" is used when the individual does not receive both food and shelter. 20 C.F.R. § 416.1140. It also applies to persons receiving in-kind support and maintenance while living their own household or in a non-medical institution. 20 C.F.R. § 416.1141(a), (b). Under this rule, SSA presumes that any food or shelter received is worth a maximum value, as opposed to determining the actual dollar value. This maximum value is equal to one-third of the individual's benefit rate plus $20 (the general exclusion of unearned income not based on need described above). The presumed value rule is a rebuttable presumption, which can be rebutted by showing that the actual amount paid for the food or shelter received, or its current market, is less than the presumed value. 20 C.F.R. § 416.1140(a)(2).

d. Deeming of Income

Deeming is the term SSA uses when it considers another person's income—such as the income of a claimant's spouse or, if the claimant is a child, the income of the child's parent—to be the claimant's income. 20 C.F.R. § 416.1160. As with other types of income, deemed income is considered both to determine eligibility and the amount of the benefits. 20 C.F.R. § 416.1160(b). It does not matter whether the "deemed" income is actually available to the claimant because spouses or parents are expected to use part of their income toward the claimant's care. 20 C.F.R. § 416.1160(a)(1)–(2). The rules for deeming income from spouses and parents not eligible for SSI are discussed below. Rules also exist for deeming income from "essential persons" who have lived with an SSI recipient since the program was enacted, 20 C.F.R. § 416.222, or from a recipient's sponsor, if the recipient is a non-citizen. 42 U.S.C. § 1382c(f)(3)–(4); 20 C.F.R. § 416.1160(a)(3)–(4).

Generally, three steps are followed in deeming income. First, SSA calculates the total amount of earned and unearned income of the person whose income is being deemed, applying various exclusions similar to those used with regard to a claimant's income. Second, an amount is allocated for any ineligible children in the household. Finally, certain additional deeming rules are applied depending on the category of individual whose income is to be deemed. 20 C.F.R. § 416.1160(c). The regulations also address situations where the one-third reduction and presumed value rules for in-kind support and maintenance interact with the deeming rules. *See* 20 C.F.R. § 416.1148(a).

The income and resources of any child claimant under the age of 18 living in the same household as a parent who is not eligible for SSI will be deemed to include any income and resources of that parent (or the spouse of the parent). 42 U.S.C. § 1382c(f)(2)(A); 20 C.F.R. § 416.1160(a)(2). *See also* 20 C.F.R. § 416.1165. Parents' income may not be deemed, however, if the child is disabled and eligible for medical assistance under certain home care plans after having been institutionalized. 42 U.S.C. § 1382c(f)(2)(B); 20 C.F.R. § 416.1165(i). In addition, SSA may determine that it would be inequitable under the circumstances to deem income from a parent. 42 U.S.C. § 1382c(f)(2)(A).

If there is only one eligible child, any of the parents' remaining current monthly income will be deemed to be the child's unearned income. 20 C.F.R. § 416.1165(e)(1). If there is more than one eligible child, the parental income will be divided and deemed equally among the eligible children. 20 C.F.R. § 416.1165(e)(2). If deeming income to one eligible child reduces the child's benefits to zero (effectively making the child ineligible), any income beyond that attributed to the first child will be deemed available to any other eligible children. 20 C.F.R. § 416.1165(e)(3).

2. RESOURCES REQUIREMENTS

Supplemental Security Income resource limits serve to restrict eligibility to persons with effectively no disposable assets, with certain specific exceptions. Thus, an applicant or recipient is limited to non-excludable resources that do not exceed $2,000 in value (couples can have up to $3000 in non-excludable resources). 20 C.F.R. § 416.1205. The same resource limits also apply to child claimants. Thus, resources may not exceed $2,000 in value if the child is living with one parent or $3,000 if the child is living with both parents (or with the parent and a spouse). 20 C.F.R. § 416.1202(b). Once an individual satisfies this limit, the value of any resources below that limit has no effect on the amount of benefits awarded.

Resources are defined as cash or other liquid assets, or any real or personal property that an individual or his or her spouse owns and could convert to cash to be used for support and maintenance. 20 C.F.R. § 416.1201(a). Liquid resources include cash and financial instruments convertible to cash within 20 days; non-liquid resources include all personal and real property that is not cash and cannot be converted to cash within 20 days. For the most part, both are evaluated according to their equity value. 20 C.F.R. § 416.1201(b). Among items excluded, subject to various limits and exceptions, are a home that serves as the individual's principal place of residence; most household goods and personal effects; an automobile, if used for transportation; resources necessary for a blind or disabled person to fulfill an approved plan for achieving self-support; disaster relief assistance; and burial spaces and certain funds up to $1,500 for burial expenses. 20 C.F.R. §§ 416.1210, 1216. The proceeds from the sale of a home excluded from the individual's resources will also be excluded from resources to the extent they are intended to be used and are, in fact, used to purchase another home. The new home must be similarly excludable and purchased within 3 months of the date of receipt of the proceeds. 20 C.F.R. § 416.1212(e). Funds held in financial institution accounts, such as savings and checking accounts or certificates of deposit, are also considered to be a resource if the funds can be used for the individual's support and maintenance. Determinations about whether the funds can be used in this way depend upon whether the account is held individually or jointly. 20 C.F.R. § 416.1208.

The value of property essential to self-support is also typically not counted towards the value of an individual's resources. This includes real and personal property used in a trade or business; non-business income-producing property (houses or apartments for rent, land other than home property, etc.); and property used to produce goods or services essential to an individual's daily activities. There are detailed rules for counting income-producing property that is essential to self-support, as well as nonbusiness property used to produce goods or services. 20 C.F.R. §§ 416.1222, 1224. Resources, other than those used as part of a trade or business, must be non-liquid in order to be considered essential to self-support. 20 C.F.R. § 416.1220.

Similar to the ways in which income from an ineligible spouse or parent may be deemed available to a claimant or beneficiary, the resources of an ineligible spouse or parent may be deemed resources of their spouse or child. 20 C.F.R. § 416.1202. As with income, the resources will be deemed regardless of whether they are actually available to the individual. Deemed resources are subject to the same exclusions as those of a claimant or beneficiary.

Determinations about the availability, value, and excludability of resources are made at the beginning of the month. Changes in the value of resources that occur during a month will not be counted until the beginning of the next month. Similarly, if an individual receives an item in cash or in kind during a month, it will be evaluated under the income-counting rules during that month but will not be subject to the rules for counting resources until the beginning of the next month. Receipts from the sale, exchange, or replacement of a resource continue to be counted as a resource and are not considered income, regardless of when the change takes place. *See* 20 C.F.R. § 416.1207. Under certain circumstances, an individual may dispose of a limited amount of resources that exceed the limits set for in the regulations in order to become eligible for benefits. *See* 20 C.F.R. § 416.1207(e). Generally, resources must be sold at fair market value. *See* 20 C.F.R. § 416.1246 (rules applied when sale is for less than market value).

C. OLD AGE COVERAGE

Old age was a major part of the original coverage of the Social Security Act of 1935 for both social insurance and public assistance benefits. Old age benefits have remained a central part of what has become the Old Age, Survivors, and Disability Insurance program (OASDI). As a result of expansions to Social Security Act coverage over time, including the creation of the Supplemental Security Income (SSI) program in the early 1970s, a broad range of benefits are available today on the basis of old age under both OASDI and SSI.

As explained in more detail in Chapter 3, there are two separate age requirements in the OASDI program for persons fully insured on the basis of their own earnings—one for early retirement, beginning at age 62 (or 60 in the case of widow(er)s), and the other for full retirement. 42 U.S.C. § 402(a). The age for full retirement has been undergoing a gradual extension from the traditional age of 65 to

67. *See* 42 U.S.C. § 416(*l*). There is no similar change underway for the early retirement age. 42 U.S.C. § 416(*l*)(2). The old age threshold for SSI has always been the traditional retirement age of 65. 42 U.S.C. § 1382c(a)(1)(A).

D. DISABILITY COVERAGE

Disability benefits are available through the Old Age, Survivors, and Disability Insurance (OASDI) program and the Supplemental Security Income (SSI) program. OASDI disability benefits are available not only persons who are insured on the basis of their own work record (often referred to as "wage earners"), but also their spouses (after they reach a certain age) and their adult children (so long as they became disabled before a certain age). The SSI program provides disability benefits to both adults and children under the age of 18. As explained later in this chapter and also in Chapter 3, persons seeking OASDI disability benefits as a wage earner's dependent or survivor must meet—in addition to the insured-status requirements for the wage earner—certain relationship-to-wage-earner requirements.

The disability requirement is the same for all claimants under both programs, except for children under the age of 18 applying for SSI benefits. Persons seeking disability benefits under the OASDI program and adults seeking disability benefits under the SSI program must show that they are unable to engage in "substantial gainful activity" as the result of a "medically determinable" physical or mental impairment that has lasted for, or is expected to last, at least one year (or expected to result in death), taking into account the claimant's age, level of education, and prior work experience. 42 U.S.C. §§ 423(d)(1), 1382c(a)(3)(A). There is a separate SSI disability standard for children under the age of 18, which is intended to measure "disability" in the special context of younger age. *See* 42 U.S.C. § 1382c(a)(3)(C) These disability standards are discussed at length in Chapters 4–7.

1. CONTINUING ELIGIBILITY

Once an individual has been found to be disabled and entitled to benefits, payments continue unless and until SSA determines that the recipient is no longer eligible. There are a number of special circumstances that can trigger ineligibility apart from no longer meeting the requirements for receiving disability benefits, including fraud or having provided incomplete or incorrect information. *See* 42 U.S.C. §§ 423(f), 405(u)(1); 20 C.F.R. § 404.1594(e). In addition, SSI recipients can become ineligible if they come to have income or resources above the maximum allowable amount. The most common basis for finding recipients no longer eligible for disability benefits—and the one most often contested by the recipient—is that they are no longer disabled. The standard for terminating benefits on that basis is discussed in detail in Chapter 4.

There are, of course, circumstances where the recipient obviously is no longer disabled, either because the disabling condition had improved or the recipient returned to work reflecting substantial gainful activity. (As explained in Chapter 5, minimal levels of work may not result in disqualification.) This may come to SSA's attention when reported by the recipient, as required under 20 C.F.R. §§ 404.1588, 416.988, or in the course of a "continuing disability review" (CDR). Even recipients who have returned to otherwise disqualifying work may remain eligible if the return to work qualifies as a "trial work period." CDRs and trial work periods are discussed immediately below.

a. Continuing Disability Reviews (CDR)

The Social Security Act mandates review of ongoing disability cases in order to determine continuing eligibility for benefits. 42 U.S.C.A. § 421(i); *see also* 20 C.F.R. §§ 404.1589, 404.1590, 416.989, 416.990. The Act requires that CDRs be conducted every three years for all beneficiaries, except for those whose disabilities were determined to be permanent. *See* 42 U.S.C.A. § 421(i)(1). In addition, SSA policy is to review administrative hearing decisions on an essentially random basis. 20 C.F.R. §§ 404.969(b)(1), 416.1469(b)(1).

After a case is chosen for review, the file is sent by SSA to the relevant state agency for further action, which then notifies the recipient that a review has been undertaken. (As explained in Chapter 8, state agencies are charged with determining disability for both OASDI and SSI benefits.) The notice includes a form requesting information on the recipient's current ability to work and medical providers. *See generally* 20 C.F.R. §§ 404.1589, 416.989. If the information is not current or sufficiently detailed, a consultative medical examination may be ordered. 20 C.F.R. §§ 404.1593(c), 416.993(c). If SSA decides that a recipient is no longer disabled on the basis of the record, it sends a notice to the recipient that benefits will be terminated unless additional information establishing continuing disability is sent within the next 10 days. *See* 20 C.F.R. §§ 404.1594, 404.1595, 416.994, 416.995, 416.1331(b). The notice must include a statement of the evidence upon which the decision to terminate was based. 20 C.F.R. §§ 404.1595(a), 416.995. A claimant's benefits can be suspended for failure to cooperate with a request for additional information and can be terminated after twelve months of suspension if the claimant continues not to cooperate. 20 C.F.R. §§ 404.1587, 416.992.

b. Trial Work Period

Recipients of OASDI disability benefits, including surviving spouses, widows and widowers, and disabled adult children, are entitled to a nine-month "trial work period" during which they can test their ability to work without losing their eligibility for benefits or having their payments suspended. *See generally* 42 U.S.C. §§ 422(c), 423(a); 20 C.F.R. § 404.1592. The trial work period rules apply only after becoming entitled to benefits. 20 C.F.R. § 404.1592(e); SSR 82–52 (1982). In other words, any work performed before becoming eligible for benefits will be considered in determining whether a claimant is able to engage in substantial gainful activity. *See* 20 C.F.R. § 404.1592(d)(2)(iii). Recipients are entitled to only a single trial work period during any one period of eligibility for benefits. 20 C.F.R. § 404.1592(c). However, the nine months do not have to be consecutive. 20 C.F.R. § 404.1592(a).

Although SSA may not consider any work performed during the trial work period as evidence that a recipient's disability has ended, it may use proof of work during a trial work period as evidence that the disability ended after the end of the trial work period. 20 C.F.R. § 404.1592(a). Moreover, benefits may be terminated during the trial work period if other evidence not related to work done during the trial work period shows that a disability has ended. 20 C.F.R. §§ 404.1592(a), 404.1592(e)(3). Such evidence must be separate from proof that the recipient engaged in substantial gainful activity during the work period. Hancock v. Barnhart, 206 F. Supp. 2d 757, 766, 81 Soc. Sec. Rep. Serv. 561 (W.D. Va. 2002) (claimant's own testimony concerning his ability to work during trial work period can be considered, as opposed to "evidence of work itself"); *cf.* Love v. Heckler, 564 F. Supp. 195, 198, 2 Soc. Sec. Rep. Serv. 789 (W.D. N.C. 1983) (administrative law judge based decision on eight months of employment during trial work period and not on independent medical evidence).

There is no parallel provision in the Supplemental Security Income program. However, SSI recipients who work despite a disabling impairment may be eligible for special cash benefits and continuing Medicaid coverage. Their gross income, while exceeding the amount that ordinarily represents substantial gainful activity, must be too low to provide benefits and services comparable to those they would receive without those earnings. *See* 42 U.S.C.A. § 1382h(a)(1); 20 C.F.R. §§ 416.260–269. This special eligibility status for SSI recipients that return to work is intended to remove disincentives to work, much like a trial work period.

c. Reentitlement Period

As further encouragement for OASDI disability benefit recipients to work, regulations authorize a 36-month "reentitlement period" upon completion of a trial work period to avoid beneficiaries losing their eligibility if they cannot continue working. *See generally* 20 C.F.R. § 404.1592a. During that period, SSA will determine that disability ceased for persons engaging in substantial gainful employment during the reentitlement period, but will pay benefits for the first three months even though the person is working. After those three months and for the remained of the reentitlement period, benefits will continue to be paid for any months during which the person does not engage in substantial gainful activity. In addition, beneficiaries who stop working altogether during the reentitlement period can be reinstated without having to reapply. 20 C.F.R. § 404.1592a(a)(2)(i).

2. PERIOD OF DISABILITY

Closely related to, but separate from, eligibility for OASDI disability benefits is a "period of disability" (often referred to as a "disability freeze"). The purpose of a period of disability is to establish, for various administrative purposes, that a claimant or beneficiary was disabled at that time—regardless of whether the person was also eligible to receive cash benefits. A period of disability can be used, for example, to toll quarters of coverage used to apply the 20/40 requirement for attaining disability insured status, which has the effect of extending the date at which a claimant may be eligible for disability benefits. *See* 20 C.F.R. § 404.131(a).

In order to be entitled to a period of disability, one must also be insured for disability for that period and disabled according to the Social Security disability standard. 42 U.S.C. § 416(i)(2)(A); 20 C.F.R. § 404.320(b). An application for a period of disability must be filed within 12 months after the period ended. 20 C.F.R. § 404.320(b)(3). A period of disability can also be helpful when calculating the amount of benefits. As explained further in Chapter 7, the primary insurance amount (PIA) formula on which OASDI benefit amounts are based removes periods of disability from the calculation, rather than treating that period as including potentially harmful no-work quarters. And the five-month waiting period—applicable to most claims for disability benefits—does not apply to anyone who was entitled to benefits or to a "period of disability" during the five years prior to the month the claimant again became disabled. 20 C.F.R. § 404.315(a)(4).

E. DEPENDENT AND SURVIVORS COVERAGE

Old Age, Survivors, and Disability Insurance (OASDI) provides a wide variety of secondary benefit payments to spouses, children, and even parents of wage earners, all based on the wage earner's earnings record. The overriding purpose of these secondary benefits is to provide a source of income to those people most likely to have relied on the wage earner for support.

As explained in Chapter 1, secondary benefits were first included in the Social Security Act in 1939 at a time when social policy assumed males as breadwinners and their wives as dependents—but has since accommodated cultural shifts to provide full benefits for dependent husbands and widowers as well. Most recently, SSA extended coverage of spouse benefits to same-sex couples following recent Supreme Court decisions on same-sex marriage. Thus, subject to certain conditions, spouses (and divorced spouses), surviving spouses (and surviving divorced spouses), parents, and children of insured wage earners may be eligible for old age or disability benefits on the basis of the worker's earnings record. Eligibility requirements for these programs are discussed in detail in Chapter 3.

There is no "survivors" concept in the Supplemental Security Income (SSI) program. While the death of an SSI recipient may affect the amount of a family member's income and resources and therefore affect that person's financial eligibility, the fact that someone applying for SSI had been dependent on a deceased recipient is not independently relevant.

CHAPTER 3

ELIGIBILITY CRITERIA FOR OLD AGE AND SURVIVORS BENEFITS

As noted in Chapter 2, eligibility requirements for benefits under the two key benefit titles of the Social Security Act—Title II, governing the Old Age, Survivors, and Disability Insurance Program (OASDI), and Title XVI, governing the Supplemental Security Income Program (SSI)—include both financial and personal criteria. The financial criteria for OASDI and SSI eligibility—insurance status for the former program, limited income and resources for the latter—were covered in some detail in that chapter. This chapter covers the personal criteria for the old-age programs under both titles and the survivors benefit programs under Title II. The personal criteria for the disability programs under both titles are covered separately and in significantly more detail in Chapters 4–6.

This chapter is divided into two sections, covering first old age benefits and then survivors benefits. The section on old age programs discusses the retirement age requirements for OASDI benefits for wage earners and the age requirement for SSI benefits for financially qualified individuals. It also covers issues relating to proof of age for both types of benefits. The section on OASDI survivors benefits discusses the eligibility criteria for secondary benefits paid to certain survivors and dependents of covered workers. Persons eligible for survivors benefits can include a wage earner's spouse (including some former spouses), children, and parents. The section highlights key issues relevant to different categories of survivors: for spouses' and widow(er)s' benefits, who qualifies as a spouse or widow(er) and the evidentiary requirements for proving marriage; for children's insurance benefits, the types of relationships that qualify for entitlement in this category, the requirement that the child be dependent on the insured worker, and the evidence required to prove the parent-child relationship and dependency; and for benefits based on one's status as a parent, special requirements for entitlement to "mother's and father's benefits" for caretaker parents of a wage earner's child and "parent's benefits" for a wage earner's parents.

A. OLD AGE BENEFITS

While both OASDI and SSI provide benefits on the basis of old age, the two programs differ in substantial ways that reflect the differences between social insurance and public assistance. As explained in Chapter 2, OASDI is a social insurance program and therefore OASDI old age benefits are structured as retirement benefits for persons who worked and paid Social Security taxes in a sufficient amount and over a sufficiently long period of time to become "insured" under that program. SSI, on the other hand, is a public assistance program and therefore SSI old age benefits are available to all older persons with limited income and resources, independent of any work history. Consistent with the social insurance/public assistance distinction between the two programs, the amount of an OASDI benefit is determined by a formula that is based in part on the amount of Social Security taxes paid. SSI benefits, on the other hand, are calculated to meet basic financial needs. The methods for calculating the amount of OASDI and SSI benefit payments are discussed in detail in Chapter 7.

Although both OASDI and SSI provide benefits based on age, the age requirements for the two programs are slightly different. Because OASDI old age benefits are designed to insure against wage loss due to old age, the age requirement for benefits under that program are based on the concept of retirement. There is a similar, but simpler, age requirement for SSI old age benefits.

1. OASDI RETIREMENT AGE

OASDI has two different age requirements, allowing insured wage earners to opt for either early or full retirement. Until recently, the full retirement age was 65—the same age established for old age benefits in the original Social Security Act (which was based, in turn, on the age set in the nineteenth century for the first modern Social Security system in Germany). However, beginning in 2003, the full retirement age increased gradually over a period of six years to 66. The full retirement age began increasing again in 2020 from 66 to 67, also over a period of six years. The Act sets out a schedule that lists at what age full retirement benefits may be received. *See* 42 U.S.C. §§ 402(a), 416(*l*); 20 C.F.R. § 404.2(c)(4). The schedule is based on the year a claimant reached the age of 62 (which is, as explained below, the youngest age that qualifies for early retirement). Thus, as a practical matter, the full retirement age has been 66 since 2009 (that is, for persons who reached the age of 62 in 2005); starting in 2021 (that is, for persons who reached the age of 62 in 2017), the full retirement age will begin to creep up to 67; and by 2027 (that is, for persons who reached the age of 62 in 2022), the full retirement age will be 67.

A second option is to receive early retirement benefits, which are available to insured wage earners as early as age 62. 42 U.S.C. § 402(a)(2); 20 C.F.R. § 404.2(c)(4). However, for persons who choose to retire before full retirement age, benefits are reduced by a fraction of a percent for each month of retirement before full retirement age. On the other hand, if an individual retires only after reaching full retirement age, the amount of monthly payments increase to make up for the months when the individual was not receiving benefits. These rules and others concerning the amount of OASDI benefits are explained in detail in Chapter 7.

2. SSI AGE REQUIREMENT

SSI old age benefits are available at age 65. 42 U.S.C. § 1381. Congress has not increased the age requirement for SSI benefits since the program began and there is no option to receive a lesser amount at an earlier age.

3. PROOF OF AGE

Individuals applying for OASDI or SSI old age benefits must provide, with limited exceptions, proof that shows their date of birth. 20 C.F.R. §§ 404.715(a), 416.801. The type of evidence required is somewhat different, however, for the two programs. OASDI regulations distinguish between "preferred" and "other" evidence, while SSI regulations are more detailed and complete.

For OASDI, preferred evidence includes a birth certificate, hospital birth record, or a religious record showing the claimant's date of birth. In order for these records to constitute preferred evidence, they must be recorded before age 5. If such records are not available, the claimant will be asked to provide other evidence of age, such as an original family bible or family record, school records, census records, a statement signed by the physician or midwife who was present at the claimant's birth, insurance policies, a marriage record, a passport, an employment record, a delayed birth certificate, or an immigration or naturalization record. *See* 20 C.F.R. § 404.716.

For SSI, the requirements for proof of age are more comprehensive. SSA gives the highest probative value to a public record of birth or a religious record of birth or baptism established or recorded before the claimant reached age 5. If this is unavailable, the claimant must submit other evidence of age similar to those allowed for OASDI, such as a school record, original family bible or other family record, church record of baptism or confirmation while a child or young adult, marriage record, military record, delayed birth certificate, physician's or midwife's record of birth, immigration or naturalization record, or passport. In addition, SSI regulations provide explicitly that in determining the probative value of these other forms of evidence, consideration will be given to when the documents were established or recorded and the circumstances under which they were established or recorded. *See* 20 C.F.R. §§ 416.802, 803. At the same time, SSI regulations also provide for expedited adjudication of certain old age benefit claims. Thus, if an applicant alleges that he or she is at least 68 years old and submits any documentation supporting this allegation that is at least 3 years old—and if there is no evidence to the contrary—no further evidence of age will be required. *See* 20 C.F.R. §§ 416.801, 806.

In most instances, proof of age is straightforward and uncontested. Nonetheless, sometimes the usual simple forms of documentation are not available. In such cases the claimant's age can be in dispute, often with competing evidence supporting two different birthdates. *See, e.g.*, Collier v. Apfel, 91 F.Supp.2d 904, 906, 68 Soc. Sec. Rep. Ser. 463 (W.D. Va. 2000) (court-ordered birthdate entered more than 50 years after alleged date rejected in favor of Census data from when claimant was 7 years old; upheld because "[a] reasonable mind might accept such rationale . . . even if the court determines that the contrary result is also supported by substantial evidence.").

B. SURVIVORS BENEFITS

As noted at the beginning of this chapter, eligibility for OASDI survivors benefits always begins with a "wage earner" upon whose earnings record—and insured status—other family members may, under certain circumstances, claim benefits as well. Benefits provided to wage earners' survivors and dependents include retirement and disability benefits for dependent and surviving spouses, retirement benefits for surviving parents, disability benefits for dependent and surviving children, and general allowances for dependent and surviving children and their caretaking parents. This section discusses the basic eligibility requirements for dependent and survivor benefits, apart from the insured status of the wage earner on whose earnings record the claim is based (discussed already in Chapter 2) and the requirements for establishing disability (which are discussed in Chapters 4–6). Claims based on three different family relationships with the wage earner are covered separately below: wage earners' dependent and surviving spouses, their children, and their parents.

1. SPOUSES AND WIDOW(ER)S BENEFITS

In general terms, the Social Security Act provides benefits to spouses or widow(er)s of insured workers who retire, become disabled, or die. Spouses constitute by far the largest number of secondary benefit recipients. Unlike with other family relationships providing the basis for secondary OASDI benefits, independent proof of dependency is not required to receive spouses benefits. Instead, dependency is presumed. (As noted in Chapter 7, the extent of spouses' or widow(er)s' dependency is address in the various rules on the amount of benefits they receive, including the amount of benefits they may be entitled to on the basis of their own earnings records.)

This section looks first at the eligibility requirements for dependent spouses of retired or disabled workers. Next, it discusses the requirements for widows and widowers of insured workers. Finally, it examines the evidence required to prove the existence of a marriage or other spousal relationship between the claimant and wage earner.

a. Eligibility Requirements for Spouses

Generally, wives or husbands of wage earners are considered to be a "spouse" for purposes of receiving secondary benefits if married to the wage earner for at least one year at the time the application was filed or if they are the parent of the wage earner's child. In addition to current spouses, former spouses divorced from the wage earner may be entitled to benefits if the marriage to the wage earner lasted at least ten years and the divorced spouse-claimant is unmarried. 42 U.S.C. § 416(a)–(b), (f). As explained below with respect to proof of marriage, spouses of same-sex marriages are now covered as well.

A spouse can receive OASDI old age benefits starting at the age of 62, 42 U.S.C. § 402(a); however, spouses can begin receiving benefits at any age if they are caring for the wage earner's child—so long as the child is younger than 16 or disabled and entitled to child's disability benefits. 42 U.S.C. § 402(b)–(c). As explained further below, eligibility for benefits as the parent caretaker of a wage earner's child does not extend to divorced spouses.

b. Eligibility Requirements for Widow(er)s

As with spouses of retired wage earners, spouses of deceased wage earners must meet certain statutory requirements in order to qualify for widow(er)'s secondary benefits. Surviving spouses qualify if they were married to the wage earner for at least nine months before the wage earner died or, if married less than nine months, they are the parent—or, with some qualifications, the adopted parent—of the wage earner's child (or if the deceased wage earner adopted the surviving spouse's child before the child turned 18). 42 U.S.C. § 416(c), (g); 20 C.F.R. § 404.335. In addition, they must not be remarried and must have reached the age of 60. Surviving spouses are also eligible for disability benefits, which they can start receiving at age 50. 42 U.S.C. § 402(e)(1)(B), (f)(1)(B); 20 C.F.R. § 404.335(c). The disability requirement for these and other Social Security disability benefits are discussed in Chapter 4.

When survivors benefits were first included in the Social Security Act, there were separate dependency requirements for a widower's benefits that did not apply to a widow's benefits. That distinction was declared unconstitutional in Weinberger v. Wiesenfeld, 420 U.S. 636 (1975). *See also* Califano v. Goldfarb, 430 U.S. 199 (1977) (invalidating requirement that widowers—but not widows—prove dependency in order to receive surviving spouses benefits). Congress eventually removed all of the Act's gender-based distinctions. *See* Social Security Amendments of 1977, Pub. L. No. 95–216, § 334, 91 Stat. 1509, 1544; Social Security Amendments of 1983, Pub. L. No. 98–21 §§ 301–310, 97 Stat. 65, 109–18.

c. Proof of Marriage or Other Spousal Relationship

The Social Security Administration determines spousal relationships based on whether the courts of the state in which the wage earner is or was domiciled at the time an application for benefits is filed would find that the claimant and the wage earner were validly married, either at the time the claim was filed or at the time the wage earner died. Following the Supreme Court's decisions in United States v. Windsor, 570 U.S. 744, 133 S. Ct. 2675 (2013) and Obergefell v. Hodges, 576 U.S. 644, 135 S. Ct. 2584 (2015), holding the Defense of Marriage Act and state law bans on same-sex marriage unconstitutional, SSA now recognizes same-sex marriages in every state. Moreover, SSR 17–1p (2017) effectively allows for reopening of denials based on the fact that the marriage in question was between members of the same sex.

The spousal requirement can also be met if the claimant would have the same status as a spouse with respect to personal property under the intestate law in the state in which the insured individual was domiciled at the time of the application or the wage earner's death. 20 C.F.R. § 404.345. In addition, a spousal relationship can be established via a "deemed valid marriage" when it can be established that the claimant in good faith went through a marriage ceremony that would have been valid but for a legal impediment not known to the claimant at the time. 20 C.F.R. § 404.346.

Federal regulations provide detailed guidance regarding the types of evidence that can be used to establish various types of spousal relationships and when such evidence is required. Any individual who applies for spouses benefits must provide evidence of the marriage, including where and when the marriage took place. The type of evidence requested depends on whether the marriage was a ceremonial marriage, a common-law marriage, or a marriage deemed valid. 20 C.F.R. § 404.723.

A "ceremonial marriage" is one that follows procedures set by law in the state or foreign country where it took place. This can include a marriage that follows certain tribal or foreign customs. If a ceremonial marriage is claimed, SSA will request signed statements from the spouse and the insured regarding the time and location of the marriage. If other evidence creates doubt as to whether a ceremonial marriage took place, SSA may request other documentation, including copies of the public or religious marriage records, certified statements as to the marriage, or the original marriage certificate. If these types of "preferred evidence" are not obtainable, the claimant will be asked for an explanation why this is the case, a signed statement of the individual who conducted the marriage ceremony, and any other probative evidence of the marriage. 20 C.F.R. § 404.725.

A "common-law marriage" is a marriage considered valid under certain state laws even though no formal ceremony took place. It is a marriage between two persons who are free to marry, who consider themselves married, live together, and in some states, meet certain other requirements. *But see* Ayuso-Morales v. Secretary, 677 F.2d 146 (1st Cir. 1982) (widow benefits not available because common law marriage not recognized under the law of Puerto Rico). Preferred evidence of this type of marriage includes signed statements of both parties, if they are still alive, or of blood relatives, explaining why the person who signed the statement believes that a marriage existed. If this preferred evidence cannot be obtained, SSA will request an explanation why this is the case as well as any other convincing evidence of the marriage. 20 C.F.R. § 404.726.

Finally, as mentioned earlier a "deemed valid marriage" is one that would have been valid but for a legal impediment not known to the claimant at the time. If this is asserted, the regulations specify certain types of preferred evidence, including documentary evidence of the ceremonial marriage or signed statements by the wage earner or purported spouse stating that he or she went through the marriage ceremony in good faith and his or her reasons for believing the marriage was valid. In addition, if reasonable doubt exists as to the marriage, the claimant may be asked to produce signed statements from others showing how the purported marriage took place in good faith or evidence that the parties were living together when the application for benefits was filed or when the wage earner died. 20 C.F.R. § 404.727.

2. CHILD'S BENEFITS

In addition to spouses, certain dependent and surviving children of insured wage earners are entitled to secondary OASDI benefits. Wage earners' children who may be entitled to benefits include dependent natural children, legally adopted children, stepchildren, grandchildren, and step grandchildren. *See* 20 C.F.R. § 404.354. This section looks first at how various qualifying parent-child relationships are defined. Next, it discusses age limits and dependency requirements for different categories of child's benefits. Finally, it examines the types of evidence needed to prove qualifying parent-child relationships and, when required, the child's dependence on the wage earner.

a. Parent-Child Relationship

Most children who qualify for OASDI secondary benefits are classified as "natural children" of the wage earner, which includes any child with the same inheritance rights as the wage earner's biological child. In making this determination, SSA looks to the intestate law on personal property of the state where the wage earner is domiciled at the time the application is filed; if the wage earner is deceased, it will look to the laws of the state where the wage earner was domiciled at the time of death. 20 C.F.R. § 404.355(a)(1), (b)(1).

There are also other ways to qualify as a wage earner's natural child. One is considered a natural child if the wage earner and the child's mother or father went through a ceremony that would have resulted in a valid marriage but for a legal impediment. Even if the child's mother or father had not married the wage earner, the child will be deemed the wage earner's natural child if the wage earner had acknowledged the child in writing, had been decreed by a court as the parent of the child, or had been ordered by a court to contribute to the support of the child. Finally, an applicant can submit other forms of evidence to prove a parent-child relationship, including evidence that the wage earner was either living with the child or contributing to the child's support at the time the application was filed (or, with respect to deceased wage earners, at the time they died). 20 C.F.R. § 404.355(a)(2)–(4).

In addition to natural children, other categories of wage earners' children may be entitled to receive secondary benefits. These include the insured's legally adopted children, stepchildren, grandchildren, step grandchildren, and equitably adopted children. The requirements for eligibility based on these categories are defined by statute and set out in detail in the regulations. *See* 42 U.S.C. § 416(e); 20 C.F.R. §§ 404.356–359.

b. Age Limits

Children of insured wage earners who have died or are receiving old age or disability benefits are entitled to benefits up to the age of 18, or 19 if still "a full-time elementary or secondary school student." 42 U.S.C. § 402(d)(1)(B). A student attending a traditional school, receiving instruction through home schooling, or participating in an independent study education program will be eligible, so long as the educational program is in accordance with state law where the child resides. The student must be attending school full-time carrying a full-time subject load (according to the institution's standards or those set by the state), for at least 13 weeks. A student will remain eligible during a period of nonattendance or part-time attendance if this period lasts no more than 4 consecutive months, is not due to expulsion or suspension from school, and the student shows an intention to resume studies full-time at the end of the period. Finally, students are not eligible for benefits if they are being paid by an employer who has requested or required the student to attend school. *See* 20 C.F.R. §§ 404.367, 368.

During the time that a child is eligible for benefits, the child's caretaker parent is entitled to a parent's benefit if the wage earner is deceased. These "mother's and father's benefits" are available only if the widow(er)-parent is otherwise not entitled to a surviving spouse benefit. Parent benefits are discussed in greater detail later in this chapter.

Child's benefits may extend beyond the age of 18, subject to certain other dependency-related requirements. The current dependency requirements are discussed in the next section.

c. Dependency Requirement

If the primary wage earner is living, the child must be dependent on the wage earner at the time the application was filed. If the primary wage earner has died, the child must have been dependent at the time of the wage earner's death. Dependency is assumed for claimants who are a wage earner's "natural child." 20 C.F.R. § 404.361(a). The same is true for children adopted before the wage earner became eligible for old age or disability benefits. 20 C.F.R. § 404.462(a). However, claimants with other types of relationships to the wage earner—including equitably adopted children, stepchildren, grandchildren, and step grandchildren—are required to satisfy additional conditions. Depending on the type of relationship, child claimants may be asked to show that they lived with the wage earner at a specific time, that the child received "contributions for support" from the wage earner, or that the wage earner provided at least "one-half support" to the child. 20 C.F.R. §§ 404.360–365. *See also* 20 C.F.R. § 404.366 (defining "living with" "contributions for support" and "one-half support").

One other way the Social Security Act effectively imposes a dependency requirement for child claimants is by requiring that they be unmarried in order to receive child's benefits, with certain limited exceptions. 42 U.S.C. § 402(d)(1)(B), (d)(5); 20 C.F.R. § 404.352(b)(4).

d. Proof of Parent-Child Relationship and Dependency

An application for children's secondary benefits must be supported by evidence of the child's qualifying relationship to the wage earner-parent. 20 C.F.R. § 404.730. If the claimant is the natural child of the wage earner, a copy of the child's public or religious birth record made before age 5 will be requested; if it shows the same last name for the child and the parent, the record will be convincing evidence of the parent-child relationship. However, more evidence must be presented if such a record is unobtainable or if other evidence calls into question whether the claimant is the wage earner's natural child. Acceptable evidence includes a statement signed by the wage earner attesting to the relationship (or copies of any court orders declaring that the claimant is the wage earner's natural child or requiring the wage earner to provide child support) or sufficient proof that the claimant would be able to inherit the wage earner's personal property under the applicable state's intestacy laws. 20 C.F.R. § 404.731.

If the claimant is the wage earner's stepchild, regulations require proof of the relevant parent-child relationship as well as the child's parent's marriage to the wage earner. *See* 20 C.F.R. § 404.732. Regulations provide more specific guidance on the type of evidence required where the child was adopted, either legally or equitably. 20 C.F.R. §§ 404.733, 734.

The proof required to show dependency is determined by the type of relationship between the claimant-child and the insured wage earner. As noted earlier, proof of dependency is not required if the claimant is the "natural child" of the wage earner. If the claimant is adopted, SSA may require a signed statement "by someone who knows the facts" that confirms the relationship. The claimant may also be asked to produce a signed statement "by someone in a position to know" showing when and where the child lived with the wage earner, as well as information regarding the support that the child received. Similar regulatory provisions govern the evidentiary requirements for establishing dependency in other types of relationships. *See* 20 C.F.R. § 404.736.

Disputed claims for survivors benefits typically involve questions about the existence (or non-existence) of the relevant family relationship between the claimant and the wage earner. Most often, the critical relationship is that between a claimant child and his or her wage-earner parent. The most common disputed issues are the paternity of a wage-earner father and the extent of a parent's (usually the father's) support for the child. *See*, e.g., Jones v. Chater, 101 F.3d 509, 52 Soc. Sec. Rep. Ser. 244 (7th Cir. 1996) (failure to prove that wage earner was providing "regular and substantial support" to child claimant when he died.)

Child's benefits may also be available to posthumously conceived children, but only if they would be entitled to inherit under state law. Astrue

v. Capato, 566 U.S. 541, 132 S. Ct. 2021 (2012) (rejecting argument that posthumous biological child is automatically eligible; benefits denied because child born 18 months after death of wage earner would not inherit under applicable state law). *See also* MacNeil v. Berryhill, 869 F.3d 109 (2d Cir. 2017) (child ineligible because would not inherit under applicable New York intestacy law).

e. Dependency and Disabled Adult Children

Although dependency is measured most often according to specific circumstances existing at the time a claimant applies for benefits, certain standard external conditions come into play as well. The most obvious is age; after a certain age, children are considered independent and therefore are no longer eligible for child's benefits. Dependency is more open-ended for disabled children. As discussed in Chapter 4, if a child of a wage earner becomes disabled before reaching the age of 22, the "child" can continue to receive child's disability benefits as a dependent of the wage earner so long as they remain disabled. However, wage earners' disabled children are considered dependent only so long as they are unmarried, except that a child already receiving benefits will remain dependent after marrying someone also eligible for benefits. 42 U.S.C. §§ 402(d)(1)(D), 402(d)(5); 20 C.F.R. § 404.350(d). *See also* Crane v. Sullivan, 993 F.2d 1335, 41 Soc. Sec. Rep. Ser. 214 (8th Cir. 1993) (child's insurance benefits are available to married adult children only if they apply prior to marriage).

3. PARENTS BENEFITS

There are two instances in which a parent can be eligible as such for OASDI benefits on the basis of another person's earning record. First, as noted earlier, widow(er)s of insured wage earners may qualify for "mother's and father's insurance benefits" if they are the caretaker parent of a deceased wage earner's child under the age of 16. *See* 42 U.S.C. § 402(g). However, eligibility for benefits as the parent caretaker of a wage earner's child does not extend to divorced spouses. Nor does it extend to a parent who was not married to the wage earner. The Supreme Court upheld these distinctions in Mathews v. De Castro, 429 U.S. 181 (1976) and Califano v. Boles, 443 U.S. 282, 99 S. Ct. 2767 (1979). (As explained earlier, the children themselves are entitled to child's benefits until they reach the age of 18, or 19 if they are in school full-time.)

Second, under certain limited circumstances a deceased wage earner's parent may be entitled to secondary benefits. In order to qualify for this type of benefit, parents must be at least 62 years old and must be able to show that they were receiving one-half of their financial support from the wage earner at the time of death. Parent's benefits may also be available to a wage earner's stepparents (if the marriage to the wage earner's natural parent took place before the wage earner turned 16) and adopting parents (if the wage earner was adopted before the age of 16). *See* 42 U.S.C. § 402(h)(1), (h)(3); 20 C.F.R. § 404.370.

CHAPTER 4

ELIGIBILITY CRITERIA FOR DISABILITY BENEFITS

The Social Security Act sets out two different disability standards that apply to current claims for benefits. Both are discussed generally in this chapter and then discussed in greater detail in Chapters 5 and 6.

The most important disability standard—by far—is the standard that applies to all current claims for disability benefits under the Old Age, Survivors, and Disability Insurance (OASDI) program, including claims by wage earners and their surviving spouses and disabled children 18 years of age or older, and all claims for Supplemental Security Income (SSI) disability benefits by adults. The Social Security Act defines "disability" for all of those programs as the "inability to engage in any substantial gainful activity by reason of any medically determinable physical or mental impairment which can be expected to result in death or which has lasted or can be expected to last for a continuous period of not less than 12 months." 42 U.S.C. § 423(d)(1)(A); *see also* 42 U.S.C. § 1382c(a)(3)(A).

A second, separate disability standard applies to SSI claims on behalf of children under the age of 18. The definition of disability for the purposes of child's SSI benefits differs from the general standard noted above in that it focuses on whether a child "has a medically determinable physical or mental impairment, which results in marked and severe functional limitations," 42 U.S.C. § 1382c(a)(3)(C)(i), as opposed to the "inability to engage in substantial gainful activity."

The difference between these two standards—the general standard that applies to all OASDI claims and to SSI claims by adults and the special SSI standard that applies only to claims by children under the age of 18—is seen most dramatically in how they are implemented by the Social Security Administration. Claims for benefits under the general standard are evaluated by a 5-step "sequential evaluation process," which includes the use of a listing of qualifying impairments but also allows an individualized assessment of the claimant's medical and vocational capacity to work. Claims by children under the special SSI child's disability benefits standard are evaluated by means of a shorter version of the sequential evaluation process that lays greater emphasis on the claimant's condition meeting or equaling the requirements of a similar listing of qualified impairments. The two disability standards are alike, however, in a number of respects: both require that the disability result from a medically determinable physical or mental impairment, and both require that the impairment has lasted, or is expected to last, at least 12 months—or is expected to result in death. The implementation of both standards and the operation of the sequential evaluation process are discussed in detail in Chapter 5. Special issues of disability determination under both standards are covered in Chapter 6.

A. DISABILITY STANDARD FOR ADULTS

As mentioned above, the general disability standard applicable to OASDI claims by wage earners, their surviving spouses, and their children 18 years of age or older, as well as by adults under the SSI program, is stated in the Social Security Act as the "inability to engage in any substantial gainful activity" resulting from a medically determinable physical or mental impairment that has lasted or can be expected to last for at least a year, or can be expected to result in death. 42 U.S.C. § 423(d)(1)(A). The disability standard for SSI adult claims has slightly different introductory language, with the standard phrased in terms of an individual who is "unable to engage in any substantial gainful activity." 42 U.S.C. § 1382c(a)(3)(A). The substance of the two standards is the same, however, and they are interpreted consistently as being essentially identical. *See* Bowen v. Yuckert, 482 U.S. 137, 140 (1987) (stating that both titles of the Social Security Act define "disability" as the inability to engage in substantial gainful activity); Perez v. Chater, 77 F.3d 41, 46 (2d Cir. 1996).

In effect, the general disability standard has three separate components: first, a severity requirement defined as the "inability to engage in any substantial gainful activity"; second, an origin requirement which specifies that the disability must be based on a "medically determinable physical or mental impairment"; and third, a duration requirement which limits eligibility to cases where the disability "can be expected to result in death or . . . has lasted or can be expected to last for a continuous period of not less than 12 months." 42 U.S.C. § 1382c(a)(3)(A). Each of these requirements must be met; for example, a short-term disability, no matter how severe, will not establish eligibility for benefits.

The disability standard further clarifies the severity requirement by specifying that an individual meets the standard for disability "only if his physical or mental impairment or impairments are of such severity that he is not only unable to do his previous work but cannot, considering his age, education, and work experience, engage in any other kind of substantial gainful work which exists in the national economy." 42 U.S.C. §§ 423(d)(2)(A), 1382c(a)(3)(B). Moreover, the disability standard focuses on a claimant's ability to perform work, not on the ability to obtain employment. Thus, the Act specifies that a claimant's ability to perform substantial gainful activity is to be determined "regardless of whether such work exists in the immediate area in which he lives, or whether a specific job vacancy exists for him, or whether he would be hired." 42 U.S.C. §§ 423(d)(2)(A), 1382c(a)(3)(B). The ultimate question is whether the claimant is able to perform substantial gainful work that exists in the "national economy," defined as "work which exists in significant numbers either in the region where he lives or in several regions of the country." 42 U.S.C. §§ 423(d)(2)(A), 1382c(a)(3)(B).

The Act sets out a more generous interpretation of the "inability to engage in substantial gainful activity" for OASDI claimants over the age of 55 whose disability is based on blindness. *See* 42 U.S.C. § 423(d)(1)(B) ("requiring skills or abilities comparable to those of any gainful activity in which he has previously engaged with some regularity and over a substantial period of time"). Blindness is a separate and independent basis of eligibility for SSI. *See* 42 U.S.C. § 1382c(a)(1)(A).

In evaluating a claim against the disability standard, SSA must consider all of a claimant's impairments in combination. As set forth in the Act, the "combined impact" of a claimant's physical and mental impairments must be taken into account throughout the disability determination process. 42 U.S.C. § 423(d)(2)(B). *See also* 20 C.F.R. §§ 404.1523, 416.923.

1. DETERMINING A BENEFICIARY IS NO LONGER DISABLED

Closely tied to the disability standard is a provision in the Social Security Act that specifies the basis for determining that someone who once met the standard is no longer disabled. Two conflicting approaches were litigated in the 1980s: requiring a showing of "medical improvement" sufficient to establish that a beneficiary was no longer disabled, as opposed to allowing benefits to be terminated whenever a beneficiary no longer met the statutory definition of disability. Congress resolved the conflict in 1984 amendments to the Act. Under the Act as amended, disability benefits can be terminated if "there has been any medical improvement in the [claimant's] impairment or combination of impairments (other than medical improvement which is not related to the [claimant's] ability to work)" and the claimant can engage in substantial gainful activity. 42 U.S.C. §§ 423(f)(1), 1382c(a)(4)(A)(i). There are, however, three exceptions that allow termination without a showing of medical improvement: if there is new medical evidence and a new assessment of the claimant's residual functional capacity that shows the claimant has benefited from medical or vocational therapy or technology related to his or her ability to work; if the claimant has, in fact, undergone vocational therapy related to his or her ability to work; or if new or improved diagnostic techniques or evaluations establish that the claimant's impairment or combination of impairments was not as disabling as had been found at the last disability determination. 42 U.S.C. §§ 423(f)(2)–(3), 1382c(a)(4)(A)(i). Finally, benefits can be terminated without a showing of medical improvement or proof of the claimant's ability to engage in substantial gainful activity if the claimant is, in fact, engaging in substantial gainful activity, if the prior determination of disability was obtained fraudulently, or if substantial evidence from the record of the prior determination—or new evidence relating to that determination—establishes that it was made in error. 42 U.S.C. §§ 423(f)(4), 1382c(a)(4)(C). *See also* 20 C.F.R. §§ 404.1594, 416.994.

Federal regulations implementing the medical improvement standard clarify that the exceptions are to be applied narrowly. *See* 50 Fed. Reg. 50118, 50123 (December 6, 1985) ("The language in the revised rules has been extensively changed to clarify our original intent that these exceptions only apply in the limited circumstances described by the statute and discussed in the legislative history."); 20 C.F.R. §§ 404.1594(d), 416.994(d) ("The law provides for certain limited situations when your disability can be found to have ended even though medical improvement has not occurred, if you can engage in substantial gainful activity."). The medical improvement standard applies equally in "closed period" cases, where the issue is whether a claimant was disabled for a finite period of time, as well as those involving a "period of disability." *See* Shepherd v. Apfel, 184 F.3d 1196, 1198, 63 Soc. Sec. Rep. Ser. 125 (10th Cir. 1999) (citing 42 U.S.C. § 423(f) and 20 C.F.R. § 404.1594(b)(1)). (As explained in Chapter 2, one can establish a "period of disability" that may affect one's insured status for OASDI benefits by meeting the requirements for eligibility apart from whether one would receive cash benefits for all or part of that period.)

When a beneficiary appeals a decision to terminate benefits, the issue on appeal is whether the beneficiary was disabled not at the time the initial decision to terminate was made, but rather at any time through the date of the final decision on appeal. SSR 13–3p (2013). For a typical case in which a termination of benefits was affirmed, see Glenn v. Shalala, 21 F.3d 983, 986 (10th Cir. 1994) ("In connection with the statute and pertinent regulations, it is important to note the critical findings of the ALJ here concerning the claimant's alleged improvement. In his written decision, the

ALJ found there has been medical improvement by claimant related to her ability to perform work-related activities and that she is capable of performing her past relevant work; therefore, he found that she no longer continues to be under a disability within the meaning of the Act."). *See also* SSR 18–1p, n. 20 (2018) (an SSI claimant can also be determined to have had a closed period of disability when the claimant was disabled for at least 12 continuous months and his or her disability ceased after the month of filing, but prior to the date of adjudication).

B. DISABILITY STANDARD FOR CHILDREN

There are two categories of disability benefits available to children in the Social Security Act: OASDI benefits for wage earners' adult disabled children, and SSI benefits for children under the age of 18. The disability standard for OASDI child's benefits is the same as the standard discussed in the previous section for adults. *See* 42 U.S.C. § 402(d)(1)(B). As explained in Chapter 3, dependent children of wage earners are eligible for benefits up to the age of 18 or 19 (if enrolled full-time in school) without regard to disability. Therefore, a wage earner's child would apply for disability benefits only after reaching the age of 18; in other words, disability is an eligibility requirement for OASDI child's benefits only once a "child" is an adult.

1. SSI DISABILITY STANDARD FOR CHILDREN UNDER THE AGE OF 18

Under the SSI program, by contrast, disability benefits are paid to persons with limited income and resources at any age. Accordingly, the SSI program uses a separate child's disability standard for claimants under the age of 18. Over the years, there has been a substantial amount of difficulty and controversy regarding the implementation of the disability standard for SSI child's benefits, in part because the base notion of disability under the Social Security Act—the inability to work at a job—does not adapt well to the special circumstances of disabled children (and particularly so for very young children). The current operative language in the Act, revised in 1996, provides that children are considered disabled for purposes of SSI if they have "marked and severe functional limitations," as opposed to being unable to engage in substantial gainful activity. Consistent with the adult disability standard, a child SSI claimant must show that these functional limitations are due to medically determinable physical or mental impairments that have lasted or can be expected to last for at least 12 months (or can be expected to result in death). *See* 42 U.S.C. § 1382c(a)(3)(C); 20 C.F.R. § 416.906.

2. OASDI CHILD'S BENEFITS: PROOF OF DISABILITY BEFORE THE AGE OF 22

While the disability standard for child's OASDI benefits is the same as that used for disability claims by adults, child claimants must also prove that they met the standard before the age of 22. 42 U.S.C. § 402(d)(1)(B); 20 C.F.R. § 404.350(a)(5). This is not a problem for claimants who apply before or shortly after they become 22 years old. Often, however, there is a substantial time lag before a child applies for benefits. In such cases, the status of the child's disability during the intervening years can be critical. *See, e.g.,* Palomo v. Commissioner, 579 F.Supp.2d 84, 137 Soc. Sec. Rep. Serv. 529 (D.D.C. 2008) (applied for child disability benefits in 2000; few records and only three exhibits from prior to twenty-second birthday in 1974). Apart from problems with obtaining proof that may be stale, one must prove that the disabling impairment existed continuously from the alleged onset date to the date from which benefits are sought. *See, e.g.*, Miller v. Shalala, 859 F. Supp. 297, 300, 45 Soc. Sec. Rep. Ser. 457 (S.D. Ohio 1994) (34-year-old claimant not disabled continuously since age 22).

Although child's benefit claims by adult children are assessed according to the adult disability standard, SSA has recognized that "young adults" may be evaluated somewhat differently than older adults. Basically, it evaluates disability for claimants between the ages of 18 and 25 in a similar way as it does for those considered "older adolescents" in the SSI program (between the ages of 12 and 18). *See* SSR 11–2p (2011) (setting out special rules for evaluating evidence of functioning from school programs, community experiences, psychosocial supports, structured settings, and other types of extra help and accommodations).

C. TREATMENT OF DISABILITY DECISIONS BY OTHER AGENCIES

Disability benefit determinations by agencies other than SSA for benefit programs utilizing statutory disability standards different from those in the Social Security Act may be relevant in a Social Security disability benefits claim. While current medical evidence regulations from 2017 clearly distance SSA's disability determination process from that of other agencies, a determination of disability by another agency can be important evidence. Clearly, SSA is not bound by such determinations. As explained in 20 C.F.R. §§ 404.1504, 416.904: "Because a decision by any other governmental agency or a nongovernmental entity about whether you are disabled, blind, employable, or entitled to any benefits is based on its rules, it is not binding on us and is not our decision about whether you are disabled or blind under our rules.". At the same time, the agency "will consider all of the supporting evidence underlying the other governmental agency or nongovernmental entity's decision that we receive as evidence in your claim" in the same manner as any other evidence. *Id.*

The most common parallel disability decisions relevant to Social Security disability benefit claims are those that concern claims for veterans disability benefits. The United States Department of Veterans Affairs (VA) provides two types of disability benefits: Veterans Compensation and Veterans Disability Pension (often referred to as veterans disability). To receive Veterans Compensation, the claimant's disability must be service connected. Therefore, if a claim is denied because the VA found that the disability did not result from a service-related activity, the VA's decision to deny benefits would have no bearing on a claim for Social Security benefits. On the other hand, caselaw makes it clear that a VA finding of disability for purposes of non-service-connected Veterans Disability Pension benefits must be considered by SSA when determining disability. (The question of whether or to what extent the 2017 medical evidence regulations supersede pre-existing circuit caselaw is discussed in Chapter 9).

A significant amount of caselaw developed prior to the publication of the 2017 regulation on the question of how much weight should be given to VA decisions. Since current regulations continue to acknowledge that SSA will consider evidence underlying determinations by other agencies, those cases remain relevant. As the court stated in Joseph v. Commissioner, 741 Fed. Appx. 306 (6th Cir. 2018), shortly after the 2017 regulation was published: "The basis for this regulation is sound: different rules applied by other agencies 'may limit the relevance of a determination of disability made by another agency.' Still, we have clarified that an ALJ must at least consider a VA's disability decision and explain reasons for the weight she assigns to it." (citing a 2013 case and referencing a 2006 Ruling.) Thus, for example, the Fifth Circuit has stated that VA decisions are entitled to "great weight." Johnson v. Sullivan, 894 F.2d 683, 686, 28 Soc. Sec. Rep. Serv. 397 (5th Cir. 1990). *See also* McCartey v. Massanari,

298 F.3d 1072, 1076, 82 Soc. Sec. Rep. Serv. 530 (9th Cir. 2002) (given the "marked similarity" between the two programs, ALJs "must ordinarily give great weight to a VA determination of disability"). Other courts have stated that a VA disability decision is "critically relevant," Fowler v. Califano, 596 F.2d 600, 603 (3d Cir. 1979), "entitled to serious consideration," Champion v. Califano, 440 F. Supp. 1014, 1019 n. 9 (D.D.C. 1977), and "persuasive evidence," Williams v. Mathews, 456 F. Supp. 1125, 1129 (M.D. La. 1978). But some courts have been more cautious. *See, e.g.*, Baca v. Department of Health and Human Services, 5 F.3d 476, 480, 42 Soc. Sec. Rep. Serv. 301 (10th Cir. 1993) ("entitled to weight and must be considered"); Bird v. Comm'r of Soc. Sec. Admin., 699 F.3d 337, 343, 185 Soc. Sec. Rep. Serv. 20 (4th Cir. 2012) (while VA determination given "substantial weight," given differences in standards and circumstances "an ALJ may give less weight to a VA disability rating when the record before the ALJ clearly demonstrates that such a deviation is appropriate."); Pelkey v. Barnhart, 433 F.3d 575, 579 (8th Cir. 2006) ("should consider" but "not bound").

Another common claim is that a denial of Social Security benefits is not consistent with disability findings by state workers' compensation agencies. This argument usually fails because of the significant difference between the two programs' purposes and standards. *See, e.g.*, Mortise v. Astrue, 713 F.Supp.2d 111, 125 (N.D.N.Y. 2010)("ALJ was correct granting the disability findings "little weight," because they were formed in a Workers' Compensation context.);

Rosado v. Shalala, 868 F.Supp. 471, 473 (E.D.N.Y.1994)("Although plaintiff's doctors had checked off that plaintiff was disabled on forms sent to the Workers' Compensation Board, the standards which regulate workers' compensation relief are different from the requirements which govern the award of disability insurance benefits under the Act.") (citing Coria v. Heckler, 750 F.2d 245, 247 (3d Cir.1984)).

A different issue is raised by simultaneous applications for both unemployment and disability benefits, given that an application for Social Security disability benefits asserts that one is unable to engage in substantial gainful activity while an application for unemployment insurances asserts the ability to work. Such dual applications may raise questions of credibility. *See, e.g.*, Smith v. Colvin, 756 F.3d 621, 625 (8th Cir. 2014) ("Applying for unemployment benefits adversely affects credibility, although it is not conclusive, because an unemployment applicant 'must hold himself out as available, willing and able to work.') (quoting Jernigan v. Sullivan, 948 F.2d 1070, 1074 (8th Cir.1991)); Schmidt v. Barnhart, 395 F.3d 737, 745 (7th Cir. 2005) ("[W]e are not convinced that a Social Security claimant's decision to apply for unemployment benefits and represent to state authorities and prospective employers that he is able and willing to work should play absolutely no role in assessing his subjective complaints of disability.") On the other hand, in Ghanim v. Colvin, 763 F.3d 1154, 1164 (9th Cir. 2014) the court rejected the ALJ's discounting of the claimant's testimony because he received unemployment benefits after the alleged onset date of his disability. Noting that while receipt of unemployment benefits can cast doubt on a claim of disability where the claimant declined benefits within about a month of onset date, the court concluded that "rather than undercut his claim of disability, this prompt refusal of unemployment benefits supports it." *See generally*, Memorandum from U.S. Chief Administrative Judge Frank A. Christaudo, "*Receipt of Unemployment Insurance Benefits by Claimant Applying for Disability Benefits-INFORMATION,*" Nov. 15, 2006, Reference: 07-11 ("This is a reminder that the receipt of Unemployment Insurance Benefits does not preclude the receipt of Social Security disability benefits. The receipt of Unemployment Benefits is only one of many factors that must be considered in determining whether the claimant is disabled. *See* 20 C.F.R. §§ 404.1512(b) and 416.912(b).").

CHAPTER 5

DISABILITY DETERMINATION PROCESS

As discussed in Chapter 4, the general disability standard governing adult claims for disability benefits under both the Old Age, Survivors, and Disability Insurance (OASDI) and Supplemental Security Income (SSI) programs, although relatively sophisticated, is quite simple and straightforward: benefits are provided to people who, as the result of a physical or mental impairment, cannot perform a basic level of work activity at a job they have held in the past or at any other job that they could be expected to hold, given their age, education, and prior work history. The disability standard for SSI child's benefits is a little less concrete, but still perfectly understandable: benefits are provided to children under the age of 18 with a physical or mental impairment resulting in "marked and severe" functional limitations.

The administrative challenge for the Social Security Administration is applying these standards effectively and efficiently to millions of Social Security and SSI disability claims each year, of which hundreds of thousands are contested to one degree or another. Accordingly, SSA promulgated a set of regulations that lay out a "sequential evaluation process" for determining whether a claimant is disabled. (Earlier Social Security regulations had used the term "sequential evaluation process" and that term is still widely used.) A distinctive 5-step process is used for applying the general disability standard applicable to all disability claims under the OASDI program and all adult claims under the SSI program. A truncated version of the full 5-step process is used for applying the separate disability standard applicable to claims for SSI benefits by children under the age of 18.

The sequential evaluation process provides the framework for this chapter. The next section describes the process generally and how it is used for both adult and child claims. Subsequent sections discuss its component parts in greater detail, including the key issues raised at each step. The focus is on the 5-step process for adult claims, with additional comment on the truncated process for child claims where relevant. The chapter concludes with a brief discussion of a separate extended process, similar to the sequential evaluation process, used when disability benefits are terminated on medical grounds.

A. SEQUENTIAL EVALUATION PROCESS

The sequential evaluation process used for disability claims under the OASDI program and for adult SSI claims tests a claimant's evidence of disability at five distinct steps, each of which raises different factual and legal issues relative to a finding of disability. The process operates like a flow chart, as seen in the figure below. At each step, depending on the facts, the claim is either resolved with a finding that the claimant is disabled or not disabled, or, if neither finding can be made, the process continues to the next step. For evaluations that reach the fifth step, the process ends there—again, depending on the facts—with a finding that either the claimant is disabled or is not disabled. 20 C.F.R. §§ 404.1520, 416.920. There are, however, two limited situations where the regulations adjust the sequential evaluation process for certain claims. *See* 20 C.F.R. §§ 404.1520(h), 414.920(h) (providing for an "expedited" move from Step 3 to Step 5, skipping Step 4); 20 C.F.R. §§ 404.1520(g)(2), 404.1652, 416.920(g)(2), 416.962 (directing a finding of disabled for claimants with particularly significant vocational limitations).

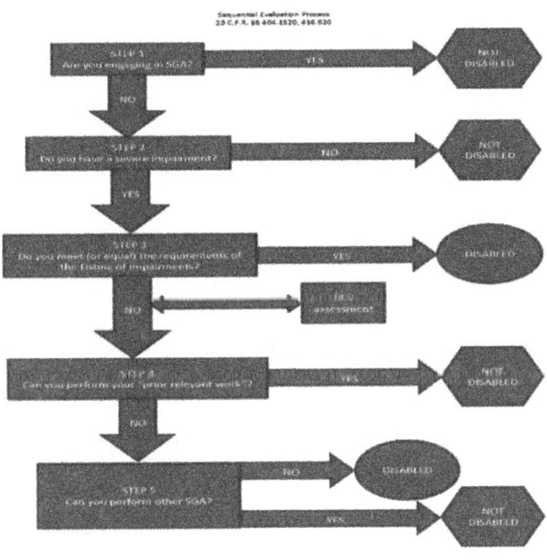

In effect, the sequential evaluation process poses a series of questions as it moves along the five steps:

STEP 1: The question at Step 1 is whether the claimant is performing substantial gainful activity. 20 C.F.R. §§ 404.1520(a)(4)(i), 416.920(a)(4)(i). If so, the claimant is considered not disabled regardless of their medical condition and the process ends there. 20 C.F.R. §§ 404.1520(b), 416.920(b).

STEP 2: If the claimant is not currently engaging in substantial gainful activity, the process moves to Step 2, where the question is whether the claimant has a "severe" physical or mental impairment that significantly limits their ability to perform work. To qualify as a "severe" impairment at this step, it must also meet the duration requirement set out in the Social Security Act; that is, it must have lasted 12 month or be expected to last at least 12 months or to result in death. 20 C.F.R. §§ 404.1520(a)(4)(ii), 404.1520(c), 416.920(a)(4)(ii), 404.920(c). If not, the claimant is considered not disabled and the process ends there. (As discussed later in this section, SSA must consider the combined effect of claimants' impairments, if they have more than one.)

STEP 3: If the claimant does have a severe impairment and meets the duration requirement, the evaluation process continues on to Step 3. The question there is whether the claimant's medical condition meets or equals the criteria for one of the disabling impairments set out in the Social Security Administration's Listing of Impairments. 20 C.F.R. §§ 404.1520(a)(4)(iii), 404.1520(d), 416.920(a)(4)(iii), 416.920(d). If so, the process ends with a finding that the claimant is disabled (regardless of age, work experience, or education).

STEP 4: If the claimant's impairment does not meet or equal the requirements of the Listing of Impairments the claim continues to Step 4, which asks a medical-vocational question: whether the claimant is prevented from performing their past relevant work. 20 C.F.R. §§ 404.1520(a)(4)(iv), 404.1520(e)–(f), 416.920(a)(4)(iv), 416.920(e)–(f). If not, the claimant is considered not disabled and the process stops there.

STEP 5: If the claimant is prevented from performing their past relevant work, the process reaches the fifth and final step, which asks whether—considering the claimant's residual functional capacity, age, education, and prior work experience—they can perform other substantial gainful work that is available in significant numbers in the national economy. 20 C.F.R. §§ 404.1520(a)(4)(v), 404.1520(g), 416.920(a)(4)(v), 416.920(g). If such other work is available, the claimant is not disabled; if not, then the claimant is disabled.

The first three steps of the process allow for relatively quick determinations by focusing on relatively narrow issues. The last two steps—determining whether the claimant can perform past relevant work and, if not, determining whether the claimant can perform other work which is available in the economy—look more broadly by incorporating an assessment of the claimant's "residual functional capacity" (RFC) and various vocational factors into the analysis. A claimant's RFC is a measure of the extent to which limitations resulting from claimants' physical and mental impairments affect their ability to work; it is an evaluation of "what [the claimant] can still do despite [those] limitations." *See* 20 C.F.R. §§ 404.1545(a), 416.945(a). In determining a claimant's RFC level and throughout the process, SSA will consider the combined effect of multiple impairments. RFC and the combinations of impairments are discussed in more detail later in this chapter.

The Supreme Court described the sequential evaluation process as follows in Bowen v. Yuckert, 482 U.S. 137, 153, 17 Soc. Sec. Rep. Serv. 661 (1987):

> Step one determines whether the claimant is engaged in 'substantial gainful activity.' If he is, disability benefits are denied. . . . If he is not, the decisionmaker proceeds to step two, which determines whether the claimant has a medically severe impairment or combination of impairments. . . . If the claimant does not have a severe impairment or combination of impairments, the disability claim is denied. If the impairment is severe, the evaluation proceeds to the third step, which determines whether the impairment is equivalent to one of a number of listed impairments that the

> Secretary acknowledges are so severe as to preclude substantial gainful activity. . . . If the impairment meets or equals one of the listed impairments, the claimant is conclusively presumed to be disabled. If the impairment is not one that is conclusively presumed to be disabling, the evaluation proceeds to the fourth step, which determines whether the impairment prevents the claimant from performing work he has performed in the past. If the claimant is able to perform his previous work, he is not disabled. . . . If the claimant cannot perform this work, the fifth and final step of the process determines whether he is able to perform other work in the national economy in view of his age, education, and work experience. The claimant is entitled to disability benefits only if he is not able to perform other work.

Generally, claimants have the burden of proof on the issue of disability. *See* 42 U.S.C. § 423(d)(5)(A) ("An individual shall not be considered to be under a disability unless he furnishes such medical and other evidence of the existence thereof as the Commissioner of Social Security may require"); *see also* 20 C.F.R. §§ 404.1512(a), 416.912(a). This applies generally with regard to the sequential evaluation process as well; however, case law makes it clear that upon proof that a claimant cannot perform prior work at Step 4, the burden shifts to the Social Security Administration to prove that the claimant can perform other work available in the national economy at Step 5. As the Court explained in Bowen v. Yuckert, *supra*: "the [Social Security

Administration] bears the burden of proof at step five, which determines whether the claimant is able to perform work available in the national economy. But the Secretary is required to bear this burden only if the sequential evaluation process proceeds to the fifth step." 482 U.S. at 146 n. 5. *See also* Pass v. Chater, 65 F.3d 1200, 1203 (4th Cir. 1995) ("The applicant bears the burden of production and proof during the first four steps of the inquiry. If he or she is able to carry this burden through the fourth step, the burden shifts to the Secretary in the fifth step to show that other work is available in the national economy which the claimant could perform.") This shift in the burden of proof is discussed in more detail when Steps 4 and 5 are covered later in this chapter.

When followed fairly and correctly, the sequential evaluation process is an effective way to reach decisions in accordance with the words and goals of the statutory disability standard. As noted earlier, the first three steps are particularly efficient to the extent that they can direct a finding of disabled or not disabled without a lengthy review of the record. Thus, claimants who are actually engaging in "substantial gainful activity" or have no "severe" impairments are denied quickly and relatively easily at Steps 1 or 2; those with impairments that meet (or equal) the limited, strict criteria set forth in the SSA's Listing of Impairments are granted benefits quickly and relatively objectively at Step 3. The last two steps take on the closer cases—those that cannot be resolved fully at one of the first three steps—and address the more complex medical-vocational aspects of the disability standard. Step 4 is still relatively focused; claimants who can still perform jobs that they held in the past—jobs that, by definition, are within their vocational competence—are denied benefits on that ground. Only at step 5 does the process deal with the open-ended, ultimate question of whether the claimant can perform any jobs at all, given their age, education, and work experience. (As discussed later in this chapter, there are other special rules and guidelines that assist with step 5 decisions).

The sequential evaluation process is used throughout the administrative process and is fully accepted by the courts as a proper framework for analysis of a disability claim. *See, e.g.*, Combs v. Commissioner of Social Security, 459 F.3d 640, 649 (6th Cir. 2006) ("The entire five-step sequential evaluation process has been designed to regulate adjudicatory conduct for the purpose of making adjudication of claims efficient and flexible."); Dugas v. Astrue, 2009 WL 1780121 (E.D. Tex. June 22, 2009) ("Administrative adjudicators of social security disability claims utilize a five-step, sequential evaluation process prescribed by regulation and approved by courts as a fair and just way for determining disability applications in conformity with the Social Security Act and as contributing to uniformity and efficiency in such determinations."). Moreover, courts review ALJ decisions according to how they applied the process and failure to follow the process is considered legal error. *See* Hill v. Colvin, 753 F.3d 798, 801 (8th Cir. 2014) ("An ALJ commits legal error if [he or she] fails to follow the sequential evaluation process"). *See also* Mitchell v. Schweiker,

551 F. Supp. 1084, 1087–88 (W.D. Mo. 1982) ("It is important for the [administrative law judge] to follow the orderly framework set out in the [sequential evaluation regulations] to ensure uniformity and regularity in outcome as well as fairness to the claimant.").

The sequential evaluation process also provides a straightforward and effective means for courts to review individual claims for benefits. *See, e.g.*, Plummer v. Apfel, 186 F.3d 422, 428–29, 63 Soc. Sec. Rep. Ser. 264 (3d Cir. 1999) (summarizing the five steps of the process and reviewing its application to the claimant at each step). Judicial review and federal courts' oversight of SSA's administrative process are discussed in detail in Chapter 8.

1. THE SEQUENTIAL EVALUATION PROCESS FOR CHILD SSI CLAIMS

As noted earlier and in Chapter 4, claims for SSI benefits on behalf of disabled children under the age of 18 are assessed according to a separate disability standard. The current standard, enacted as part of 1996 reforms, provides that a child is disabled for purposes of SSI if the child "has a medically determinable physical or mental impairment, which results in marked and severe functional limitations, and which can be expected to result in death or which has lasted or can be expected to last for a continuous period of not less than 12 months." 42 U.S.C. § 1382c(a)(3)(C)(i). While this standard includes the familiar requirement that a child claim be based on a "medically determinable physical or mental impairment" that "can be expected to result in death or which has lasted or can be expected to last for a continuous period of not less than 12 months," SSA uses a modified version of the sequential evaluation process to determine disability for Child's SSI claims designed to implement the special "marked and severe functional limitations" severity standard for that program. Before describing that process, some background about how the sequential evaluation process was used for child SSI claims before the 1996 reforms will be helpful.

Federal benefits were first provided for children with disabilities in 1974 when the federal-state public assistance program for the aged, blind and disabled (AABD) was replaced by the federal SSI program and responsibility for that program was given to SSA. At that time, the Social Security Act provided that children were disabled for purposes of the SSI program if they "suffer[ed] from any medically determinable physical or mental impairment of comparable severity" to an impairment that would qualify as disabling under the adult program. 42 U.S.C. § 1382c(c)(3)(A) (1974). Reasoning that the fourth and fifth steps of the sequential evaluation process, with their focus on work activity, were not applicable to claims by children, SSA simply cut off the sequential evaluation process for child SSI claims after the first three steps. As a result, children could receive SSI only if they had an impairment, or combination of impairments, that met or equaled either the requirements of the general (Part A) or special children's (Part B) Listing of Impairments. 20 C.F.R.

§ 416.923 (1974). (SSA added Part B to the Listing of Impairments to account for certain medical conditions unique to children that were not included in Part A, recognizing that it may not be appropriate to limit the determination of children's disabilities to the general Listing of Impairments.)

SSA's 3-step process for Child SSI claims was challenged, beginning in the 1980s, on the ground that it was inconsistent with the "comparable severity" language in the disability standard for children as set out in the Social Security Act. The basic argument was that limiting disability determinations to the first three steps of the sequential evaluation precluded a finding of disability for children with impairments comparable to those of adults who would be found disabled at Steps 4 or 5 of the full sequential process. Some courts upheld SSA's approach, noting that the agency was entitled to deference when interpreting the statute and that adopting the 3-step process was within its broad rule making power. *See, e.g.*, Powell By and Through Powell v. Schweiker, 688 F.2d 1357, 1360–61 (11th Cir.) , *reh'g denied,* 694 F.2d 727 (11th Cir. 1982); Hinckley on Behalf of Martin v. Secretary of Health and Human Services, 742 F.2d 19 (1st Cir. 1984). Other courts rejected SSA's implementation of the statutory language. The Third Circuit, for example, declined to follow Hinckley because the Listing of Impairments ignores functional consequences of impairments, yet "only impaired ability to function . . . results in disability." Zebley by Zebley v. Bowen, 855 F.2d 67, 74 (3d Cir. 1988).

The Supreme Court resolved the split and invalidated the 3-step process in Sullivan v. Zebley, 493 U.S. 521, 110 S. Ct. 885, 28 Soc. Sec. Rep. Serv. 367 (1990). The Court noted first that the criteria set out in the Listing of Impairments are more restrictive than the "comparable severity" disability standard in the Act. Specifically, it found that the Listing does not cover all possible impairments; for those medical conditions covered in the Listing, the criteria listed are set at a higher level of severity that requires that claimants be precluded from "any gainful activity" rather than from just "substantial gainful activity" as set out in the Act; the Listing does not provide for any individualized assessment of the effects of an impairment, given the claimant's age, education, and work experience; and claimants with unlisted impairments, or a combination of impairments that do not equal the criteria set out for a listed impairment, are excluded. 493 U.S. at 533–534. The Court thus concluded that "no set of listings could ensure that child claimants would receive benefits whenever their impairments are of 'comparable severity' to ones that would qualify an adult for benefits under the individualized, functional analysis contemplated by the statute and provided to adults by the Secretary." 493 U.S. at 539.

The Social Security Administration issued a complex set of regulations for child SSI claims designed to conform the sequential evaluation process with the ruling in *Zebley*, adding an age-appropriate "individualized functional assessment" to determine whether those functional limitations imposed a level of disability comparable to that set out in the adult standard. *See* 20 C.F.R. §§ 416.924, 924e (1995). Those regulations were short lived, however, as Congress repealed the Social Security Act's "comparable severity" disability standard for children a few years later and substituted the current standard, thereby effectively reversing the Supreme Court's decision in *Zebley*. *See* Personal Responsibility and Work Opportunity Reconciliation Act of 1996. Pub. L. No. 104–193, 110 Stat. 2105 (1996). SSA followed up on the 1996 amendments with the current sequential evaluation process for determining disability for children, which is essentially a more flexible version of the truncated pre-*Zebley* 3-step process. *See* 20 C.F.R. § 416.924.

As was the case initially, the first two steps of the current 3-step sequential evaluation process for child's SSI claims operate in the same manner as do the first two steps of the 5-step process for adult claims. Benefits are denied if the claimant is engaging in "substantial gainful activity" (Step 1) or does not have a "severe" impairment (Step 2). After that, the process for children deviates substantially. As with the adult process, the process for children process poses a series of questions as it moves along the three steps:

STEP 1: The question at Step 1 is whether the child is actually performing substantial gainful activity. If so, the child is considered not disabled—regardless of their medical condition—and the process ends. 20 C.F.R. § 416.924(b).

STEP 2: If the child is not currently engaging in substantial gainful activity, the process moves to Step 2, which asks whether the child has a severe impairment (or combination of impairments) that significantly limits their ability to perform work. If not, the child is considered not disabled and the process ends there. 20 C.F.R. § 416.924(c).

STEP 3: If the child does have a severe impairment and meets the same duration requirement applied to adult claims, the evaluation process continues on to a third and final step. While the sequential evaluation process for children does end at Step 3, the third step in the Child's SSI sequential evaluation process is less restrictive than is Step 3 for adult claims in one important respect. Children will be found disabled at Step 3 not only if they have an impairment or combination of impairments that meets or equals the requirements of the Listing of Impairments, but also if the impairment(s) "functionally equals" the requirements of the Listing. 20 C.F.R. § 416.924(d).

The Child's SSI sequential evaluation process is used only for periods when claimants are, or were, under the age of 18. For claimants that reach age 18 after filing a disability claim but before a decision is made by SSA, the process for children will be used for the period during which the claimant was under 18 and the adult process will be used for the period beginning with the day the claimant reached age 18. 20 C.F.R. § 416.924(f).

SSA has recognized that a child's chronological age can be an important factor in evaluating an impairment beyond simply being under the age of 18. Thus, there are special rules acknowledging the need to treat various chronological age categories differently when assessing the capacity of children at various steps in the child's SSI sequential evaluation process. For example, age is a consideration when determining the severity of an impairment and when comparing the claimant's impairment to a listing that includes specific age categories. *See* 20 C.F.R. § 416.924b. *See also* 20 C.F.R., Part 404, Subpart P, Appx. 1 (Listings) § 100.00A (Listing for low birth weight and failure to thrive, which applies only from birth to the age of one for low birth weight and from birth to the age of three for failure to thrive). For some child claimants born prematurely (at less than 37 weeks' gestation), a corrected chronological age may be used in the evaluation to adjust for any discrepancy between developmental age and chronological age. 20 C.F.R. § 416.924b(b). Rules identifying and recognizing limits of specific categories of chronological age for purposes of evaluating disability exist also for adults at Step 5 of the adult sequential evaluation process, which are discussed later in this chapter.

2. COMBINATION OF IMPAIRMENTS

Each step of the sequential evaluation process, other than Step 1, requires an assessment of the claimant's alleged physical or mental impairment—or combination of impairments. Although the Social Security Act conditions eligibility on work incapacity resulting from "any medically determinable physical or mental impairment," the definition of disability has long been interpreted to include the inability to engage in substantial gainful activity resulting from a combination of impairments as well. Following some controversy about combining impairments at Step 2, the Act was amended to state specifically that a combination of impairments can satisfy the severity requirement of the sequential evaluation process. *See* Social Security Disability Benefits Reform Act of 1984, PL 98–460 § 4(a)(1), 98 Stat. 1794 (1984); 42 U.S.C.A. § 423(d)(2)(B). *See also* 20 C.F.R. §§ 404.1523(b), 416.923(b) (in determining medical severity SSA "will consider the combined effect of all of [a claimant's] impairments without regard to whether any such impairment, if considered separately, would be of sufficient severity.").

Social Security regulations also state clearly that combining impairments is also required at any other point in the sequential evaluation process where the claimant alleges disability due to the combined effect of more than one impairment. 20 C.F.R. §§ 404.1523(c), 416.923(c) ("If we do find a medically severe combination of impairments, the combined impact of the impairments will be considered throughout the disability determination process."). Similarly, the general regulation on the sequential evaluation process refers regularly to "impairment(s)." *See* 20 C.F.R. §§ 404.1520, 416.920. *See also* Barrett v. Barnhart, 355 F.3d 1065, 1068–69, 94 Soc. Sec. Rep. Serv. 7 (7th Cir. 2004) (evidence of arthritis, obesity, numbness and pain in arm; "all too characteristically, the administrative law judge failed to consider the applicant's medical situation as a whole").

Combinations of impairments can present different issues depending on which step in the sequential evaluation process a combination of impairments is presented. The treatment of combinations of impairments at various steps is discussed in further detail later in this chapter when those steps of the process are covered.

B. SIMPLIFIED DENIAL AT STEPS 1 AND 2: SUBSTANTIAL GAINFUL ACTIVITY, MINIMUM DURATION, AND SEVERITY

As mentioned in the previous section, the first two steps of the 5-step sequential evaluation process are designed to provide adjudicators with simple and efficient criteria for finding that, in the most obvious cases, a claimant is not disabled. Step 1 focuses on the concept of "substantial gainful activity" (often referred to as SGA). Persons who, at the relevant time, are actually engaging in substantial gainful activity are obviously not unable to perform "substantial gainful activity"—the key criterion for a finding of disability under the statute—and therefore are not eligible for benefits. Step 2 goes a little further than the first step and looks to see whether those claimants who are not currently engaging in substantial gainful activity have at least a minimal physical or mental impairment that has lasted, or is expected to last, at least one year—the minimum severity and duration criteria set out in the Act. Claimants who do not have a severe impairment cannot possibly meet the statutory requirement and therefore are not eligible for benefits. That does not mean, however, that claimants who have a "severe impairment" that has lasted, or is expected to last, at least one year are eligible for benefits; satisfying the minimal requirements at Step 2 just allows the claim to continue through the rest of the sequential evaluation process.

The first part of this section examines the concept of substantial gainful activity and how it is incorporated into Step 1 of the sequential evaluation process. (Substantial gainful activity is also discussed later in this chapter since it is used to assess a claimant's capacity to work at Steps 4 and 5 as well.) The second part of the section discusses the minimum severity and duration requirements that form the substance of Step 2.

1. STEP 1: SUBSTANTIAL GAINFUL ACTIVITY (SGA)

"Substantial gainful activity" is the measure of the minimum level of work activity that the Social Security Act considers necessary for an individual to be self-sustaining. If a claimant's capacities are such that they cannot perform at that minimum level—that is, cannot perform substantial gainful activity—then a finding of disability is warranted. *See* 20 C.F.R. §§ 404.1571, 416.971.

Substantial gainful activity is defined as work activity that is both substantial and gainful. Substantial work activity is defined in turn as any work activity that involves doing significant physical or mental activities, even when it is done part-time, for a lower wage, or with more limited responsibilities than work the claimant may have performed in the past. 20 C.F.R. §§ 404.1572(a), 416.972(a). While there is no doubt that part-time work can amount to substantial gainful activity at Step 1, it may not be substantial gainful activity at other steps of the sequential evaluation process. As mentioned earlier, in addition to being at the heart of any Step 1 analysis—where the focus is on whether any current work, or work-like, activity amounts to substantial gainful activity—substantial gainful activity is also a key factor at the end of the sequential evaluation process. At Step 5, for example, the question is whether claimants can perform other work that exists in the national economy, given their age, education, and prior work experience. Not only must there be other jobs in the economy that a claimant can perform, but those jobs must amount to substantial gainful activity. As explained later in this chapter when discussing Step 5, part-time work is not considered to be substantial gainful activity at that point in the sequential evaluation process—and proof that a claimant whose claim reaches Step 5 could do part-time work is not sufficient to support a finding of non-disability.

Gainful work activity is defined as work activity that is done, or usually done, for pay or for profit—even if it is not done in a work setting or does not actually result in profit for the claimant. 20 C.F.R. §§ 404.1572(b), 416.972(b). On the other hand, the ability to do a certain amount of "non-work" activity should not by itself establish the ability to engage in substantial gainful activity. Activities not generally considered to be substantial gainful activity include taking care of oneself, doing household tasks, hobbies, therapy, school attendance, club activities, and social programs. *See* 20 C.F.R. §§ 404.1572(c), 416.972(c). As one court has stated, the "[a]bility to drive an automobile, participate in some community affairs, attend school, or do some work on an intermittent basis does not necessarily establish that a person is able to engage in 'substantial gainful activity,' but such activity may be considered by SSA, along with medical testimony, in determining the right of a claimant to disability payments under the Act." Markham v. Califano, 601 F.2d 533, 534 (10th Cir. 1979). *See also* Cohen v. Secretary, 964 F.2d 524, 37 Soc. Sec. Rep. Ser. 341 (6th Cir. 1992) (attending law school classes for 3 ½ hours three days per week and doing homework approximately two hours per day, continuing ballroom dancing on a limited basis, and talking on the phone for two to three hours per week for a national support group did not establish the ability to perform SGA).

The Social Security Act authorizes SSA to promulgate regulations that "prescribe the criteria for determining when services performed—or earnings derived from services—demonstrate an individual's ability to engage in substantial gainful activity." 42 U.S.C. § 423(d)(4)(A). Thus, 20 C.F.R. §§ 404.1573, 416.973 set out criteria for measuring the nature of the work a claimant performs, how well it is done, and whether it is done under special conditions. Work that requires the use of an individual's experience, skills, supervision and responsibilities, or that contributes substantially to the operation of a business, tends to show that the individual has "the ability to work at the substantial gainful activity level." 20 C.F.R. §§ 404.1573(a), 416.973(a). On the other hand, work that involves "minimal duties that [make] little or no demands on [the claimant] and that are of little or no use to [the] employer, or to the operation of a business if [the claimant is] self-employed," tends to show that it is not substantial gainful activity. 20 C.F.R. §§ 404.1573(b), 416.973(b).

One of the key factors that SSA considers in determining whether claimants are engaged in substantial gainful activity is the amount of their earnings. Social Security regulations list amounts of earnings for given years that indicate the capacity to perform SGA; if a claimant's earnings exceed the amount listed for the relevant period, the work activity ordinarily is considered substantial and gainful. *See generally* 20 C.F.R. §§ 404.1574, 416.974. The amount of earnings that will trigger this presumption is adjusted yearly to account for national average wage growth. For the year 2021, earnings amounting to an average of $1,310 per month or more will ordinarily show that the work was substantial gainful activity. Prior to 2001, the regulations included both a lower and an upper threshold so that if a claimant's earnings were less than the low amount listed for the relevant period, the work activity ordinarily was considered not substantial and gainful; if an individual's earnings fell between those values, SSA would consider additional information, including work done by comparable, unimpaired individuals. 20 C.F.R. § 404.1574(b)(2)(i), (b)(6)(i), (b)(6)(iii) (2000). Current regulations do not include a lower threshold and SSA now generally will not consider information in addition to earnings unless there is other evidence indicating that the claimant, despite low earnings, may be engaged in substantial gainful activity. 20 C.F.R. §§ 404.1574(b)(2)(ii), 416.974(b)(2)(ii).

Although the value of an individual's earnings is used as a guide in determining if the work is substantial gainful activity, the key issue is whether the individual has the physical or mental capacity to earn at the requisite level. The regulations thus establish only a presumption that work is substantial gainful activity if the claimant earned more than the stated amount, and that presumption is rebuttable by the claimant. *See* 20 C.F.R. §§ 404.1574(a)(1), 416.974(a)(1) ("Generally, in evaluating your work activity for substantial gainful activity purposes, our primary consideration will be the earnings you derive from the work activity. We will use your earnings to determine whether you have done substantial gainful activity unless we have information from you, your employer, or others that shows that we should not count all of your earnings."). Thus, claimants who earn the listed amount or more may still be able to show that they are not, in fact, capable of engaging in substantial gainful activity. *But see* Dukes v. Barnhart, 436 F.3d 923, 927 (8th Cir. 2006) ("Because he is engaged in substantial gainful activity and has failed to rebut the presumption created by his earnings, Dukes is ineligible to receive SSI benefits."). While SSA has maintained that the post-2001 regulations eliminated a similar presumption that a claimant is not engaging is substantial gainful activity when earnings fall below the stated amount, some courts have effectively continued to follow the pre-2001 rule by applying a rebuttable presumption in those circumstances. *See, e.g.*, Copeland v. Colvin, 771 F.3d 920, 925–27, 210 Soc. Sec. Rep. Serv. 435 (5th Cir. 2014) (citing unpublished opinions to the same effect in the Third and Tenth Circuits).

When calculating a claimant's earnings, only the amounts actually earned, as opposed to the amounts actually received, are considered; that is, SSA should consider only the reasonable value of the work performed and exclude any earnings that exceed that value. 20 C.F.R. §§ 404.1574(a)(2), 416.974(a)(2). Therefore, the regulations detail special situations where SSA may determine that the full amount of an individual's earnings should not be used to determine if the work performed amounted to substantial gainful activity, such as when an individual's earnings are being effectively subsidized. 20 C.F.R. §§ 404.1574(a)(2)–(3), 416.974(a)(2)–(3). For example, if a person does simple tasks under close and continuous supervision, SSA will look at the amount of the wages paid but it will also determine whether the individual was being paid more than the reasonable value of the actual services performed, and will then subtract the amount of that difference from the person's gross earnings to determine if the work was, in fact, substantial gainful activity. *See* 20 C.F.R. §§ 404.1574(a)(2), 416.974(a)(2); Rossello v. Astrue, 529 F.3d 1181, 132 Soc. Sec. Rep. Serv. 462

(D.C. Cir. 2008) (earnings were subsidized where claimant worked for her uncle performing only simple, basic tasks under close supervision by family members and for which she would not otherwise have been hired).

SSA regulations specify further various circumstances it will consider to determine if a claimant is working under special conditions that may indicate that the work is not substantial gainful activity, such as where the claimant is given special assistance while performing work tasks or is allowed to work "at a lower standard of productivity or efficiency." 20 C.F.R. §§ 404.1573(c)(1), 404(c)(5), 416.973(c)(1), 416(c)(5). Other examples of special conditions include situations in which claimants "required and received special assistance," were "allowed to work irregular hours or take frequent rest periods," were provided "special equipment" or assigned "work especially suited" to the claimant's impairment," could work only under "specially arranged circumstances," worked at a "lower standard of productivity or efficiency" than others, and were able to work only "because of family relationship, past association with [their] employer, or [their] employer's concern for [their] welfare." *See generally* 20 C.F.R. §§ 404.1573(c), 416.973(c). Thus, treating earnings above SSA guidelines as dispositive and not considering all examples of special conditions relevant to a claimant's case can be grounds for remand. *See, e.g.*, Cardew v. Comm'r of Soc. Sec., 896 F.3d 742, 748, 258 Soc. Sec. Rep. Serv. 536 (6th Cir. 2018) (claimant worked in a short-term, highly accommodated summer internship his cousin had arranged for him; noting that examples of special conditions are often "difficult, if not impossible, to quantify in a subsidy analysis" and "are not factors but rather non-exclusive 'examples' that can show the claimant does not have the ability to do substantial gainful activity.").

The threshold amount set out in the regulations as presumptively demonstrating the ability to engage in substantial gainful activity is subject to certain deductions. Thus, an individual can deduct from the earnings calculation the reasonable costs of impairment-related work expenses, including payments for drugs and medical services used to control the effects of a claimant's impairments. 20 C.F.R. §§ 404.1576(c), 416.976(c); Allen v. Astrue, 2009 WL 2253815, 143 Soc. Sec. Rep. Serv. 873 (D.S.D. 2009). These costs are deductible even if the assistance is also needed by the individual to carry out normal daily functions that are unrelated to work. *See* 20 C.F.R. §§ 404.1576(a), 416.976(a).

The earnings guidelines are also not dispositive in demonstrating what is not substantial gainful activity. For example, even where an employee's wages are not substantial according to the guidelines, if there is other evidence indicating that the claimant was engaged in substantial gainful activity or that a claimant was in the position to control the amount of wages paid, SSA may consider whether the work performed is "comparable to that of unimpaired people in [the employee's] community who are doing the same or similar occupations as their means of livelihood, taking into account the time, energy, skill, and responsibility involved in the work." 20 C.F.R. §§ 404.1574(b)(3)(ii)(A), 416.974(b)(3)(ii)(A). SSA may also rely on evidence that the employee's work is clearly worth more than the substantial gainful activity amounts provided for the particular calendar year in the earnings guidelines based upon the prevailing pay scales in the employee's community. 20 C.F.R. §§ 404.1574(b)(3)(ii)(B), 416.974(b)(3)(ii)(B). Thus, where an employee-claimant had no significant earnings SSA can point to other evidence in the record to establish that claimant was engaged in substantial gainful activity. *But see, e.g.*, Le v. Astrue, 540 F.Supp.2d 1144, 1148–51, 131 Soc. Sec. Rep. Serv. 102 (C.D. Calif. 2008) (other than SSA's assertion that claimant's work as a rice farmer constituted past relevant work, the ALJ made no effort to rebut the presumption against substantial gainful activity; even if the earnings presumption did not apply, claimant's prior work would still not be qualify because there was no evidence of the prevailing pay scales for rice farmers in claimant's community or any evidence that unimpaired people in her community performed comparable work as rice farmers for profit).

Similarly, if claimants are self-employed SSA will consider the work activities they have performed and their value to the business to determine whether they engaged in substantial gainful activity. 20 C.F.R. §§ 404.1575(a), 416.975(a). SSA regulations provide three tests for determining whether self-employment qualifies as substantial gainful activity. A self-employed claimant will be found to have engaged in

SGA "if you render services that are significant to the operation of the business and receive a substantial income from the business"; if the claimant's work activity, including working hours, skills, duties, and responsibilities, are "comparable to that of unimpaired individuals in your community who are in the same or similar businesses as their means of livelihood"; or if the work activity "although not comparable to that of unimpaired individuals, is clearly worth the amount shown in [the Commissioner's Earnings Guidelines] when considered in terms of its value to the business, or when compared to the salary that an owner would pay to an employee to do the work you are doing." 20 C.F.R. §§ 404.1575(a)(2)(i)–(iii), 416.975(a)(2)(i)–(iii). If the individual's work is substantial gainful activity under test one, the ALJ need not apply tests two and three. If not, then the remaining tests are applied to see if it is SGA under one of the other two. Thus, in a case involving a self-employed rice farmer, Le v. Astrue, 540 F.Supp.2d 1144, 131 Soc. Sec. Rep. Serv. 102 (C.D. Calif. 2008), the claimant did not receive a substantial income nor was there evidence in the record that rice and produce she grew would amount to a substantial income; there was no evidence that her work activity was comparable to that of unimpaired persons in her community who earned wages or other substantial income as rice farmers or from other similar occupations; nor was there evidence to support a finding that her work was clearly worth wages amounting to the SSA's earning guidelines, in terms of its value to the farm or based upon what an employer would ordinarily pay a rice farmer. The court therefore determined that there was a "lack of conclusive evidence as to the comparability of the required factors" to show that the claimant performed substantial gainful activity. 540 F.Supp.2d at 1151 (referencing 20 C.F.R. §§ 404.1575(a)(2), 416.975(a)(2) and quoting SSR 83–34 (1983)).

a. Illegal Activity

Both the Social Security Act and applicable federal regulations state directly that illegal activity can also constitute substantial gainful activity. *See* 42 U.S.C. §§ 423(d)(4)(B), 1382c(a)(3)(E); 20 C.F.R. §§ 404.1571, 416.971. Thus, any work activity, legal or illegal, may be evidence that an individual can work. SSA considers not just the income earned in such activities, but also the claimant's ability to run an illicit operation and avoid apprehension by the authorities. *See, e.g.,* Dotson v. Shalala, 1 F.3d 571, 575–77, 42 Soc. Sec. Rep. Serv. 17 (7th Cir. 1993); Hart v. Sullivan, 824 F. Supp. 903, 905–07, 41 Soc. Sec. Rep. Serv. 451 (N.D. Cal. 1992). *See also* Speaks v. Secretary of Health and Human Services, 855 F. Supp. 1108, 1112, 45 Soc. Sec. Rep. Serv. 52 (C.D. Cal. 1994) (prostitution constitutes substantial gainful activity).

This does not mean, however, that all profitable illegal activity will count as substantial gainful activity. *See, e.g.,* Corrao v. Shalala, 20 F.3d 943, 948–49, 44 Soc. Sec. Rep. Ser. 150 (9th Cir. 1994) (claimant purchased small amounts of heroin for others, receiving some for his own use; "there is no indication of initiative, organization, responsibility, or physical or mental exertion by [the claimant] as is required for SGA"). *Cf.* Jones v. Shalala, 21 F. 3d 191, 44 Soc. Sec. Rep. Serv. 291 (7th Cir. 1994) (petty theft earnings of $60 per day was substantial gainful activity).

2. STEP 2: MINIMUM DURATION AND SEVERITY

The Social Security Act requires not only that a claimant be unable to engage in any "substantial gainful activity," but also that this inability to work result from a "medically determinable physical or mental impairment which can be expected to result in death or which has lasted or can be expected to last for a continuous period of not less than 12 months." *See* 42 U.S.C. § 423(d)(1)(A); 20 C.F.R. §§ 404.1509, 416.909. Both components of this requirement—that the impairment be medically determinable and that it has lasted for a continuous period of 12 months (or is expected to last at least 12 months or to result in death)—have been incorporated, along with a minimum severity requirement, into Step 2 of the sequential evaluation process. Thus, in order to proceed past the second step claimants must show that they have a medically determinable "severe" impairment that has lasted 12 months or can be expected to last at least 12 months or to result in death. Claimants whose impairments are not "medically determinable," are of short duration, or are "non-severe" will be denied. 20 C.F.R. §§ 404.1520(a)(4)(ii), 416.920(a)(4)(ii). The type of proof required to show that an impairment is medically determinable is discussed later in Chapter 8 on Social Security practice.

a. 12-Month Duration Requirement

The duration requirement is usually not much of an issue since in many cases the impairments in question will have already lasted at least 12 months by the time disability is evaluated. Although relatively rare, there are circumstances where proof that a claimant meets this threshold requirement can be critical. *See, e.g.*, Karlix v. Barnhart, 457 F.3d 742, 748, 113 Soc. Sec. Rep. Serv. 28 (8th Cir. 2006) (issue whether impairment met the requirement of the Listing of Impairments; impairment failed to meet the duration requirement); Hoadley v. Astrue, 503 F.Supp.2d 466, 489 123 Soc. Sec. Rep. Serv. 85 (D.Conn. 2007) (ALJ did not have to consider a mental impairment that was raised at the hearing because it failed to meet the duration requirement). A dispute as to whether the duration requirement has been met is most likely to arise where the claim relies on proof that the impairment, while not yet having lasted 12 months, is expected to last for at least 12 months or result in death. *See, e.g.*, McDonald v. Bowen, 818 F.2d 559, 562, 17 Soc. Sec. Rep. Serv. 758 (7th Cir. 1986) ("an individual may be declared disabled on the basis of an expectation of a twelve-month impairment").

Although there is some ambiguity in the terms of the statute as to whether the duration requirement applies to both the existence of the impairment and the inability to engage in substantial gainful activity,

SSA takes the position that it applies to both. *See* SSR 82–52 (1982). The Supreme Court, applying its interpretive rule of Chevron U.S.A. Inc. v. Natural Resources Defense Council, Inc., 467 U.S. 837, 104 S. Ct. 2778 (1984), approved SSA's reading in Barnhart v. Walton, 535 U.S. 212, 79 Soc. Sec. Rep. Serv. 1 (2002). The Court also considered whether the duration requirement could be satisfied where a claimant had a qualifying impairment at the time of application that could be expected to preclude gainful activity for at least 12 months but, in fact, returned to work before 12 months had passed. SSA regulations say no and the Court agreed, describing the agency's position as follows: "[SSA] reads the term 'expected to last' as applicable only when the 'inability' has not yet lasted 12 months. In the case of a later Agency determination—where the 'inability' did not last 12 months—the Agency will automatically assume that the claimant failed to meet the duration requirement. It will not look back to decide hypothetically whether, despite the claimant's actual return to work before 12 months expired, the 'inability' nonetheless might have been expected to last that long." 467 U.S. at 215.

Although the duration requirement is met most clearly in cases where the claimant had already been disabled for at least 12 months at the time of adjudication, a "symptom-free" period during the time preceding the adjudication does not necessarily preclude a finding that the requirement has been met. This is true particularly where the claim involves a mental impairment. *See, e.g.*, Lebus v. Harris, 526 F. Supp. 56, 61 (N.D. Cal. 1981) ("While the mere existence of symptom-free periods may negate a finding of disability when a physical impairment is alleged, symptom-free intervals do not necessarily compel such a finding when a mental disorder is the basis of the claim. Unlike a physical impairment, it is extremely difficult to predict the course of mental illness."); Pagan v. Bowen, 862 F.2d 340, 346, 24 Soc. Sec. Rep. Serv. 20 (D.C. Cir. 1988) (periodic psychotic episodes without single episode lasting 12 months); Dreste v. Heckler, 741 F.2d 224, 226, 6 Soc. Sec. Rep. Serv. 208 (8th Cir. 1984) ("It is inherent in psychotic illnesses that periods of remission will occur."). It can apply, however, to physical impairments as well. *See, e.g.*, Lester v. Chater, 81 F.3d 821, 833, 50 Soc. Sec. Rep. Serv. 536 (9th Cir. 1995) (claimant had some relief from back pain for a brief period of time; "Occasional symptom-free periods—and even sporadic ability to work—are not inconsistent with disability.").

As discussed earlier, SSA considers the effect of a combination of impairments throughout the disability determination process. This applies with respect to the duration requirement as well. However, a claimant cannot combine two or more unrelated medically determinable impairments to fulfill the 12-months duration requirement. If neither of two sequentially developed impairments is alone expected to last for 12 months, then the duration requirement is not met, even though the two, in combination, would last for the 12-month period. 20 C.F.R. §§ 404.1523(a), 416.923(a); Landis v. Colvin, 2017 WL 1035680 (N.D. Ala. March 17, 2017). The same is true for concurrent, combined impairments; each one of a set of impairments that are claimed together to establish disability must meet the duration requirement. *See* Rhodes v. Barnhart, 2004 WL 856467, 96 Soc. Sec. Rep. Serv. 177 (N.D. Ill. April 20, 2004) (surgery for fractured knee, problems with shoulders, and surgery to repair a hernia; duration requirement not met, citing 20 C.F.R. § 404.1522(a)).

b. Severity Requirement

By far the most frequently contested Step 2 finding is whether the claimant has a severe impairment (or combination of impairments) allowing the claim to move on to Step 3. The issue has been confused by the use of the term "severe" in the regulations to describe the required finding at this step. In practice, anyone with a minimally serious, greater-than-slight impairment (or combination of impairments) passes through this step relatively easily.

As set out in the sequential evaluation regulations, the claimant must have an impairment that "significantly limits his or her physical or mental ability to do basic work activities," without taking into consideration of the claimant's age, education, and work experience. 20 C.F.R. §§ 404.1520(c), 416.920(c). *See also* 20 C.F.R. §§ 404.1522(a), 416.922(a) ("An impairment or combination of impairments is not severe if it does not significantly limit your physical or mental ability to do basic work activities"). Basic work activities are defined as "the ability and aptitudes necessary to do most jobs," including physical functions such as walking, standing, sitting, or handling; capacities for seeing, hearing, and speaking; and use of judgment. 20 C.F.R. §§ 404.1522(b), 416.922(b). Thus, when administered correctly Step 2 denials are reserved for only those claimants with the most obviously non-severe impairments; that is, claims that are so obviously unwarranted that they can and should be denied quickly and easily without having to proceed through the rest of the sequential evaluation process.

When SSA originally proposed establishing a severity requirement, it expressed its view that Congress intended that predominant importance be given to medical factors when making disability determinations. *See* 43 Fed. Reg. 55349, 55350 (November 28, 1978). The problem with determining severity on medical evidence alone at Step 2, however, is its potential for abuse by precluding the implementation of the full sequential evaluation process in cases where the claimant might be found to be disabled later in the process on the basis of vocational factors in combination with evidence of medical impairment. A denial on the basis of non-severity can be particularly unfair when a claimant is relatively old and has a limited amount of education and work experience. In such cases, the severity requirement can block consideration of the potentially significant impact of age, education, and work experience on the claimant's ability to work at Steps 4 and 5. For these reasons, there was a great deal of controversy concerning the validity and interpretation of the new severity requirement in the mid-1980s—even though it replaced a regulation that already required claimants to demonstrate only that their impairment was not slight. *See* 20 C.F.R. § 404.1502(a) (1968).

Advocates and others raised concerns in the early 1980s that the Step 2 threshold severity requirement, intended to screen out only frivolous claims, was being used to deny claims that might well be approved at later steps in the process. In a 1985 Ruling, which was published in part to "reflect certain circuit court decisions that have taken issue with the [Social Security Administration's] previously stated definition of 'not severe' impairments," SSA indicated that a finding of non-severity could be made only when "the evidence establishes only a slight abnormality(ies) which has no more than a minimal effect on a claimant's ability to do basic work activities" and cautioned that "[g]reat care should be exercised in applying the not severe impairment concept." SSR 85–28 (1985). Despite this Ruling, the circuit courts of appeals were split on whether the severity regulation was consistent with the language and legislative history of Social Security regulations governing disability determinations. The Supreme Court upheld the requirement in Bowen v. Yuckert, 482 U.S. 137, 17 Soc. Sec. Rep. Ser. 661 (1987), noting that "both the language of the Act and its legislative history support the Secretary's decision to require disability claimants to make a threshold showing that their 'medically determinable' impairments are severe enough to satisfy the regulatory standards." 482 U.S. at 145. *See also id.* at 153 (characterizing Step 2 as "identifying at an early stage those claimants whose medical impairments are so slight that it is unlikely they would be found to be disabled even if their age, education, and experience were taken into account.").

In an influential concurring opinion, Justice O'Connor noted concerns that "this facially valid regulation has been applied systematically to deny benefits to claimants who do meet the statutory definition of disability." Noting further that the Act "does not permit the Secretary to deny benefits to a claimant who may fit within the statutory definition without determining whether the impairment prevents the claimant from engaging in either his prior work or substantial gainful employment that, in light of the claimant's age, education, and experience, is available to him in the national economy," she concluded: "Only those claimants with slight abnormalities that do not significantly limit any "basic work activity" can be denied benefits without undertaking this vocational analysis." 482 U.S. at 157–58 (O'Connor, J., concurring). Later cases have relied consistently on both *Yuckert* and SSR 85–28 to reaffirm a "de minimis" severity requirement at Step 2 of the sequential evaluation process. As the court noted in Dixon v. Shalala, 54 F.3d 1019, 1030 (2d. Cir. 1995): "Since the Court's decision in *Yuckert*, at least seven circuits have followed Justice O'Connor's lead and held that Step 2 may do no more than screen out de minimis claims." The Sixth Circuit has used slightly different language to make the same point, perhaps more forcefully: "The severity requirement may still be employed as an administrative convenience to screen out claims that are 'totally groundless' solely from a medical standpoint." Higgs v. Bowen, 880 F.2d 860,

863, 26 Soc. Sec. Rep. Serv. 296 (6th Cir. 1988). *See also* Carpenter v. Astrue, 537 F.3d 1264, 1266, 134 Soc. Sec. Rep. Serv. 520 (10th Cir. 2008) (citing O'Connor concurrence); Stevens v. Berryhill, 404 F.Supp.3d 933, 944 (M.D. Pa. 2019) (same)

As with the minimum duration requirement, SSA "will consider the combined effect of all of [a claimant's] impairments without regard to whether any such impairment, if considered separately, would be of sufficient severity." 20 C.F.R. §§ 404.1523, 416.923. Thus, the limitations of even slight "non-severe" impairments must be combined to determine whether they are cumulatively severe and thus exceed the de minimis threshold. *See, e.g.*, Bailey v. Sullivan, 885 F.2d 52, 61 (3d Cir. 1989) ("*Yuckert* reinforced the notion that the SSA concept of disability is functional, rather than technical, thus supporting the common-sense realization that the combined effect of nonsevere medical conditions can cause a functional impairment that meets the statutory definition of disability.") As one court noted, precluding a finding of a severe impairment at Step 2 by combining the effects of non-severe impairments would be how "[i]n much the same way, a mathematician might prove that because two does not equal four, two plus two never equals four." Dixon v. Heckler, 589 F. Supp. 1494, 1508 (S.D.N.Y. 1984).

C. SIMPLIFIED GRANT: STEP 3 AND THE LISTING OF IMPAIRMENTS

The third step in the sequential evaluation process involves the application of the Social Security

Administration's Listing of Impairments. As discussed earlier in this chapter, in order to arrive at this third step claimants must have already demonstrated that they are not engaging in substantial gainful activity (Step 1) and have a medically determinable "severe" impairment—or combination of impairments—that has lasted, or is expected to last, at least 12 months or result in death (Step 2). If so, a claimant's impairments are compared at Step 3 to criteria set out in the Listing. If an impairment meets the requirements of a listed impairment, then the claimant is considered to be disabled; if not, a claimant can still be found to be disabled at this step if the same or other impairments, alone or in combination, are the "medical equivalent" of a listed impairment. 20 C.F.R. §§ 404.1520(d), 416.920(d). If the claimant has no impairment or combination of impairments that meet or equal the requirements of the Listing, the sequential evaluation process continues to the final two steps which address a claimant's ability to perform past jobs or any other jobs in the national economy. The final two steps of the sequential evaluation process are discussed later in this chapter.

Step 3 thus serves as an efficient way to decide strong medical claims relatively quickly, without having to consider a claimant's vocational history and capacity. The logic is simple: an impairment that meets the strict criteria of a listed impairment can be recognized and evaluated early in the disability determination process and at relatively little cost. Step 3 is most efficient when the claimant meets the requirements of a clearly diagnosed impairment. Step 3 evaluations become somewhat more involved when a claimant does not have an impairment that meets the listing requirements but has an impairment or combination of impairments that could be the "medical equivalent" to a listed impairment. Medical equivalence is discussed in detail later in this Section.

The key practical distinction of using the Listing of Impairments at Step 3 is that a finding of disability based on the Listing relies exclusively on medical proof and does not consider the claimant's vocational capacity. Deciding claims based on relatively objective medical evidence using specific medical criteria gives the process a level of efficiency and professional legitimacy. On the other hand, it is possible that someone who meets the requirements of a listed impairment could actually go to work. In effect, Step 3 eligibility gives a limited number of potential claimants the option of choosing to accept disability benefits rather than work despite a Listing-level impairment. Of course, someone who does work despite having a Listing-level impairment would be found ineligible at Step 1, so long as the work constituted substantial gainful activity.

The Listing is used somewhat differently for OASDI and adult SSI claims than it is for SSI claims on behalf of children under the age of 18. As explained in Chapter 4, all disability claims under the OASDI program proceed according to the adult disability standard set out in the Social Security Act, as do claims by adults under the SSI program.

Claims for SSI disability benefits on behalf of children under the age of 18, on the other hand, are evaluated according to a different disability standard that relies more heavily on the Listing of Impairments. *Compare* 20 C.F.R. § 404.1525 (OASDI) *with* 20 C.F.R. § 416.925 (SSI). For child SSI claims, the Listing is applied first in the same manner as with adult claims (except, as explained below, there is an additional set of listings that apply only to children). But if the medical evidence fails to show impairments that meet or equal the requirements of the Listing, the claim then proceeds to an evaluation unique to the Child SSI program: whether the child's impairments are the "functional equivalent" of a listed impairment. Functional equivalence in the Child's SSI program is discussed later in this section, after coverage of Step 3 for adult claims.

1. APPLYING THE LISTING AT STEP 3

The Listing of Impairments, published as an appendix to the federal OASDI and SSI regulations, is divided into two parts: Part A and Part B. *See generally* 20 C.F.R., Part 404, Subpart P, Appx. 1 (Listings). Claims for OASDI and adult SSI benefits are evaluated using only Part A. Part A may be used also to evaluate SSI benefits for children under the age of 18 "if the disease processes have a similar effect on adults and children." 20 C.F.R. §§ 404.1525(b)(1), 416.925(b)(1). Part B is designed to evaluate diseases or impairments that are found generally only in children, as well as those that may have a different effect on children and adults even where the diagnosis is the same. As explained by the Social Security Administration at the time Part B was promulgated, Part B corresponds to Part A "for those impairments common to both adults and children . . . with modifications of the adult criteria, where necessary, to take into account the different impact on children. In addition, [Part B] contains impairments that are generally seen only in children." 42 Fed. Reg. 14705, 14706 (March 16, 1977). When evaluating the disability of a child under age 18, Part B is used first; if the medical criteria of Part B do not address all aspects of the child's impairments, then Part A is used as well. 20 C.F.R. § 416.925(b)(2).

Part A of the Listing is divided into 14 sections; many, but not all, of the categories of impairments are the same in Part B. Each section of the Listing covers a different major body system (*e.g.*, musculoskeletal, gastrointestinal, or cardiovascular systems), and each is divided into two parts. The first part of each section is an introduction to the body system covered in that section. The introduction defines terms used in that section and may spell out exact medical findings necessary to meet particular listings. The second part of most sections is the "Category of Impairments," which sets out individual impairments and the medical findings necessary to show that a claimant with that impairment is disabled. The number of impairments varies, from just one (congenital disorders that affect multiple body systems) to more than 15 (cancer). Section 9 of the Listing, covering endocrine disorders, works differently. Instead of a group of listed impairments with qualifying criteria it sets out an introductory section that explains how various disorders are to be evaluated, including cross-references to listings under other body systems.

The listings for mental disorders also follow a somewhat different approach, with the criteria for meeting the listing set out in three "Parts" (A, B, and C). As with the other categories of impairments, claimants must first show that they have a medically determinable mental impairment by documenting certain signs and symptoms enumerated in a Part A of the listing. Then they must demonstrate certain functional limitations outlined either in a Part B or, for some, they can demonstrate an alternative basis for establishing functional limitations set out in a Part C. Five of the eleven listings require claimants to meet the following Part B criteria: an "extreme" limitation of one—or "marked" limitation of two—of four areas of mental functioning (understand, remember, or apply information; interact with others; concentrate, persist, or maintain pace; or adapt or manage oneself). Another five listings require meeting either the Part B criteria or those set out in a Part C: the relevant mental disorder is "serious and persistent" with a medically documented history of its existence over a period of at least 2 years, together with evidence of both "medical treatment, mental health therapy, psychosocial support(s), or a highly structured setting(s) that is ongoing and that diminishes the symptoms and signs of your mental disorder" and "marginal adjustment, that is, you have minimal capacity to adapt to changes in your environment or to demands that are not already part of your daily life." *See generally* 20 C.F.R., Part 404, Subpart P, Appx. 1 (Listings) § 12.00. Within the category of mental impairments, the listing for intellectual disability (formerly labeled "mental retardation") is structured separately. To qualify, a claimant must satisfy one of two sets of criteria in unique Parts A and B that focus on intellectual and adaptive functioning or a combination of IQ score and deficits in adaptive mental functioning (the same areas set out above in Part B for other mental impairments). 20 C.F.R., Part 404, Subpart P, Appx. 1 (Listings) § 12.05.

The criteria for all of the categories of impairments in the Listing are quite strict, as they are intended to identify persons whose medical condition alone precludes them from engaging in "any gainful activity." The "any gainful activity" standard—also referred to as "per se disability"—is a regulatory standard distinct from the general statutory disability standard that looks to the ability to engage in "substantial gainful activity" and also takes into account the claimant's age, education, and prior work experience. *See generally* 20 C.F.R., Part 404, Subpart P, Appx. 1 (Listings). The Supreme Court discussed the difference between the criteria in the Listing and the general disability standard in Sullivan v. Zebley, 493 U.S. 521 (1990), discussed at length earlier in this chapter, in ruling that then-existing SSA regulations cutting off the sequential evaluation process at Step 3 for Child SSI claims were contrary to the Social Security Act:

> [T]he listings in several ways are more restrictive than the statutory standard. First, the listings obviously do not cover all illnesses and abnormalities that actually can be disabling. . . . Second, even those medical conditions that are covered in the listings are defined by criteria setting a higher level of severity than the statutory standard, so they exclude claimants who have listed impairments in a form severe enough to preclude substantial gainful activity, but not quite severe enough to meet the listings level—that which would preclude any gainful activity. Third, the listings also exclude any claimant whose impairment would not prevent any and all persons from doing any kind of work, but which actually precludes the particular claimant from working, given its actual effects on him—such as pain, consequences of medication, and other symptoms that vary greatly with the individual and given the claimant's age, education, and work experience. Fourth, the equivalence analysis excludes claimants who have unlisted impairments, or combinations of impairments, that do not fulfill all the criteria for any one listed impairment. Thus, there are several obvious categories of claimants who would not qualify under the listings, but who nonetheless would meet the statutory standard.

493 U.S. at 533–34.

There is relatively little case law dealing with specific listed impairments, probably because close or difficult cases tend to be resolved later in the sequential evaluation process. Strong claims that should be granted at Step 3 based on the Listing are, for the most part, resolved with a finding of disability. On the other hand, if it isn't clear from readily available medical evidence that a claimant meets the requirements of one or more of the listed impairments, the safe approach is to pass the claim on to Steps 4 and 5. And if the claim is granted eventually at Step 5, as often is the case when an impairment is close to meeting the requirements of the Listing, the failure to find that the impairment met the listing becomes moot. However, in order for Step 3 to fulfill its efficiency role in the sequential evaluation process SSA must be ready to make a finding of disability whenever the medical evidence shows that a claimant has met the requirements of the Listing. Thus, claimants with a Listing-level impairment must be found eligible even if other evidence shows that they could perform work they have done in the past and therefore would be found not disabled at Step 4. *See, e.g.*, Ambers v. Heckler, 736 F.2d 1467, 1468, 5 Soc. Sec. Rep. Ser. 383 (11th Cir. 1984) ("claimant meets the listing, she is entitled to benefits regardless of the fact that she may be able to hold gainful employment as she did in the past.").

One area of significant circuit court caselaw on Step 3 and the Listing of Impairments involves the articulation and adequate reasoning requirements for ALJ decisions assessing whether claimants' medical proof meets, or is medically equivalent to, the criteria of a listed impairment. An ALJ who omits an applicable listing or provides no more than a superficial analysis commits reversible error. Rather "[i]n considering whether a claimant's condition meets or equals a listed impairment, an ALJ must discuss the Listing by name and offer more than a perfunctory analysis of the Listing." Kastner v. Astrue, 697 F.3d 642, 647, 184 Soc. Sec. Rep. Serv. 401 (7th Cir. 2012); *see also* Radford v. Colvin, 734 F.3d 288, 295, 197 Soc. Sec. Rep. Serv. 28 (4th Cir. 2013) (ALJ summarily concluded that claimant's impairment did not meet or equal a listed impairment, but provided no explanation other than that he "considered, in particular," a variety of listings, including the spinal listing, and noted that state medical examiners had also concluded "that no listing [was] met or equaled"; "[t]his insufficient legal analysis makes it impossible for a reviewing court to evaluate whether substantial evidence supports the ALJ's findings" or undertake a "meaningful review" of the findings.); Burnett v. Commissioner of Social Sec. Admin., 220 F.3d 112, 120, 70 Soc. Sec. Rep. Serv. 604 (3d Cir. 2000) (ALJ's mere conclusory statement, without mentioning any specific listed impairments or explaining his reasoning, is a "hopelessly inadequate step three ruling" beyond meaningful judicial review; on remand ALJ should "explain his findings at step three, including an analysis of whether and why [the claimant's] impairments, or those impairments combined, are or are not equivalent in severity to one of the listed impairments."). As discussed in Chapter 8, failure to address or explain the application of Listing criteria is common basis for reversal and remand on appeal. *See, e.g.*, Clifton v. Chater, 79 F.3d 1007, 1009, 50

Soc. Sec. Rep. Serv. 413 (10th Cir. 1996) (ALJ's mere summary statement that a claimant's condition does not meet or equal a listing, without identifying the relevant listed impairments, discussing the evidence, or explaining his reasoning, reflects a "bare conclusion" that is beyond meaningful review).

a. Overview of the Listing Criteria for Musculoskeletal and Cardiovascular System Impairments

This section discusses briefly the main criteria in the Listing of Impairments for two of the most commonly applied listings, those for claims involving musculoskeletal and cardiovascular system impairments.

Musculoskeletal impairments are evaluated under Section 1 of the Listing of Impairments. *See generally* 20 C.F.R., Part 404, Subpart P, Appx. 1, § 1.00 (Listings). The focus is on conditions that affect functional abilities, such as the use of hands and arms, feet and legs, or the spine. Typically, these functional abilities are considered compromised when a claimant cannot walk and/or perform fine and gross movements effectively. The conditions listed include major dysfunction of a joint, disorders of the spine, amputation, fracture, and injuries to soft tissue. Rheumatoid arthritis is covered within the Immune System listings. *See* 20 C.F.R., Part 404, Subpart P, Appx. 1, § 14.09 (Listings).

Musculoskeletal impairments are not only among the most commonly alleged bases for disability benefits but are also often difficult to prove, as they require clear and convincing medically documented proof that the often-detailed listings criteria have been met. Thus, all of the listings except for soft tissue injury require: a documented medical need for a walker, bilateral canes or bilateral crutches or a wheeled and seated mobility device involving use of both hands; an inability to use one upper extremity to independently initiate, sustain and complete work-related activities involving fine and gross movements, and a medically documented need for a one-handed, hand-held assistive device that requires the use of the other upper extremity or a wheeled and seated mobility device involving use of one hand; or an inability to use both upper extremities to the extent that neither can be used to independently initiate, sustain, and complete work-related activities involving fine and gross movements. With respect to the need for assistive devices, the Listing defines "documented medical need" as "evidence from a medical source that supports your medical need for an assistive device for a continuous period of at least 12 months" which must also "describe any limitation(s) in your upper or lower extremity functioning and the circumstances for which you need to use the assistive device." 20 C.F.R., Part 404, Subpart P, Appx. 1, § 1.00C.6.a. Fractures, for example, are covered under two listings: fractures of the femur, tibia, pelvis, or one or more tarsal bones, and fracture of an upper extremity. Both are disabling if they do not heal within a 12-month period and produce functional limitations on mobility or gross and fine movements proven at the level and with the documentation set out above. *See* 20 C.F.R.,

Part 404, Subpart P, Appx. 1, §§ 1.06, 1.07 (Listings). For almost all of these listings, the required detailed criteria must be present simultaneously, or within "a close proximity of time" (meaning within a consecutive 4-month period), to satisfy the level of severity needed to meet the listing. 20 C.F.R., Part 404, Subpart P, Appx. 1, § 1.00C.7.b.

Cardiovascular impairment results from one or more of four consequences of heart disease: chronic heart failure or ventricular dysfunction; discomfort or pain due to myocardial ischemia; syncope, or near syncope, due to inadequate cerebral perfusion from any cardiac source, and central cyanosis due to right-to-left shunt, reduced oxygen concentration in the arterial blood, or pulmonary vascular disease. *See* 20 C.F.R., Part 404, Subpart P, Appx. 1, § 4.00A (Listings). The listings place more emphasis on functional limitations, as opposed to diagnosis, which increases the importance of a claimant's response to a therapy regimen prescribed by the claimant's treating physician. Accordingly, a longitudinal record of therapy and observations over a period of at least three months will "usually" be required to make a determination. 20 C.F.R., Part 404, Subpart P, Appx. 1 § 4.00B.1 (Listings).

The introduction to the cardiovascular listings includes a detailed discussion of the objective tests that SSA may require when evaluating disabilities arising from the cardiovascular system. An electrocardiogram (ECG, referred to sometimes also by the German abbreviation EKG) is perhaps the most important type of laboratory test used in examining the cardiovascular system. These tests, as well as some others, are important enough that under certain circumstances SSA will purchase them in order to make a disability determination. On the other hand, SSA will not purchase cardiac catheterization studies, an invasive test that evaluates coronary arteries by injecting contrast dye into them, but the results will be considered as part of the evaluation process. *See generally* 20 C.F.R., Part 404, Subpart P, Appx. 1, § 4.00C (Listings).

Specific listed cardiovascular impairments include ischemic heart disease, recurrent arrhythmias, cardiac transplantation, aneurysm of the aorta or its major branches, and peripheral vascular disease. Among the more important listed cardiovascular system impairments is chronic heart failure. *See* 20 C.F.R., Part 404, Subpart P, Appx. 1, § 4.02 (Listings). The listing includes a series of detailed tests and findings. It must be documented by appropriate imaging and must result in at least one category of functional effects, such as the inability to initiate, sustain, or complete activities of daily living. Although not given its own listing, the preface to this section of the Listing recognizes obesity as a contributing factor to cardiovascular impairments. *See* 20 C.F.R., Part 404, Subpart P, Appx. 1, § 4.00I(1) (Listings). As discussed further below, obesity can also be considered in determining medical equivalence to a listed impairment.

2. MEDICAL EQUIVALENCE TO A LISTED IMPAIRMENT

For those claims where the record does not support a finding of disability based on the requirements of a particular listing in the Listing of Impairments, Step 3 offers a second option: a finding of "medical equivalence" to a listed impairment. Medical equivalence findings are an option at Step 3 for all OASDI and SSI claims and range from being almost as straightforward as a finding that an impairment meets the requirements of a listing to being far more complex and obscure. However, because of the separate disability standard for SSI claims on behalf of children under the age of 18—and in particular the introduction of the concept of "functional equivalence" for those claims—the regulations governing the operation of the sequential evaluation process for the SSI program relative to findings of medical equivalence differ somewhat from those governing the OASDI program. *See generally* 20 C.F.R. § 404.1526 (OASDI); 20 C.F.R. §§ 416.926, 416.926a (SSI). Most significantly, for OASDI and adult SSI claims a finding that a claimant does not meet or equal the requirements in the Listing of Impairments results in the claim moving on to an evaluation of the impact of various vocational factors at the fourth and fifth steps of the sequential evaluation process. For child SSI claims, on the other hand, the claim will be denied unless the child can show that their impairment either meets the requirements of the Listing or is the medical or functional equivalent of a listed impairment.

Functional equivalence for child SSI claims is discussed later in this section.

Medical equivalence can be found in one of three ways. First, if the claimant has an impairment included in the Listing of Impairments but the medical evidence does not match the criteria set out in the listing for that particular impairment, the impairment will be considered medically equivalent if other medical findings related to the impairment are at least of equal medical significance to those set out for the listed impairment. Second, if a claimant has an impairment that is not included in the Listing of Impairments, medical findings relative to the unlisted impairment will be compared to those required for a similar listed impairment to determine whether the medical findings relative to the unlisted impairment are at least of equal medical significance to those set out for the selected listed impairment. And finally, if the claimant has a number of impairments, none of which meet or equal the requirements of any listed impairment, the medical findings for all of the claimant's impairments will be combined to determine whether the combined medical findings are at least of equal medical significance to those set out for a "closely analogous" listed impairment. 20 C.F.R. §§ 404.1526(a)–(b), 416.926(a)–(b).

As with findings that an impairment meets the requirements of a listing, medical equivalence findings are based exclusively on medical evidence. This evidence, which includes symptoms, signs, and laboratory findings, must be supported by medically acceptable diagnostic techniques. When assessing a claim for medical equivalence, SSA will also consider the medical opinion of its medical or psychological consultants. 20 C.F.R. §§ 404.1526(b), 416.926(b).

The most common—and most difficult—medical equivalence claims are those that involve a combination of impairments, especially when pain and subjective complaints are involved. First of all, one must pull together a variety of otherwise insufficient medical findings relating to what are often quite different types of medical conditions. And then those findings must not only be shown to establish listings-level severity (that is, preclude engaging in "any gainful activity"), but they must also be tied somehow to a "closely analogous" listed impairment. Proof of medical equivalence based on a combination of otherwise non-qualifying impairments must be presented precisely and effectively. In such cases, a medical expert can be particularly helpful. *See, e.g.,* Aubuchon v. Barnhart, 403 F. Supp. 2d 152, 160, 108 Soc. Sec Rep. Ser. 438 (D. Mass. 2005) (medical advisor called by the ALJ to testify at the hearing concluded that the combination of claimant's back and liver impairments "constituted medical equivalency" to the liver listing (listing 5.05) and that testimony was unrebutted; "the clamant should have been deemed automatically disabled at step three."). Thus, SSA policy requires that a decision of medical equivalence at the ALJ level (and at the Appeals Council level, when the Appeals Council makes the decision) include one of three specified types of expert opinion in the record: a prior administrative medical finding from a

Medical or Psychological Consultant from the initial or reconsideration adjudication levels supporting the medical equivalence finding; Medical Expert evidence, which may include testimony or written responses to interrogatories, obtained at the hearing level supporting the medical equivalence finding; or a report from the Appeals Council's medical support staff supporting the medical equivalence finding. SSR 17–2p (2017).

An important limitation on proof of medical equivalency is that additional pain—even an extraordinary amount from other impairments—cannot be considered separately when pain is already one of the criteria for the listed impairment relative to which a claimant wishes to show medical equivalence. *See* Marciniak v. Shalala, 49 F.3d 1350, 1353–54, 47 Soc. Sec. Rep. Ser. 146 (8th Cir. 1995).

a. Medical Equivalence and Obesity

Obesity is a special case with respect to proof of medical equivalence. Until 2000, obesity was a listed impairment measured by a combination of the claimant's height and weight. However, when SSA removed obesity as a separate listing, the agency made it clear that a claimant's height and weight could be considered in determining medical equivalence. *See* SSR 00–3p (2000), SSR 02–1p (2002). *See also* Diaz v. Commissioner, 577 F.3d 500, 145 Soc. Sec. Rep. Serv. 486 (3d Cir. 2009). Thus, current SSA policy provides that while not a listed impairment, "obesity may increase the severity of a coexisting or related impairment(s) to the extent that the combination of impairments medically equals a listing" and "in cases involving obesity, fatigue may affect the person's physical and mental ability to sustain work activity." SSR 19–2p (2019).

3. FUNCTIONAL EQUIVALENCE TO A LISTED IMPAIRMENT (FOR CHILD SSI CLAIMS ONLY)

As noted earlier, child SSI claims will be denied if the requirements of the Listing of Impairments are not met, unless the claimant can show that their impairment (or combination of impairments) is the medical equivalent of a listed impairment—or, according to special rules only for Child SSI claims, is the "functional equivalent" of a listed impairment. In other words, the disability determination process for child SSI claims ends at Step 3 of the sequential evaluation process with the Listing of Impairments; eligibility must be based on either proof that meets the criteria for a listed impairment or a finding medical equivalence or functional equivalence. As noted in Chapter 4 and earlier in this chapter, this more limited sequential evaluation process for determining disability results from the different statutory standard used for child SSI claims.

The process for determining functional equivalence for children is set out in detail in federal regulations. *See* 20 C.F.R. § 416.926a. The process calls for assessing a child's functional limitations resulting from physical or mental impairments, including impairments that are not considered to be severe. Functional limitations may include what the child cannot do—or has difficulty doing—at home, at school, and in the community. 20 C.F.R. § 416.926a(a). The child's functioning is assessed according to six domains: "(i) acquiring and using information; (ii) attending and completing tasks; (iii) interacting and relating with others; (iv) moving about and manipulating objects; (v) caring for yourself; and, (vi) health and physical well-being." 20 C.F.R. § 416.926a(b)(1). *See also* SSR 09–3p (2009); Roelandt ex rel. Roelandt v. Apfel, 125 F. Supp. 2d 1138, 1146–48, 72 Soc. Sec. Rep. Serv. 168 (S.D. Iowa 2001) (functional equivalence found for 8-year-old child with adjustment disorder with mixed disturbance of emotions and conduct, attention deficit hyperactivity disorder, and fetal alcohol exposure). Separate subsections of the regulations describe each domain, provide examples of the activities that are assessed within each domain, and provide examples of functional limitations within each domain. *See* 20 C.F.R. § 416.926a(g)–(*l*).

An impairment or combination of impairments will be deemed functionally equivalent to the listings if they result in "marked" limitations in two domains of functioning or an "extreme" limitation in one domain of functioning. 20 C.F.R. § 416.926a(a). A "marked" limitation is "a limitation that is 'more than moderate' but 'less than extreme' "; the impairment must "seriously interfere" with the child's "ability to independently initiate, sustain, or complete activities." 20 C.F.R. § 416.926a(e)(2)(i). *See also* Bradley o/b/o Y.T.B. v. Berryhill, 305 F. Supp. 3d 460 (W.D. N.Y. 2018) (case remanded due to ALJ's "largely-unexplained" determination that child claimant, who had difficulty with all core academic subjects, had less than "marked" limitations with respect to acquiring and using information.); Slusser ex rel. Gill v. Apfel, 85 F.Supp.2d 634, 637–38, 67 Soc. Sec. Rep. Serv. 406 (W.D.Va.2000) ("this court has consistently held that performance within the first percentile establishes the existence of a marked limitation. . . . Inasmuch as [the claimant] has clearly established the presence of marked limitations in two broad areas of development and/or function, the court concludes that plaintiff has met the burden in establishing that his impairments functionally equal a listed impairment"). An "extreme" limitation is "a limitation that is 'more than marked' "; the impairment must "very seriously" interfere with the child's "ability to independently initiate, sustain, or complete activities." 20 C.F.R. § 416.926a(e)(3)(i).

When assessing both marked and extreme limitations, standardized test scores are used to compare the child's functioning in a specified domain with the functioning of other children in the same domain. However, the regulations state specifically that SSA "will not rely on any test score alone" and that the agency "will consider [a child's] test scores together with the other information we have about [the child's] functioning, including reports of classroom performance and the observations of school personnel and others." 20 C.F.R. § 416.926a(e)(4). Finally, the regulations also provide some examples of impairments that functionally equal the listings. *See* 20 C.F.R. § 416.926a(m) (ranging from a documented need for a major organ transplant, such as a liver, to "[a]ny physical impairment(s) or combination of physical and mental impairments causing complete inability to function independently outside the area of one's home within age-appropriate norms.").

D. RESIDUAL FUNCTIONAL CAPACITY (RFC)

As noted earlier, the Social Security Act's definition of disability is centered on the notion of work incapacity. The various steps of the sequential evaluation process for determining disability are designed to assess a claimant's work capacity in different contexts, but any determination that a claimant is or is not disabled based on work capacity must conform to the "ability to perform substantial gainful activity" measure of the statutory disability standard. A claimant's "residual functional capacity" (often referred to as RFC) is a measure of what that claimant, despite the existence of a severe impairment, can still do in a work setting. *See* 20 C.F.R. §§ 404.1545(a), 416.945(a). RFCs can be an important tool is assessing claimants' ability to perform substantial gainful activity.

RFC assessments come into play in the last two steps of the sequential evaluation process: determining whether the claimant can perform past relevant work (Step 4), and, if not, determining whether the claimant can perform other work available in the national economy (Step 5). RFC is not involved at Step 1 because it considers only actual work activity, nor at Step 2 that focuses exclusively on impairments. RFC is also not a factor at Step 3, not only because the Listing of Impairments focuses primarily on medical factors with only limited use of functional criteria, but also because claimants that meet the strict requirements in the Listing are likely to have little or no residual capacity for work. In other words, the sequential evaluation process regulations incorporate RFC assessments only at the fourth and fifth steps of the process because an assessment of a claimant's residual functional capacity is relevant only for those with severe impairments that do not meet or equal the requirements of the Listing of Impairments. *See* 20 C.F.R. §§ 404.1520(e)–(f), 416.920(e)–(f). The determination of a claimant's RFC is particularly important in cases decided at Step 5 through the use of SSA's Medical-Vocational Guidelines. In such cases, the difference between one level of RFC and another can be the difference between automatic findings of disability and non-disability. Steps 4 and 5 are covered in detail in the next two sections of this chapter.

RFC determinations are based on claimants' physical and mental limitations and how they affect their ability to work. Although the regulations state that RFC determinations also involve consideration of sensory restrictions and other non-exertional limitations, the major emphasis is on physical exertional limitations such as sitting, standing, walking, lifting, carrying, pushing, and pulling. *See* 20 C.F.R. §§ 404.1545(b), 416.945(b). Indeed, the various levels of RFC specified in the regulations—sedentary work, light work, medium work, heavy work, and very heavy work—are defined in the regulations in terms of "physical exertion requirements." 20 C.F.R. §§ 404.1567, 416.967. Thus, the basic requirements for sedentary work are the ability to lift a maximum of 10 pounds at one time, lift or carry light objects occasionally, such as files or small tools, and walk or stand occasionally; light work requires the ability to lift a maximum of 20 pounds at one time and the ability to carry or lift frequently objects that weigh up to 10 pounds; medium work requires the ability to lift a maximum of 50 pounds at one time, and to lift or carry frequently objects weighing up to 25 pounds; heavy work requires lifting a maximum of 100 pounds at a time and carrying or lifting frequently up to 50 pounds; very heavy work requires lifting a maximum of over 100 pounds at a time and carrying or lifting frequently over 50 pounds. Persons who can perform any one of these RFC levels are assumed to be able to perform all lighter levels as well. 20 C.F.R. §§ 404.1567(a)–(e), 416.967(a)–(e).

SSA issued a major Ruling in 1996 on assessing RFC at Steps 4 and 5 of the sequential evaluation process. SSR 96-8p (1996). The Ruling clarifies that an RFC is an administrative assessment of a disability claimant's "remaining ability to do sustained work activities in an ordinary work setting on a regular and continuing basis," meaning 8 hours a day 5 days a week, or the equivalent. *Id.* While the Ruling notes that only limitations attributable to medically determinable impairments can be considered, it emphasizes that RFC assessments must address claimants' exertional and nonexertional capacities.

RFC assessments are quite easy when the facts correspond exactly to the specific exertional requirements for sedentary, light, medium, heavy, and very heavy work. The more difficult cases involve questions as to whether the claimant can perform the full range jobs at the relevant RFC level, especially when multiple functional requirements are at issue. *See generally* SSR 96–9p (1996). A frequent issue is the extent to which a claimant can sit or stand. *See, e.g.*, Shiner v. Heckler, 608 F. Supp. 481, 484–85, 9 Soc. Sec. Rep. Ser. 878 (D.Mass.1985) (claimant able to stand only one-half hour before feeling pain and discomfort, sit for only a shorter period, and could "probably" lift a 20-pound turkey "If I had to"; "a determination that a claimant is able to perform sedentary work 'must be predicated upon a finding that the claimant can sit most of the day, with occasional interruptions of short duration.' ") (quoting Benko v. Schweiker, 551 F. Supp. 698, 704 (D.N.H. 1982)). Findings in this regard must be specific. *See, e.g.*, Arnett v. Astrue, 676 F.3d 586, 590 (7th Cir.2012) (RFC assessment that did not include how often the claimant must be able to sit and stand insufficiently specific; "An RFC must be specific about the required frequency of standing and sitting.") (citing SSR 96–9p).

E. STEP 4: ABILITY TO PERFORM PAST RELEVANT WORK

Step 4 is the first of the final two steps of the Social Security Administration's sequential evaluation process. Together, Steps 4 and 5 address two related questions. The question at Step 4 is whether the claimant can perform past relevant work. As explained earlier, persons who can perform past relevant work are, by definition, not disabled and therefore ineligible for benefits. The question at Step 5 is whether a claimant who cannot perform past relevant work can perform other work available in the national economy. If they can, they are also ineligible for benefits. Thus, only claimants who cannot perform both their past relevant work and any other work in the national economy will be found to be disabled. *See* 20 C.F.R. §§ 404.1560(b)–(c), 416.960(b)–(c).

Step 4 leads to a finding of non-disability if a claimant can perform "past relevant work" regardless of whether that particular work is available to the claimant. (As explained in Chapter 4, the Social Security Act specifies a claimant's ability to perform substantial gainful activity is to be determined "regardless of whether such work exists in the immediate area in which he lives, or whether a specific job vacancy exists for him, or whether he would be hired." 42 U.S.C. §§ 423(d)(2)(A), 1382c(a)(3)(B)). The logic behind this step in the sequential evaluation process is that a claimant's ability to perform a prior job demonstrates that the claimant still has the physical and mental capacity to hold a job within their vocational range. Of course, this makes sense as a proxy for the ability to perform substantial gainful activity only if the prior job amounted to "substantial gainful activity" and the claimant has retained the vocational capacity to perform the requirements of the job. Social Security regulations therefore provide that while work that a claimant has done in the past "shows the kind of work" that the claimant "may be expected to do," the agency will deny a claim at Step 4 only if the past work that the claimant can still do was "done within the last 15 years, lasted long enough for [the claimant] to learn to do it, and was substantial gainful activity." 20 C.F.R. §§ 404.1565(a), 416.965(a).

1. PAST RELEVANT WORK DEFINED

In most instances, there is no disagreement about which of a claimant's prior jobs qualify as past relevant work for purposes of Step 4. When there is an issue as to whether a particular job qualifies as past relevant work, three main issues tend to arise: first, whether the inquiry should focus on the requirements of a particular job, as opposed to the general type of work the claimant performed; second, how far into a claimant's vocational past SSA can go before the job is no longer relevant; and third, whether work a claimant performed for only a short period of time should be considered at all. *See e.g.*, Stahovich v. Astrue, 524 F. Supp.2d 95, 103, 126 Soc. Sec. Rep. Serv. 153 (D. Mass. 2007) ("[T]he process of determining the relevance of such prior work entails a number of subsidiary inquiries, e.g., when the particular job was done, whether it lasted long enough for a claimant to know how to do it, whether the work skills acquired continue to apply, whether the work was only 'off and on' or for brief periods of time.").

The Social Security Administration issued two Rulings relevant to the question whether past relevant work means only particular jobs the claimant had performed or if it includes other jobs of the same general type. *See generally* SSR 82–61 (1982), SSR 82–62 (1982). SSR 82–62 specifically disfavors reference to general types of jobs: "Finding that a claimant has the capacity to do past relevant work on the basis of a generic occupational classification of the work is likely to be fallacious and unsupportable." Noting that such types of jobs "may have a common characteristic," the Ruling concludes that "they often involve quite different functional demands and duties requiring varying abilities and job knowledge." On the other hand, the same Ruling provides that when comparing the physical and mental demands of a claimant's past jobs, having the RFC to perform jobs "performed in the past (either the specific job a claimant performed or the same kind of work as it is customarily performed throughout the economy) is generally a sufficient basis for a finding of not disabled." Similarly, SSR 82–61 notes that a claimant's past work "may have involved functional demands and job duties significantly in excess of those generally required for the job by other employers throughout the national economy" but then concludes that "if the claimant cannot perform the excessive functional demands and/or job duties actually required in the former job but can perform the functional demands and job duties as generally required by employers throughout the economy, the claimant should be found to be 'not disabled'." SSA relies on the United

States Department of Labor's Dictionary of Occupational Titles (DOT) to identify functional duties of various occupations as they are generally performed in the economy. *See* SSR 82–61.

Where a claimant's past work involved aspects of multiple different occupations, that work is considered a "composite" job and there is no single DOT title describing how such jobs are generally performed in the economy. Therefore, to qualify as past relevant work for purposes of Step 4 it must be the actual composite job the claimant performed, and the claimant must be able to perform all aspects of that job and its multiple responsibilities. SSR 82–61 (1982). *See also*, Armstrong v. Sullivan, 814 F. Supp. 1364, 1372, 40 Soc. Sec. Rep. Ser. 404 (W.D. Tex. 1993) (claimant, whose prior "composite job" was as cook (medium RFC) and cashier (sedentary RFC), limited to sedentary work; "Generally, an ALJ may not find a claimant capable of performing his or her past relevant job, if the claimant is not capable of performing all of the duties of that job."); Bechtold v. Massanari, 152 F. Supp.2d 1340, 1345, 75 Soc. Sec. Rep. Ser. 216 (M.D. Fla. 2001) (prior job included positions of sales clerk, file clerk, and receptionist, but receptionist position re-characterized by ALJ as telephone clerk; "Where it is clear that a claimant's past employment was a "composite job," an administrative law judge may not find a claimant capable of performing her past relevant work on the basis that she can meet some of the demands of her previous position, but not all of them.")

The reasoning behind a time period of fifteen years within which prior work is considered relevant is explained in SSA regulations as follows: "A gradual change occurs in most jobs so that after 15 years it is no longer realistic to expect that skills and abilities acquired in a job done then continue to apply. The 15-year guide is intended to insure that remote work experience is not currently applied." 20 C.F.R. §§ 404.1565(a), 416.965(a). However, this time period is not applied rigidly. Thus, SSR 82–62 (1982) provides that while it usually applies, "in some cases work performed prior to the 15-year period may be considered as relevant when a continuity of skills, knowledge, and processes can be established between such work and the individual's more recent occupations." *See also* Barnes v. Sullivan, 932 F.2d 1356, 1358, 33 Soc. Sec. Rep. Ser. 399 (11th Cir. 1991) (15-year limit "merely creates a 'presumption of inapplicability' of skills and abilities acquired in work performed outside the fifteen year period.")

The manner in which the amount of time a claimant held a past job should be considered at Step 4 is explained further in SSR 82–62: "It should have been sufficient for the worker to have learned the techniques, acquired information, and developed the facility needed for average performance in the job situation. The length of time this would take depends on the nature and complexity of the work." Clearly, work done only for a short period or off-and-on should not qualify. *See, e.g.*, Ruperto Torres v. Secretary, 791 F. Supp. 342, 343–44, 37 Soc. Sec. Rep. Ser. 549 (D.P.R. 1992) ("It was error for the ALJ to extrapolate from the three month experience of working for her cousin, that the plaintiff had acquired all the administrative, organizational, and operational skills of a secretary, because "off-and-on" positions are not considered pursuant to the regulations."); Baker v. Secretary, 955 F.2d 552, 557, 36 Soc. Sec. Rep. Ser. 280 (8th Cir. 1992) (two months on a training program for a job that the Department of Labor requires three to six months of preparation not long enough to be considered past relevant work).

2. TREATMENT OF FOREIGN AND OUT-OF-DATE JOBS

As noted earlier, the ability to perform jobs held in the past serves as a proxy for the ability to perform other similar types of jobs existing in the national economy, thereby justifying the denial of benefits at Step 4 for claimants who could still perform jobs they held in the relatively recent past. While this works well and without difficulty where a claimant worked in the United States and those jobs continue to exist, it can be more complicated where a claimant's most relevant recent employment was either in a foreign country or has since become obsolete. SSA addressed the question of the vocational relevance of past work performed in a foreign country in SSR 82–40 (1982). The Ruling rejects the idea that prior work in a foreign country is not relevant unless the same or substantially similar work exists in the United States. Drawing a distinction between the Step 4 assessment of whether a claimant can perform past work and the Step 5 assessment whether a claimant can perform other jobs in the US economy, the Ruling concludes that the consideration of past work in a foreign country is not different from that of past work in the US: "If a claimant can meet the sitting, standing, walking, lifting, manipulative, intellectual, emotional and other physical and mental requirements of a past job, he or she is still functionally capable of performing that job regardless of the fact that the individual no longer resides in the country where the past work was performed."

The question of how to treat past work that no longer exists was presented to the Supreme Court in Barnhart v. Thomas, 540 U.S. 20, 124 S. Ct. 376 (2003). The claimant, who had worked as an elevator operator, argued that the position had been automated into obsolescence and that only past work that still exists in the national economy could serve to deny eligibility at Step 4. SSA's position was that the requirement that work exist in the national economy applies only at Step 5; Step 4 looks instead to the ability to perform prior work as a matter of work capacity. Applying the doctrine of deference to an agency's regulations issued to resolve statutory silence or ambiguity in Chevron U.S.A. Inc. v. Natural Resources Defense Council, 467 U.S. 837, 843, 104 S. Ct. 2778 (1984), and various rules of statutory interpretation, the Court upheld SSA's position as a reasonable implementation of the statute. 540 U.S. at 25 ("[S]tep four can result in a determination of no disability without inquiry into whether the claimant's previous work exists in the national economy; the regulations explicitly reserve inquiry into the national economy for step five.").

F. STEP 5: ABILITY TO PERFORM OTHER WORK

1. OVERVIEW

Disability claims reach the fifth and final step of the sequential evaluation process only after passing through the first four, which means that the claimant is not working (engaging in "substantial gainful activity") (Step 1) and has a "severe" impairment (or combination of impairments) (Step 2) that does not meet or equal the requirements of the Listing of Impairments (Step 3) but does preclude the claimant for performing any of their "past relevant work" (Step 4). As the final step of the sequential evaluation process, Step 5 addresses directly the operative language of the statutory disability standard: the inability to engage in "any substantial gainful activity" due to one or more medically determinable physical or mental impairments that "are of such severity that [the claimant] is not only unable to do his [or her] previous work but cannot, considering his [or her] age, education, and work experience, engage in any other kind of substantial gainful work which exists in the national economy." *See* 42 U.S.C. §§ 423(d)(1)–(3), 1382c(a)(3)(B).

In its simplest form, Step 5 looks at claimants' residual functional capacity (RFC), age, education, and past work experience to determine if they can do any work that exists in the national economy. If so, the claimant will be found to be not disabled; if not, the claimant will be found to be disabled. 20 C.F.R. §§ 404.1520(f), 416.920(f). In practice, however, Step

5 determinations are considerably more complicated. As explained in Chapter 4, the Social Security Act specifies that the disability standard looks to the existence of work that the claimant can perform and not the likelihood that the claimant will be hired to perform that work. Moreover, the Act defines the phrase "work which exists in the national economy" as "work which exists in significant numbers either in the region where [the claimant] lives or in several regions of the country." 42 U.S.C. §§ 423(d)(2)(A), 1382c(a)(3)(B). *See also* 20 C.F.R. §§ 404.1560(c), 416.960(c). This presents significant issues of proof, discussed later in this section.

Closely related is the question of the burden of proof. As noted earlier in this chapter, if a claimant cannot perform past relevant work and thereby passes through Step 4 to Step 5, the burden shifts to the Social Security Administration to prove that the claimant can perform other work in the national economy. *See* 20 C.F.R. §§ 404.1512(b)(3), 416.912(b)(3) ("In order to determine that you are able to make an adjustment to other work, we must provide evidence about the existence of work in the national economy that you can do, given your residual functional capacity (which we have already assessed, age, education, and work experience."). When SSA first acknowledged this shift in its regulations, the agency noted that while claimants "shoulder the dual burdens of production and persuasion" through the various steps in the disability process leading up to evaluation of ability to perform past relevant work, its burden of proof at Step 5 is a burden of production. 68 Fed. Reg. 51,153,

51,155 (Aug. 26, 2003). Noting that it would be unreasonable to require claimants to show that there are no jobs in the national economy that they can perform, the agency explained that it must provide evidence that there are a significant numbers in the national economy that claimants can do, given their RFC, age, education, and work experience. *Id.* ("When the burden of production of evidence shifts to us at Step 5, our role is to obtain evidence to assist in impartially determining whether there is a significant number of jobs in the national economy you can do. Thus, we have a burden of proof even though our primary interest in the outcome of the claim is that it be decided correctly. As required by the Act, the ultimate burden of persuasion to prove disability, however, remains with you.").

Whether phrased as a burden of proof or production, the burden shifts with respect to all aspects of the question whether the claimant can perform other work existing in the national economy. Thus, Step 5 places the burden on SSA to show that there are jobs in the national economy that the claimant can perform—and that those jobs are substantial and gainful, exist in "significant" numbers, and exist "either in the region where [the claimant] lives or in several regions of the country." Central to Step 5 analysis is a claimant's vocational ability to make a "work adjustment" to new work environments and job functions required at other jobs in the economy. As explained in SSR 83–10 (1983): "The issue of whether a work adjustment is possible involves a determination as to whether the jobs whose requirements can be met provide an opportunity for adjusting to substantial and gainful work other than that previously performed. Accordingly, the issue of work adjustment is determined based on the interaction of the work capability represented by RFC (the remaining occupational base) with the other factors affecting capability for adjustment—age, education, and work experience."

a. Ability to Perform Part-Time Work

The measure of work incapacity assessed at Step 5 is, in one sense, fundamentally similar to the measure used at the first step of the sequential evaluation process. Step 1 provides that a claimant cannot be disabled if actually performing substantial gainful activity; Step 5 provides that a claimant who can perform and adjust to substantial gainful activity that exists in the national economy is also not disabled. For most purposes, Social Security regulations do not distinguish between the meaning of SGA as used in these two different contexts because in both the purpose is to determine if the claimant meets the same statutory standard. In other words, both steps aim to determine whether the clamant is able to engage in substantial gainful activity. There is, however, a substantial difference between the two steps with respect to how they treat part-time work.

As noted earlier, depending on the nature and extent of the work, part-time work can amount to substantial gainful activity thereby justifying a finding of non-disability at Step 1. The issue at Step

1 is simply whether the particular work that a claimant is engaging in amounts to SGA. *See* 20 C.F.R. §§ 404.1572(a), 416.972(a) (a claimant's work "may be substantial even if it is done on a part-time basis."). Similarly, part-time work that qualifies as substantial gainful activity can amount to past relevant work at Step 4. *See* SSR 96–8p, n.2 (1996). However, those regulations and agency guidance do not apply at Step 5. At Step 5, the question is whether a claimant, who is not working and cannot perform work done in the past, nonetheless has the capacity to other perform work on a "regular and continuing basis." SSR 96–8p (1996) (specifying that "regular and continuing basis" means 8 hours per day, 5 days per week "or an equivalent work schedule"). In other words, the measure of work capacity at Step 5 is full-time work. *See* 68 Fed. Reg. 51153, 51158 (August 26, 2003) ("in SSR 96–8p, we explain that at step 5 we consider only full-time work when we consider other work you are able to do."). *See also* Bladow v. Apfel, 205 F.3d 356, 359–60, 67 Soc. Sec. Rep. Ser. 283 (8th Cir. 2000) (noting that SSA conceded that full-time work 8 hours/day, 5 days/week is required at Step 5, per SSR 96–8p); Kelley v. Apfel, 185 F.3d 1211, 1213–15, 62 Soc. Sec. Rep. Ser. 602 (11th Cir. 1999) (same).

b. Jobs That Exist in the National Economy

In most cases, Step 5 determinations turn on the extent of functional loss due to physical and mental impairments, as well as the impact of vocational factors—age, education, prior work experience—on the claimant's ability to work. There may also be a dispute as to whether the claimant can, in fact, perform and adjust to jobs that SSA identifies as within the claimant's medical and vocational capacity. Usually this is not seriously disputed because the jobs identified are common and available in large numbers throughout the country. There are, however, instances where SSA must struggle to show that the jobs the claimant can do exist in certain regions and in significant numbers in the economy.

While the Social Security Act provides that "work which exists in the national economy means work which exists in significant numbers either in the region where such individual lives or in several regions of the country," 42 U.S.C. §§ 423(d)(2)(A), 1382c(a)(3)(B), what constitutes a significant number is not specified in the statute or in federal regulations. *But see* 20 C.F.R. §§ 404.1566(b), 416.966(b) ("Isolated jobs that exist only in very limited numbers in relatively few locations outside of the region where you live are not considered 'work which exists in the national economy'."). Neither does caselaw provide clear guidance. *Compare* Harmon v. Apfel, 168 F.3d 289, 292, 60 Soc. Sec. Rep. Ser. 267 (6th Cir. 1999)(900,000 jobs and about 700 jobs within a 75-mile radius of claimant's home sufficient; noting that regulations specify that it does not matter if work exits in the immediate area where claimants live, fact that claimant lives 70 miles from nearest metropolitan area "is a factor extrinsic to her disability and is not to be considered") (citing 20 C.F.R. § 404.1566(a)(1)) *with* Beltran v. Astrue, 700 F.3d 386, 390–91, 185 Soc. Sec. Rep. Serv. 371 (9th Cir. 2012)(1,680 jobs nationally and 135 jobs in claimant's region not a significant number; expecting claimant to find even one of 135 jobs in her region or one of 1,680 jobs scattered across several regions would "foreclose a deserving claimant from obtaining disability benefits on the basis of the existence of a few isolated jobs.").

The methods by which SSA estimates the number of jobs existing in the national economy for claims that reach Step 5—typically using government labor reports and, at hearings, with testimony of vocational experts—have come under scrutiny lately by a number of courts. These issues are discussed further below and in Chapter 9.

2. STEP 5 AND THE MEDICAL-VOCATIONAL GUIDELINES ("GRIDS")

As noted above, Step 5 determinations require an assessment of not only a claimants' physical and mental impairments but also their age, education, prior work experience—and how all of those factors affect the claimant's ability to work. The Social Security Administration uses a two-part analysis in order to decide the critical question at Step 5 consistent with the statutory disability standard: whether a claimant, who can no longer perform prior relevant work, can perform other work in the national economy. The first part is an evaluation of the work limitations caused by the claimant's medical condition, using the same residual functional capacity (RFC) assessment described earlier in relation to Step 4. Then the vocational factors of age, education, and prior work experience are brought in to decide whether, given the claimant's RFC, a significant number of jobs exist in the national economy that the claimant could perform. 20 C.F.R. §§ 404.1560(c), 416.960(c).

With the shift in burden of proof after Step 4, SSA faces the formidable task of showing that claimants who reach Step 5 can perform particular jobs that exist in significant numbers in the national economy, either in the claimant's region or in several regions of the country. In order to ease that burden, SSA published a special set of rules and tables in 1979—known as the Medical-Vocational Guidelines—that dictate findings of "disabled" or "not disabled" based on a claimant's RFC and where the claimant falls in designated categories of age, level of education, and prior work experience. The Guidelines are published as an appendix to the Social Security regulations. *See* 20 C.F.R., Part 404, Subpart P, Appx. 2.

At the heart of the Medical-Vocational Guidelines are the so-called "grids," which consist of three tables that can determine whether a claimant is or is not disabled. A claimant's RFC determines which table of the Medical-Vocational Guidelines is to be used: Table No. 1 applies to individuals whose RFC limits them to sedentary work; Table No. 2 applies to those limited to light work; and Table No. 3 applies to those limited to medium work. There are no tables for individuals still able to perform heavy or very heavy work because the Guidelines assume, in effect, that regardless of their age, education, or work experience, sufficient jobs exist in the national economy for such individuals to pursue substantial gainful activity. On the other extreme, separate regulations dictate a finding of disability for claimants with particularly significant vocational limitations. *See* 20 C.F.R. §§ 404.1562, 416.962 ("you have done only arduous unskilled physical labor"; "you are at least 55 years old, have no more than a limited education, and have no past relevant work experience"). *See also* 20 C.F.R. §§ 404.1520(g), 416.920(g). On the other hand, claimants unable to perform work at even a sedentary level are not necessarily assumed to be disabled. *See* SSR 96–9p (1996) (noting that the ability to perform less than the full range of sedentary work "reflects very serious limitations" but "does not necessarily equate with a decision of 'disabled' ").

The "grids" were developed by taking official notice of the number of unskilled jobs that exist throughout the national economy that a claimant with various medical-vocational profiles could perform at the different functional levels included in the grid tables, as supported by various government publications such as the Dictionary of Occupational Titles and the Occupation Outlook Handbook published by the U.S. Department of Labor. Based on this information, SSA developed a set of "rules" for each of the tables that correspond—with respect to the appropriate RFC—to the various combinations of age, education, and work experience claimants may present. When a claimant's vocational factors are plugged in using the table that corresponds to the claimant's RFC, a particular rule directs a conclusion that the claimant is or is not disabled. *See* 20 C.F.R., Part 404, Subpart P, Appx. 2, (Tables 1–3). For example, according to Table No. 2 (covering claimants with an RFC of "light work"), if a claimant is limited to light work, is closely approaching advanced age (defined as between the ages of 50 and 54), is illiterate, and has either no previous work experience or previous work experience limited to unskilled labor, then Rule 202.09 would direct a finding that the claimant is disabled. On the other hand, if that same individual were at least literate, then Rule 202.10 would direct a finding of not disabled.

Certain vocational factors used in the grids require further explanation. For example, SSR 20–1p (2020), provides further internal guidance on the meaning of "illiteracy" when relevant in applying the grids. Persons fall into the "illiteracy" category if they "cannot read or write a simple message" in any language, "such as instructions or inventory lists even though [they] can sign [their] name." The Ruling explains further that SSA "will generally find that an individual who completed fourth grade is able to read or write a simple message and is therefore not illiterate" unless the individual can provide "relevant evidence" of illiteracy from various delineated categories, to counter this presumption. *See also* 20 C.F.R. §§ 404.1564(b)(1), 416.964(b)(1) ("Illiteracy means the inability to read or write. We consider someone illiterate if the person cannot read or write a simple message such as instructions or inventory lists even though the person can sign his or her name. Generally, an illiterate person has had little or no formal schooling"). In the past, the illiteracy category embraced either illiteracy or the inability to communicate in English; however, effective April 27, 2020, SSA eliminated the inability to communicate in

English as an educational factor in the regulations when evaluating disability claims. *See* 85 Fed. Reg. 10586, 10587 (February 25, 2020).

Ultimately, claims that fall within the grids lead to a relatively straightforward disability determination at Step 5. However, as discussed in more detail later in this section, some cases do not fit neatly within the grids and therefore still require an individualized determination. *See* 20 C.F.R. §§ 404.1569, 416.969. *See also* 20 C.F.R. §§ 404.1569a, 416.969a.

a. Authority and Applicability of the Grids

Prior to the adoption of the Medical-Vocational Guidelines, SSA regulations provided only general, non-binding guidance for making determinations concerning a claimant's ability to perform other substantial gainful activity. Therefore, for SSA to meet its Step 5 burden of proof at an administrative hearing, testimony of a vocational expert was usually required. As a result, often similarly situated claimants were treated differently. The new Guidelines were developed in part to overcome this problem. As stated by SSA at the time they were first proposed, the Guidelines were intended to "consolidate and elaborate upon long standing medical-vocational evaluation policies"; to "make clearer to claimants and their representatives how disability is determined where vocational factors must be considered"; to "better assure the soundness and consistency of disability determinations in all claims filed regardless of the level at which adjudicated"; and to "promote better understanding and acceptance by the public and the courts of disability determinations that are made." 43 Fed. Reg. 55349 (November 28, 1978).

After the Guidelines took effect in 1979, many claimants sought to challenge them on constitutional and statutory grounds. The major challenges put forth by claimants were that the Guidelines were beyond the rule-making power of the Secretary of Health and Human Services under the Social Security Act; that the use of the Guidelines constituted a denial of due process and misapplied the official notice doctrine in violation of the Administrative Procedure Act; and that case law still required the testimony of a vocational expert. Other related arguments were that specific jobs that the claimant could perform must still be cited, that the Guidelines create an invalid irrebuttable presumption, and that the Guidelines improperly shifted the burden of proof back to claimants. *See, e.g.*, McCoy v. Schweiker, 683 F.2d 1138 (8th Cir. 1982) (beyond SSA's rulemaking power); Rivers v. Schweiker, 684 F.2d 1144 (5th Cir. 1982) (create an invalid irrebuttable presumption and improperly shift the burden of proof).

The Supreme Court addressed these and other arguments in Heckler v. Campbell, 461 U.S. 458, 1 Soc. Sec. Rep. Ser. 3 (1983). While recognizing that the Social Security Act "contemplates that disability hearings will be individualized determinations based on evidence adduced at a hearing," citing 42 U.S.C. § 423(d)(2)(A) and 42 U.S.C. § 405(b), the Court concluded that "this does not bar the Secretary from relying on rulemaking to resolve certain classes of issues. . . . [E]ven where an agency's enabling statute expressly requires it to hold a hearing, the agency may rely on its rulemaking authority to determine issues that do not require case-by-case consideration. A contrary holding would require the agency continually to relitigate issues that may be established fairly and efficiently in a single rulemaking proceeding." 461 U.S. at 467. Moreover, the Court noted specifically that "the accuracy of those facts [supporting the grid's rules] already has been tested fairly during rulemaking, [and] the rulemaking proceeding itself provides sufficient procedural protection." *Id.* at 470. While the conclusion that a claimant who fits within all of the criteria listed for a particular grid rule is or is not disabled is not subject to challenge, still subject to individualized proof are a claimant's RFC, determining which Table to apply, and the claimant's age, level of education, and prior work experience. *See id.* at 467 ("We note that the regulations afford claimants ample opportunity both to present evidence relating to their own abilities and to offer evidence that the guidelines do not apply to them.").

b. Age Category and the Grids

While *Campbell* made it clear that the Medical-Vocational Guidelines, when applicable, can be used to meet SSA's burden of proof at Step 5, the Court reserved the question of the legality of the age classification in the grids for future consideration. 461 U.S. at 464 n.8. The Eleventh Circuit took the question up in Broz v. Heckler, 721 F.2d 1297, 3 Soc.

Sec. Rep. Ser. 264 (11th Cir. 1983), a case in which its earlier decision striking down the use of the grids to deny claims at Step 5—and the application of age categories in particular—had been vacated and remanded by the Supreme Court following the decision in *Campbell*. While acknowledging that the Supreme Court's decision overruled its pre-*Campbell* ruling that the effect of age could never be a legislative fact, the court stood by its earlier rulings that age must be considered on a case-by-case basis. 721 F.2d at 1299. This is also reflected in current regulations. *See* 20 C.F.R. §§ 404.1563(b), 416.963(b) ("We will not apply the age categories mechanically in a borderline situation. If you are within a few days to a few months of reaching an older age category, and using the older age category would result in a determination or decision that you are disabled, we will consider whether to use the older age category after evaluating the overall impact of all the factors of your case."). *Compare* Daniels v. Apfel, 154 F.3d 1129, 58 Soc. Sec. Rep. Ser. 170 (10th Cir. 1998) (claimant 65 days short of 55 years of age and application of rule that dictated a finding of not disabled; not a borderline case) *with* Phillips v. Astrue, 671 F.3d 699 (8th Cir. 2012)(claimant "four months shy" of reaching the "advanced age" category; fell within a borderline situation and therefore could be evaluated under the grids according to the higher age category). Consistent with the allocation of the burden of production at Step 5, once it is determined that a claimant's age falls within a borderline, the responsibility to show that the younger age category should still apply rests with SSA. *See, e.g.*, Daniels v.

Apfel, supra, 154 F.3d at 1134 ("placing the burden on the Commissioner of determining in the first instance what age category to apply is consistent with the Commissioner's existing burdens. Application of § 404.1563[(b)] is a step-five issue, and the burden generally is on the Commissioner at step five.")

3. STEP 5 WHEN THE GRIDS ARE NOT DISPOSITIVE

As the Court noted in *Campbell*, claimants always have the opportunity to argue that the grids alone cannot dictate a finding that they are not disabled. As explained earlier, use of a particular grid rule to support a finding that a claimant is disabled is justified because SSA has taken official notice of data through rulemaking establishing that there are substantial numbers of jobs in the national economy to which persons with the age, education, and prior work characteristics for that rule can make a work adjustment. Conversely, when a claimant's vocational factors are different from those reflected in a particular rule, that rule is not substantial evidence that there are the requisite number of jobs in the national economy to which the claimant could adjust. In such cases, therefore, the grid rules are not sufficient to meet SSA's burden of proof at Step 5.

One of the most common situations taking a claim out from the exclusive use of the grids is where the claimant has non-exertional impairments or limitations. The grids take into account only exertional impairments and limitations; therefore, if a claimant suffers from a non-exertional impairment or limitation use of the grids alone may not be appropriate. As set out in the Guidelines, "Since the rules are predicated on an individual's having an impairment which manifests itself by limitations in meeting the strength requirements of jobs, they may not be fully applicable where the nature of an individual's impairment does not result in such limitations, e.g., certain mental, sensory, or skin impairments. In addition, some impairments may result solely in postural and manipulative limitations or environmental restrictions." 20 C.F.R., Part 404, Subpart P, Appx. 2, § 200.00(e). More specifically, the grid rules cannot be used conclusively to find disability or non-disability where a claimant presents only non-exertional impairments, although the agency should give "consideration to" the grid rules in such situations. 20 C.F.R., Part 404, Subpart P, Appx. 2, § 200.00(e)(1). Accordingly, where a claimant presents both exertional and non-exertional impairments and the exertional impairments alone do not direct a finding of disabled, the grid rules "provide a framework for consideration of how much the individual's work capability is further diminished in terms of any types of jobs that would be contraindicated by the nonexertional limitations." 20 C.F.R., Part 404, Subpart P, Appx. 2, § 200.00(e)(2). In such cases, "full consideration must be given to all of the relevant facts in the case in accordance with the definitions and discussions of each factor in the appropriate sections of the regulations, which will provide insight into the adjudicative weight to be accorded each factor." *Id.*

Courts differ on the extent to which the grid rules can be used as a framework or guide to find that a claimant with non-exertional impairments or limitations is not disabled without further proof. In particular, the circuit courts of appeals are also divided on the question of how significant a non-exertional limitation must be before it precludes conclusive application of the grid regulations without testimony from a vocational expert or other vocational evidence of the impact of the non-exertional condition or limitation on the base of jobs noticed in the otherwise applicable grid rule. The Fifth and Eighth Circuits mandate that in cases involving non-exertional restrictions which exceed the Step 2 *de minimis* "severity" threshold, the ALJ must obtain vocational evidence and may not simply apply the applicable exertional grid rule. *See* Loza v. Apfel, 219 F.3d 378, 398–99 (5th Cir. 2000); Brock v. Astrue, 674 F.3d 1062, 1065 (8th Cir. 2012). The Ninth Circuit, on the other hand, has found that the finding of a severe non-exertional impairment at Step 2 does not render the impairment "sufficiently severe so as to significantly limit the range of work permitted by the claimant's exertional limitations" and precludes conclusive reliance on the grid rules without vocational evidence to deny a claim. *See* Hoopai v. Astrue, 499 F.3d 1071, 1076 (9th Cir. 2007). The First Circuit has reached a similar result. *See* Ortiz v. Secretary of Health and Human Services, 890 F.2d 520, 524 (1st Cir. 1989).

The Third Circuit took a different approach in Sykes v. Apfel, 228 F.3d 259 (3d Cir. 2000). In *Sykes*, the court observed that the Supreme Court's *Campbell* decision upheld the grid against challenges that its use violated both the procedural protections of the official notice doctrine, which guaranty advance notice and the right to rebut officially noticed facts, as well as the process protections that require evidence to be adduced at the hearing. It did so noting that these procedural protections, while applicable to adjudications, are inapplicable to legislative rulemaking where there is a rulemaking proceeding available to test the facts upon which the resulting legislative rules are generated. 228 F.3d at 264–65 (citing *Campbell*, 461 U.S. at 468–70). Therefore, the court reasoned that "in the absence of the rulemaking establishing the facts of an undiminished occupational base, the Commissioner cannot determine that a claimant's nonexertional impairments do not significantly erode [a claimant's] occupational base under the medical-vocational guidelines without either taking additional vocational evidence establishing as much or providing notice to the claimant of his intention to take official notice of this fact (and providing the claimant with an opportunity to counter the conclusion)." 228 F.3d at 261.

The Third Circuit left open in *Sykes* the question whether SSA's Social Security Rulings—which purport to provide guidance on the general impact of certain non-exertional limitations on the occupational bases reflected in the grid rules—should also be exempt from the protections of these doctrines, even though not promulgated through a legislative rulemaking process pursuant to the Administrative Procedure Act. This issue was addressed in Allen v. Barnhart, 417 F.3d 396, 407, 105 Soc. Sec. Rep. Serv. 651 (3d Cir. 2005), where the court concluded "if the Secretary wishes to rely on an SSR as a replacement for a vocational expert, it must be crystal-clear that the SSR is probative as to the way in which the nonexertional limitations impact the ability to work, and thus, the occupational base." The court also opined that "the claimant should have the opportunity to consider whether it wishes to attempt to undercut the Commissioner's proffer [through the SSR] by calling claimant's own expert" and that "this requires notice in advance of the hearing" of the ALJ's intent to rely on the SSR. *Id.* at 407–08. The court remanded the case for the ALJ to determine how those limitations affected the claimant's ability to carry out basic work-related functions, noting that "[t]his can be accomplished by noting how SSR 85–15 is relevant and controlling—if indeed that is the case—or by obtaining the individualized assessment that SSR 85–15 seems to prefer by way of a vocational expert." *Id* at 408.

The most common exception to the grid's direct and conclusive application are cases with non-exertional impairments or limitations. However, there are also exceptions for cases where claimants have exertional limitations that fall between two exertional RFC categories and would garner different results under those two categories, or where individuals lack the RFC to perform even a full range of sedentary work—the least exertionally demanding category—and therefore have an RFC potentially too diminished for any grid to apply. While in practice, ALJs often eschew grid methodology entirely and resort to vocational experts for entirely unbounded, highly variable and subjective work adjustment assessments, SSA's regulations and rulings mandate resort to the grid's adjudicative framework, assumptions and methodology, even in grid exception cases. Accordingly, in such cases some courts have found that vocational evidence in conflict with assumptions underlying the grid rules must be explained. *See, e.g.*, Swenson v. Sullivan, 876 F.2d 683, 26 Soc. Sec. Rep. Serv. 29 (9th Cir. 1989) (vocational expert identified five job categories and thousands of jobs that the claimant's insured husband could perform; case remanded because "[t]he validity of that testimony is dubious because of his statement that those jobs were fewer than the jobs performable by a person deemed disabled under the grids.").

As noted earlier, each of the three grid tables in the Medical-Vocational Guidelines is designated for use in claims where claimants have a particular level of residual functional capacity (RFC). For the same reason that grid rules cannot alone dictate a finding of not disabled where the claimant's circumstances do not match the rule's relevant age, education, and prior work categories, a particular grid table cannot be used to dictate a finding of not disabled where the claimant cannot perform the full range of work activity at the designated RFC. This can be a critical issue where the only possibly appropriate RFC is sedentary work. In such cases, if the sedentary RFC table cannot be used there will be no grid rules that can alone dictate a finding of not disabled. However, as noted earlier, that does not mean that the inability to perform the full range of sedentary work requires a finding of disability. *See* SSR 96–9p (1996) (noting that there may be sufficient number of jobs a claimant can perform notwithstanding an eroded occupational base; the ALJ "must cite examples of occupations or jobs the individual can do and provide a statement of the incidence of such work in the region where the individual lives or in several regions of the country."); Haddock v. Apfel, 196 F.3d 1084, 1088–89, 65 Soc. Sec. Rep. Ser. 168 (10th Cir. 1999) (claimant's need to alternate sitting and standing limited precluded full range of sedentary work; "in a case like this one, the ALJ must find that the claimant retains a particular exertional capacity, decide whether the claimant has acquired transferable skills, identify specific jobs that the claimant can perform with the restrictions the ALJ has found the claimant to have, and verify that the jobs the claimant can do exist in significant numbers in the regional or national economies.").

G. PROCESS FOR DETERMINING DISABILITY HAS CEASED

As noted in Chapter 4, there is a separate standard in the Social Security Act for terminating disability benefits. According to that standard it is not sufficient, when terminating benefits on medical grounds, to show that a person receiving disability benefits can engage in substantial gainful activity. Disability benefits can be terminated only if "there has been any medical improvement in the [claimant's] impairment or combination of impairments (other than medical improvement which is not related to the [claimant's] ability to work)." 42 U.S.C. §§ 423(f)(1)(A), 1382c(a)(4)(A)(i)(I). Benefits can be terminated, however, if the beneficiary is actually engaging in substantial gainful activity. 42 U.S.C. §§ 423(f)(1)(B), 1382c(a)(4)(A)(i)(II). In addition, benefits can be terminated without a showing of medical improvement or proof of the claimant's ability to engage in substantial gainful activity if the prior determination of disability was obtained fraudulently, or if substantial evidence from the record of the prior determination—or new evidence relating to that determination—establishes that it was made in error. *See generally* 42 U.S.C. §§ 423(f)(4), 1382c(a)(4); 20 C.F.R. §§ 404.1594, 416.994. Medical improvement is to be measured against the beneficiary's condition at the time of the last favorable medical decision on disability. 20 C.F.R. §§ 404.1594(b)(1), 416.994(b)(1).

Because of these additional elements in the standard for terminating benefits, the usual 5-step sequential evaluation process cannot be used. In its place, the Social Security Administration published regulations setting out a separate process—patterned after the sequential evaluation process used for initial determinations—for evaluating terminations based on a finding that the claimant's disability has ceased. The process includes up to eight steps.

The first step, which is the similar to the first step of the process for determining initial eligibility, goes to whether the beneficiary is engaged in substantial gainful activity. If so, benefits will be terminated. If not, the process moves to a second step similar to the third step of the process for determining initial eligibility. The question at this step is whether the beneficiary has an impairment or combination of impairments that meets or equals the requirements of the Listing of Impairments; if so, benefits will not be terminated. If not, the process starts to move in a new direction to account for the special requirements and exceptions in the statutory standard. The next step asks whether there has been medical improvement; if not, and if none of the exceptions to the standard apply, then benefits will not be terminated. If there has been medical improvement, an evaluation is made at as to whether the improvement relates to the beneficiary's ability to work; if not, and if none of the exceptions to the standard apply, then benefits will not be terminated. If there has been no medical improvement or if any medical improvement is unrelated to the beneficiary's ability to work (and if none of the exceptions apply), benefits will be continued. If there has been a medical improvement related to the beneficiary's ability to work and if none of the exceptions apply, then the process returns to familiar ground. First, all of the beneficiary's impairments are evaluated to determine if they are severe; if not, benefits will be terminated. Then, if the beneficiary has a severe impairment or combination of impairments, a determination is made as to whether they can perform past relevant work; if so, benefits will be terminated. Finally, if the beneficiary cannot return to prior relevant work, a determination will be made as to whether they can perform other substantial gainful activity. 20 C.F.R. §§ 404.1594(f), 416.994(b)(5).

Although these steps should be followed whenever a decision is made to terminate benefits, an administrative law judge may not have to follow each step precisely as long as the judge's decision applies the analysis that they represent. *See* Lewis v. Barnhart, 201 F. Supp. 2d 918, 932 (N.D. Ind. 2002) ("the ALJ's decision, although not in the correct form, contains adequate information and analysis to satisfy the requirements of 20 C.F.R. § 404.1594(f)").

There is a slightly different set of steps for terminating a child's Supplemental Security Income benefits. *See* 20 C.F.R. § 416.994a. *See also* SSR 05–03p (2005) (clarifying how to determine whether there has been medical improvement in child's Supplemental Security Income cases where benefits were granted on the basis of functional equivalence, with different approaches listed depending on whether the original finding of disability was made before or after the disability standard was amended in 2001).

CHAPTER 6

SPECIAL ELIGIBILITY ISSUES FOR DISABILITY BENEFITS

As noted already in Chapter 4, the Social Security Act disability standard and Social Security Administration regulations include—in addition to general medical and vocational criteria for eligibility—a number of special provisions covering certain special circumstances or types of claims. Some involve statutory provisions that were enacted in order to clarify policies in areas that had proven to be problematic, such as disability based on pain (and other subjective symptoms) and disability based on drug addiction or alcoholism. Sometime special rules governing certain difficult issues are set out in federal regulations and federal case law. Often, these special statutory provisions or regulatory rules were promulgated in response to litigation challenging Social Security Administration policy in the particular area, followed sometimes by public policy debate in Congress and at SSA. This chapter covers five such special eligibility issues relevant to many disability claims: pain and other subjective symptoms, mental impairments, stress, drug addiction and alcoholism, and remediable impairments and the side effects of medication.

A. PAIN AND OTHER SUBJECTIVE SYMPTOMS

Although the Social Security Administration has long recognized that disability can result from pain and other subjective symptoms, the standard against which pain-based claims should be measured remained unclear through the early 1980s. Ambiguous agency policy led some adjudicators to require objective medical proof of subjective symptoms, including pain. Federal courts around the country weighed in on the issue, seeking to clarify that while a qualifying disability must result from a medically determinable physical or mental impairment objective proof of pain and other subjective symptoms was not required. *See, e.g.*, Wiggins v. Schweiker, 679 F.2d 1387, 1390 (11th Cir. 1982) ("The Fifth and Eleventh Circuits have emphatically rejected the notion that to be disabling subjective claims of pain must be supported by objective medical evidence or by clinical or laboratory findings."); Gallagher on Behalf of Gallagher v. Schweiker, 697 F.2d 82, 84 (2d Cir. 1983) ("The statutory definition of a disability represents a Congressional decision to provide benefits to those eligible persons whose impairment has a medically ascertainable source. That does not necessarily require determination of the complete etiology of the impairment, but it does mean, as the Act says, that the impairment must be attributable to abnormalities demonstrable by medically acceptable techniques.").

Congress eventually responded by establishing a special statutory standard in 1984 amendments to the Social Security Act that embraced a two-step process for establishing pain-based disability. Thus, 42 U.S.C. § 423(d)(5)(A) provides:

> An individual's statement as to pain or other symptoms shall not alone be conclusive evidence of disability . . .; there must be medical signs and findings, established by medically acceptable clinical or laboratory diagnostic techniques, which show the existence of a medical impairment that results from anatomical, physiological, or psychological abnormalities which could reasonably be expected to produce the pain or other symptoms alleged and which, when considered with all evidence required to be furnished . . . (including statements of the individual or his physician as to the intensity and persistence of such pain or other symptoms which may reasonably be accepted as consistent with the medical signs and findings), would lead to a conclusion that the individual is under a disability.

Although technically an "interim" standard that governs only claims decided before January 1, 1987, it remains in the United States Code and has been effectively re-codified in the Code of Federal Regulations, as described later in this section.

Under this formulation, the first step in evaluating a claim based on pain or other subjective symptoms is to determine whether the claimant has an underlying impairment (or combination of impairments) that "could reasonably be expected" to result in the pain or other subjective symptoms alleged by the claimant. This requires, for the most part, the same objective medical evidence required to prove the existence of any type of impairment.

(Weight and sufficiency of medical evidence is discussed in detail in Chapter 9.) The second step is to determine whether the claimant's pain (or other symptoms)—which must be reasonably consistent with the medical signs and findings establishing the underlying impairment—are sufficiently severe to support a disability determination under the Act. In effect, claims relying on pain or other subjective symptoms present two interrelated questions:

1. Is there objective proof of an underlying medical impairment that could reasonably be expected to produce the claimant's subjective symptoms, including pain?

2. Do the claimant's subjective symptoms, including pain—when supported by the claimant's subjective statements and other relevant evidence—prove that the underlying impairment is sufficiently severe to support a disability determination?

The requirement that there be proof of an objective underlying medical impairment that could reasonably be expected to produce the alleged pain or other subjective symptoms serves to preclude claims based on purely subjective statements. But even where claimants have the required objective proof of an underlying medical impairment that could reasonably be expected to produce the level of pain or other symptoms alleged, they can still be denied benefits if they fail to show, through subjective statements and other proof, that the underlying impairment has, in fact, produced the degree of pain alleged (and that that degree of pain supports a disability finding under the Act and the regulatory sequential evaluation process).

A few months prior to the enactment of the 1984 Amendments, the Eighth Circuit entered an order that had been agreed to by the plaintiffs and the Social Security Administration in a class action seeking enforcement of that circuit's case law regarding the use of subjective evidence of pain. Polaski v. Heckler, 739 F.2d 1320, 6 Soc. Sec. Rep. Ser. 123 (8th Cir. 1984). The court held, consistent with courts in other circuits around the country: "While the claimant has the burden of proving that the disability results from a medically determinable physical or mental impairment, direct medical evidence of the cause and effect relationship between the impairment and the degree of claimant's subjective complaints need not be produced. The adjudicator may not disregard a claimant's subjective complaints solely because the objective medical evidence does not fully support them." 739 F.2d at 1322. In a later decision in the same case, decided a few months after the 1984 amendments were enacted, the Eighth Circuit ruled that the *Polaski* settlement order was consistent with the Act as amended. Polaski v. Heckler, 751 F.2d 943, 950, 8 Soc. Sec. Rep. Serv. 178 (8th Cir. 1984).

The court in *Polaski* referred to Social Security Ruling SSR 82–58 (1982), which was one of a number of Rulings that SSA issued as policy statements to aid in guiding the evaluation of claims based on pain. Noting that the agency may have misinterpreted an example in the Ruling to require that allegations of pain must be fully corroborated by objective medical findings, the court quoted the following text of SSR 82–58: "The effects of symptoms must be considered in terms of any additional physical or mental restrictions they may impose beyond those clearly demonstrated by the objective physical manifestations of disorders. Symptoms can sometimes suggest a greater severity of impairment than is demonstrated by objective and medical findings alone." 739 F.2d at 1322, 751 F.2d at 948. SSR 82–58 was superseded in 1988 by SSR 88–13 (1988), which, after noting that SSA policy is consistent with the pain standard set out in the 1984 Amendments, explained:

> There are situations in which an individual's alleged or reported symptoms, such as pain, suggest the possibility of a greater restriction of the individual's ability to function than can be demonstrated by objective medical evidence alone. In such cases, reasonable conclusions as to any limitations on the individual's ability to do basic work activities can be derived from the consideration of other information in conjunction with medical evidence. This is consistent with court decisions which require that statements of the claimant or his/her physician as to the intensity and persistence of pain or other symptoms which may reasonably be accepted as consistent with the medical signs and laboratory findings are to be included in the evidence to be considered in making a disability determination.

SSR 88–13 and a number of subsequent Rulings on pain were also superseded or rescinded. The current relevant Ruling is SSR 16–3p (2016), which repudiated the concept of "credibility" in the sense of suggesting evaluation of witness character or general believability, as opposed to more specific testimonial supportability of the alleged symptoms, including pain. A prior Ruling, SSR 96–7p (1996) required ALJs to assess credibility when assessing the "extent to which an individual's statements about symptoms can be relied upon as probative evidence in determining whether the individual is disabled." SSR 16–3p eliminated the term "credibility" in order to clarify that a "subjective symptom evaluation is not an examination of an individual's character." *See* Coskery v. Berryhill, 892 F.3d 1, 5–8, 257, Soc. Sec. Rep. Serv. 31 (1st Cir. 2018) (applying SSR 16–3p).

1. EVALUATING PAIN-BASED DISABILITY UNDER CURRENT REGULATIONS

The majority of pain-based claims involve general allegations of pain, such as those supported by proof of musculoskeletal disorders resulting in back, neck, or shoulder pain. (Another smaller group of claims that involve largely subjective impairments and diseases that result in pain, such as fibromyalgia and complex regional pain syndrome, are discussed in the next section.) Evaluating claims based on musculoskeletal disorders and other impairments diagnosed through accepted clinical testing has become relatively routine following the passage of the Social Security Disability Reform Act of 1984 and the various Social Security Rulings that followed.

Moreover, the Social Security Administration issued regulations on evaluating pain-based claims in 1991 in an effort to clarify once and for all SSA's interpretation of the statutory mandate. These regulations state unequivocally that the agency will consider all of a claimant's symptoms, including pain, to the extent that those symptoms are reasonably consistent with the other evidence in the record—while at the same time caution that statements of pain or other symptoms alone will not be sufficient and that there must be medical proof of an underlying impairment that could reasonably be expected to have produced the alleged pain. *See* 20 C.F.R. §§ 404.1529(a), 416.929(a). *See also* 20 C.F.R. §§ 404.1529(b), 416.929(b).

The 1991 regulations also clarify that "[t]he finding that [claimants'] impairment(s) could reasonably be expected to produce [their] pain or other symptoms does not involve a determination as to the intensity, persistence, or functionally limiting effects of [those] symptoms." 20 C.F.R. §§ 404.1529(b), 416.929(b). In other words, evaluating the intensity and persistence of symptoms and how those symptoms limit a claimant's capacity for work is a separate, second step once a qualifying underlying medical impairment has been shown. The regulations then set out guidelines for evaluating the intensity, persistence, and functionally limiting effects of symptoms with both "objective medical evidence" and "other evidence" including: the claimant's daily activities; the location, duration, frequency, and intensity of the pain or other symptoms; any precipitating and aggravating factors; the type, dosage, effectiveness, and side effects of any medication for pain or other symptoms; other treatment for pain or other symptoms; any other measures to relieve pain or other symptoms; and any other factors related to functional limitations and restrictions due to pain or other symptoms. 20 C.F.R. §§ 404.1529(c), 416.929(c). (Other regulations draw a distinction, as explained further in Chapter 9, between "acceptable medical sources," who can offer opinions on the existence of a medical impairment, and "other sources" who can provide evidence only of severity and functional limitations. *See generally* 20 C.F.R. §§ 404.1513, 416.913).

Finally, 20 C.F.R. §§ 404.1529(d), 416.929(d) confirm that SSA will consider a claimant's symptoms, including pain, throughout the sequential evaluation process. As noted earlier, while it is now clear that pain and other subjective symptoms must be considered in evaluating a claim for disability benefits, the record must still show that the claimant is disabled within the meaning of the Social Security Act. As the court noted in affirming the denial of benefits in Michaels v. Apfel, 46 F.Supp.2d 126, 138, 62 Soc. Sec. Rep. Serv. 36 (D. Conn. 1999): "Disability requires more than a mere inability to work without pain. The ALJ did not discredit Plaintiff's complaints of pain entirely. He found instead that the medical evidence did not 'corroborate' his allegations of 'disabling pain.' " The 1991 regulations thus not only track the mandates of the 1984 Amendments, but they also set out detailed guidelines for processing disability claims based on pain and other subjective symptoms. For a case that reviews the lead-up to the 1984 amendments and elaborates on how the current regulations implement those amendments, see Craig v. Chater, 76 F.3d 585, 591–96, 50 Soc. Sec. Rep. Serv. 140 (4h Cir. 1996).

As noted earlier, SSA's most recent Ruling on evaluating subjective symptoms, SSR 16–3p (2016), sets out the agency's evaluation process in two steps: whether there is an underlying medically determinable physical or mental impairment (or combination of impairments) that could reasonably be expected to produce alleged symptoms, such as pain; and, if so, whether and to what extent the intensity and persistence of those symptoms limit the claimant's ability to perform work-related activities (or, in the case of a claimant for child's SSI benefits, to function independently, appropriately, and effectively in an age-appropriate manner). Nonetheless, the approach courts have used to review claims based on subjective claims continues to vary somewhat among the various circuit courts of appeal. The Ninth Circuit uses a different and somewhat more restrictive approach to ALJ evaluations of claimants' testimony regarding subjective pain, including the intensity of symptoms: "First, the ALJ must determine whether the claimant has presented objective medical evidence of an underlying impairment which could reasonably be expected to produce the pain or other symptoms alleged. If the claimant meets the first test and there is no evidence of malingering, the ALJ can only reject the claimant's testimony about the severity of the symptoms if she gives 'specific, clear and convincing reasons' for the rejection." Ghanim v. Colvin, 763 F.3d 1154, 1163 (9th Cir. 2014).

Assessing credibility when evaluating subjective symptoms is another area where there is some variation. As noted earlier, in addition to restating the process for evaluating subjective symptoms, SSR 16–3p de-emphasizes the term "credibility" in the sense of suggesting evaluation of witness character or general believability. By contrast, SSR 96–7p (1996), which was rescinded by SSR 16–3p, provided that "the extent to which an individual's statements about symptoms can be relied upon as probative evidence in determining whether the individual is disabled depends on the credibility of those statements." The Seventh Circuit has explained the change in agency policy reflected in the modified terminology:

> Recently the Social Security Administration announced that it would no longer assess the 'credibility' of an applicant's statements, but would instead focus on determining the 'intensity and persistence of [the applicant's] symptoms.' [citing SSR 16–3p (2016)]. The change in wording is meant to clarify that administrative law judges aren't in the business of impeaching claimants' character; obviously administrative law judges will continue to assess the credibility of pain assertions by applicants, especially as such assertions often cannot be either credited or rejected on the basis of medical evidence.

Cole v. Colvin, 831 F.3d 411, 414 (7th Cir. 2016).

ALJs are given great deference by the courts when making credibility determinations. *See, e.g.*, Herron v. Shalala, 19 F.3d 329, 335, 44 Soc. Sec. Rep. Ser. 51 (7th Cir. 1994) ("[s]ince the ALJ is in the best position to observe witnesses, we usually do not upset credibility determinations on appeal so long as they find some support in the record and are not patently wrong.") *See also* Jones v. Commissioner, 336 F.3d 469, 476 (6th Cir. 2003) ("ALJ's determinations of credibility great weight and deference particularly since the ALJ has the opportunity, which we do not, of observing a witness's demeanor while testifying."). At the same time, "the ALJ may not summarily discount subjective complaints of pain." Goldthrite v. Astrue, 535 F.Supp.2d 329, 337, 129 Soc. Sec. Rep. Serv. 676 (W.D.N.Y. 2008) (ALJ noted that claimant had been on welfare for seven years, was still receiving Medicaid, and had just begun receiving food stamps to support conclusion that the claimant was not credible; "on the issue of [claimant's] credibility, the ALJ showed 'a shocking distrust of the plaintiff and her motivations.' . . . The fact that the [claimant] was receiving other income from public assistance does not, by itself, mean that she is less credible when testifying about her pain." 535 F. Supp. 2d at 337–39.

There are a number of situations where ALJs are regularly reversed for inappropriate findings that a claimant's statements of pain lacked credibility. One of the most common is where ALJs apply a so-called "sit and squirm" test based on their observation of a claimant during the hearing. *See, e.g.*, Muncy v. Apfel, 247 F.3d 728, 736 (8th Cir. 2001) ("[Claimant's] failure to 'sit and squirm' with pain during the hearing cannot be dispositive of his credibility"); Bennett v. Barnhart, 288 F. Supp. 2d 1246, 1250–51 (N.D. Ala. 2003) ("The Eleventh Circuit has held that " 'sit and squirm' jurisprudence has no place in this circuit.' That is precisely what ALJ Shirley did in the present case.") (citation omitted). *But see* Powers v. Apfel, 207 F.3d 431, 436 (7th Cir. 2000) (while recognizing that "[m]any courts have condemned the "sit and squirm" test, and we are uncomfortable with it as well," court noted "we have repeatedly endorsed the role of observation in determining credibility."). Another common situation is where a claimant's ability to engage in simple activities are taken as proof that they are not in significant pain. *See, e.g.*, Vertigan v. Halter, 260 F.3d 1044, 1050 (9th Cir. 2001) (ALJ cited claimant's daily activities to discount her claims of pain. "This court has repeatedly asserted that the mere fact that a plaintiff has carried on certain daily activities, such as grocery shopping, driving a car, or limited walking for exercise, does not in any way detract from her credibility as to her overall disability. * * * A patient may [walk and swim] despite pain for therapeutic reasons, but that does not mean she could concentrate on work despite the pain or could engage in similar activity for a longer period given the pain involved.").

Other examples of successfully challenged credibility findings include those based on the fact that the claimant failed to take pain medicine without considering the total context, Jesurum v. Secretary, 48 F.3d 114, 118 (3d Cir. 1995) (claimant's failure to take medication in order to avoid aggravating her gastritis consistent with prescribing physician's recommendations), and those where the ALJ's reasoning is limited to general "meaningless boilerplate." Parker v. Astrue, 597 F.3d 920, 921–22 (7th Cir. 2010) (rejecting use of the following explanation by ALJ: "the undersigned finds that the claimant's medically determinable impairments would reasonably be expected to produce the alleged symptoms, but that the claimant's statements concerning the intensity, persistence and limiting effects of these symptoms are not entirely credible.") Issues of claimant credibility and the credibility of lay witnesses are discussed generally in Chapter 9.

2. CLAIMS BASED ON CHRONIC PAIN CONDITIONS

A second broad category of pain-based claims involves chronic pain conditions. Fibromyalgia, also known as fibrositis, is a relatively common chronic musculoskeletal pain syndrome characterized by widespread muscle pain and fatigue—without noticeable structural or inflammatory musculoskeletal abnormalities. Its cause or causes are unknown, there is no cure, and, of greatest importance to disability law, its symptoms are entirely subjective. There are no laboratory tests for the presence or severity of fibromyalgia. Other chronic pain conditions that have posed difficulties when presented as the basis for Social Security disability claims include Chronic Fatigue Syndrome, Complex Regional Pain Syndrome, interstitial cystitis (also known as "painful bladder symptom" or bladder pain symptom"), and primary headaches disorder.

Since there are no objective diagnostic techniques to prove or disprove the existence of these conditions, the first step of requiring objective proof of an underlying medical impairment cannot be satisfied. On the other hand, certain subjective symptoms have been identified as indicative of the presence of these and other similar conditions and, when documented by medical sources (particularly a claimant's treating physician), eligibility for benefits can be shown. (Special rules for evaluating and weighing the opinions of a claimant's treating physician, which are applied often in cases involving subjective symptoms, are discussed in detail in Chapter 9.) Accordingly, these types of claims are reviewed consistent with the available medical evidence. *See, e.g.*, Green-Younger v. Barnhart, 335 F.3d 99, 108, 89 Soc. Sec. Rep. Serv. 256 (2d Cir. 2003) ("a growing number of courts, including [the Second Circuit], have recognized that fibromyalgia is a disabling impairment and that 'there are no objective tests which can conclusively confirm the disease.' ") (quoting Preston v. Secretary, 854 F.2d 815, 818 (6th Cir.1988)); Sisco v. Department of HHS, 10 F.3d 739, 744, 43 Soc. Sec. Rep. Serv. 12 (10th Cir. 1993) (claimant had symptoms suggestive of chronic fatigue syndrome; fact that "there is no 'dipstick' laboratory test for chronic fatigue syndrome" did not preclude finding of disability consistent with physician's diagnosis based on recognized professional standard that included "a detailed list of symptoms, the painstaking exclusion of other possible disorders, and a thorough review of the patient's medical history.")

The courts in both *Green-Younger* and *Sisco* cited SSA guidelines—an internal memorandum and the agency's program operations manual (POMS)—for assessing the particular chronic pain conditions involved in the claims under review. SSA has also issued Rulings that serve the same purpose. For example, SSR 14–1p (2014), provides that chronic fatigue syndrome can be established as a "medically determinable impairment" when it is accompanied by certain medical signs or laboratory findings. The Ruling also explains the nature of the required medical signs and laboratory findings. *See* Deanna S. v. Commissioner, 474 F.Supp.3d 1137, 1145 (D. Ore. 2020) (fact that claimant's physician "performed limited examinations" of claimant was "not a specific and legitimate reason" to reject diagnosis of chronic fatigue syndrome; "Dr. Glen supported her opinion with a detailed explanation and references to objective clinical findings in Plaintiff's medical record. Thus, the ALJ's rejection of Dr. Glen's opinion is not supported by the substantial evidence in the record.") (citing SSR 14–1p).

SSA issued a detailed Ruling on fibromyalgia in 2012 which states that fibromyalgia is a medically determinable impairment when supported by diagnostic criteria established by the American College of Rheumatology, one of which is a history of widespread pain. *See* SSR 12–2p (2012). The Ruling also specifies that fibromyalgia can be established as a medical impairment only by proof from an "acceptable medical source" based on both the claimant's medical history and a physical exam. Noting that persons with fibromyalgia can have good and bad days and that the symptoms can "wax and wane," the Ruling cautions adjudicators to consider a longitudinal record whenever possible. Federal courts have held consistently that claims based on pain resulting from fibromyalgia cannot be denied on the basis of a lack of objective medical evidence. *See, e.g.*, Arakas v. Comm'r of Soc. Sec., 983 F.3d 83, 97 (4th Cir. 2020) ("we join those circuits by holding that ALJs may not rely on objective medical evidence (or the lack thereof)—even as just one of multiple factors—to discount a claimant's subjective complaints regarding symptoms of fibromyalgia or some other disease that does not produce such evidence.") (citing Johnson v. Astrue, 597 F.3d 409, 412, 414 (1st Cir. 2010); Green-Younger v. Barnhart, 335 F.3d 99, 108 (2d Cir. 2003); Rogers v. Commissioner, 486 F.3d 234, 248 (6th Cir. 2007); Sarchet v. Chater, 78 F.3d 305, 307 (7th Cir. 1996); Brosnahan v. Barnhart, 336 F.3d 671, 677–78 (8th Cir. 2003); Revels v. Berryhill, 874 F.3d 648, 666 (9th Cir. 2017)). *See also* Lim v. Colvin, 243 F.Supp.3d 307, 316 (E.D.N.Y. 2017) (subjective pain resulting from fibromyalgia can establish disability even without clinical findings or other objective medical evidence, citing SSR 12–2p).

Another Ruling, SSR 03–2p (2003), sets out guidelines for evaluating Reflex Sympathetic Dystrophy Syndrome (RSDS), also known as Complex Regional Pain Syndrome, Type I (CRPS). The Ruling notes that RSDS/CRPS is a medically determinable impairment—if documented by appropriate medical signs, symptoms, and laboratory findings—and then sets out a list of diagnostic criteria consisting of complaints of "persistent, intense pain that results in impaired mobility of the affected region" accompanied by certain clinical findings, such as swelling or osteoporosis. Thus, while RSDS/CRPS may be the basis for a finding of disability," the Ruling also cautions that "[d]isability may not be established on the basis of an individual's statement of symptoms alone."

SSA has also recognized interstitial cystitis (IC), also known as "painful bladder symptom" or "bladder pain symptom," as a medically determinable impairment that can support a disability finding. The Ruling notes that while some signs and findings could indicate the presence of IC, "there are no specific signs or findings that are universally accepted." It also acknowledges that "IC symptoms may vary in incidence, duration, and severity from person to person, and even in the same person." The Ruling also lists a series of non-exclusive symptoms, medical signs, and laboratory findings that can be considered to support the presence and severity of IC. *See* SSR 15–1p (2015).

Finally, a chronic headache disorder is another example of a painful condition that can be difficult to prove in the context of establishing eligibility for benefits. SSA issued a ruling in 2019 that defines "primary headache disorders" as "complex neurological disorders involving recurring pain in the head, scalp, or neck" and goes on to explain in some detail how it is diagnosed by the medical community. *See* SSR 19–4p (2019). It also explains how SSA will establish primary headache disorders as a "medically determinable impairment" with objective medical evidence from approved medical sources, noting that, as with other pain-based claims, it will not do so on the basis of subjective symptoms alone. Finally, the Ruling confirms that a primary headache disorder, while not a listed impairment, can, either alone or in combination with other impairments, equal a listed impairment.

Just as discussed above in relation to claims based on generalized pain, the credibility of the claimant's subjective symptoms can be critically important in evaluating a claim based on a chronic pain condition. Thus, a Ruling on assessing Chronic Fatigue Syndrome provides: "If objective medical evidence does not substantiate the person's statements about the intensity, persistence, and functionally limiting effects of symptoms, we consider all of the evidence in the case record, including the person's daily activities; medications or other treatments the person uses, or has used, to alleviate symptoms; the nature and frequency of the person's attempts to obtain medical treatment for symptoms; and statements by other people about the person's symptoms." SSR 14–1p (2014). The Ruling also provides that SSA "will make a finding about the credibility of the person's statements regarding the effects of his or her symptoms on functioning," and "will make every reasonable effort to obtain available information that could shed light on the credibility of the person's statements." *See also* Bridgeman v.

Astrue, 130 Soc. Sec. Rep. Serv. 190, 2008 WL 1803619 (E.D.N.C. 2008) (rejecting claimant's argument that ALJ erroneously required objective evidence of the intensity of the claimant's pain; "The ALJ's decision followed the guidelines in SSR 03–2p and relevant case law, which states that when an individual's subjective complaints are not supported by objective medical evidence, the ALJ must make a finding about the individual's credibility based on the entire medical record.").

B. MENTAL IMPAIRMENTS

Claims for disability benefits based on mental impairments are evaluated in essentially the same manner—and following the same five-step sequential evaluation process—as those based on physical impairments. This policy was reaffirmed in the mid-1980s, following a period during which the Social Security Administration took the position that only those mental impairments that met the requirements of the Listing of Impairments were severe enough to qualify for benefits—effectively eliminating Steps 4 and 5 for mental impairment-based claims. That policy was enjoined in class action lawsuits, *see, e.g.*, Mental Health Ass'n of Minnesota v. Schweiker, 554 F. Supp. 157, 1 Soc. Sec. Rep. Serv. 465 (D. Minn. 1982), aff'd in part, modified in part, 720 F.2d 965, 3 Soc. Sec. Rep. Serv. 183 (8th Cir. 1983), and a few years later SSA confirmed in a Ruling that "conclusions of ability to engage in SGA are not to be inferred merely from the fact that the mental disorder is not of listing severity." SSR 85–16 (1985). *See also* SSR 85–15 (1985) ("[T]he sequential evaluation process mandated by the regulations does not end with the finding that the impairment, though severe, does not meet or equal an impairment listed in Appendix 1 of the regulations. The process must go on to consider whether the individual can meet the mental demands of past relevant work in spite of the limiting effects of his or her impairment and, if not, whether the person can do other work, considering his or her remaining mental capacities reflected in terms of the occupational base, age, education, and work experience."); 20 C.F.R. §§ 404.1520a(a), 416.920a(a) ("The steps outlined in [the sequential evaluation process regulation] apply to the evaluation of physical and mental impairments.").

There are, however, some special provisions relating to the disability determination process for claims based on mental impairments, many of which were mandated by 1984 amendments to the Social Security Act. Thus, the Social Security Act now requires—for claims involving a possible mental impairment—that SSA make "every reasonable effort to ensure that a qualified psychiatrist or psychologist has completed the medical portion of the case review and any applicable residual functional capacity assessment." 42 U.S.C. § 421(h). In addition, Congress ordered a revision of the mental impairments section of the Listing of Impairments, with the directive that "[t]he revised criteria and listings . . . be designed to realistically evaluate the ability of a mentally impaired individual to engage in substantial gainful activity in a competitive workplace environment."). *See* Social Security Disability Benefits Reform Act of 1984, Pub. L. No.

98–460, § 5(a), 98 Stat. 1794, 1801. Another set of regulations mandate a "special technique" that must be used to evaluate the severity of mental impairments for adults and for children under the age of 18, when using Part A of the Listing of Impairments. 20 C.F.R. §§ 404.1520a(a), 416.920a(a). It includes detailed instructions for determining the degree of functional loss and for documenting how the technique was applied at each stage of the administrative process, including administrative reviews. *See* 20 C.F.R. §§ 404.1520a(b)–(e), 416.920a(b)–(e).

One aspect of the disability standard that requires special attention with respect to claims involving mental impairments is the 12-month duration requirement. As noted already in Chapter 5, claims can pass through Step 2 of the sequential evaluation process despite brief periods of remission. Courts have recognized that applying the duration requirement to mental impairments can be especially challenging due to the episodic and cyclical nature of certain mental conditions. *See, e.g.*, Andler v. Chater, 100 F.3d 1389, 1393 (8th Cir. 1996)("Although the mere existence of symptom-free periods may negate a finding a disability when a physical impairment is alleged, symptom-free intervals do not necessarily compel such a finding when a mental disorder is the basis of a claim."); Garrison v. Colvin, 759 F.3d 995, 1017 (9th Cir. 2015)("As we have emphasized while discussing mental health issues, it is error to reject a claimant's testimony merely because symptoms wax and wane in the course of treatment. Cycles of improvement and debilitating symptoms are a common occurrence, and in such circumstances it is error for an ALJ to pick out a few isolated instances of improvement over a period of months or years and to treat them as a basis for concluding a claimant is capable of working.").

1. MENTAL IMPAIRMENTS AND RESIDUAL FUNCTIONAL CAPACITY (RFC)

SSR 85–16 (1985), mentioned above, specifies the type of evidence that should be considered when determining the RFC of a claimant with mental impairments and provides examples of the types of factors that should be taken into account when analyzing the evidence, cautioning that "it is necessary to draw meaningful inferences and allow reasonable conclusions about the individual's strengths and weaknesses." *See also* Schaal v. Callahan, 993 F. Supp. 85, 93, 56 Soc. Sec. Rep. Serv. 56 (D. Conn. 1997) ("SSR 85–16 explains the importance of a residual functional capacity assessment for individuals whose mental impairments are severe but do not meet the listing requirements. The evaluation of residual functional capacity in persons suffering from mental disorders 'includes consideration of the ability to understand, to carry out and remember instructions, and to respond appropriately to supervision, coworkers, and customary work pressures in a work setting.' ") Further guidance is included at 20 C.F.R. §§ 404.1545(c), 416.945(c), which provides that, when assessing RFC, "[a] limited ability to carry out certain mental activities, such as limitations in understanding, remembering, and carrying out instructions, and in responding appropriately to supervision, co-workers, and work pressures in a work setting, may reduce [a claimant's] ability to do past work and other work."

2. PSYCHIATRIC REVIEW TECHNIQUE FORM (PRTF) AND SPECIAL TECHNIQUE

As noted above, the Social Security Administration uses a "special technique" for evaluating impairments. The regulations outlining this technique also provide that SSA will record pertinent information about the claimant's mental condition on a "standard document" at the initial decision and reconsideration levels of the administrative process. At the administrative hearing level, ALJs are required to "document application of the technique" in their decisions. *See* 20 C.F.R. §§ 404.1520a(e), 416.920a(e). The "standard document" currently used by SSA is called a Psychiatric Review Technique Form (PRTF). *See* Kohler v. Astrue, 546 F.3d 260, 266, 137 Soc. Sec. Rep. Serv. 278 (2d Cir. 2008) ("At the initial and reconsideration levels of administrative review, a medical or psychological consultant generally will complete a standard document, known as a Psychiatric Review Technique Form ("PRTF").) (citing 20 C.F.R. § 404.1520a(e)(1)).

In its explanation of major revisions to the mental impairments regulations published in 2000, SSA noted that the PRTF should not be confused with the evaluation technique outlined in the regulations; the form "simply documents application of the technique." 65 Fed. Reg. 50746, 50757 (August 12,

2000). Since then, use of the PRTF itself is not required at the administrative hearing or Appeals Council levels of review; however, administrative hearing and Appeals Council decisions must still effectively include all findings and conclusions called for in the PRFT form. *See* 20 C.F.R. §§ 404.1520a(e), 416.920a(e) ("At the administrative law judge hearing and Appeals Council levels (in cases in which the Appeals Council issues a decision), we will document application of the technique in the decision."). *See also* Kohler v. Astrue, *supra*, 546 F.3d at 266 ("While the regulations no longer require the ALJ to complete that standard form, they do require the ALJ's written decision to reflect application of the technique, and explicitly provide that the decision 'must include a specific finding as to the degree of limitation in each of the functional areas described in [the regulations]') (citing 20 C.F.R. § 404.1520a(e)(2) and 20 C.F.R. § 404.1520a(c)(3), which specifies the four functional areas central to the special technique). The Fourth Circuit, citing *Kohler*, noted that "the weight of authority suggests that failure to properly document application of the special technique will rarely, if ever, be harmless because such a failure prevents, or at least substantially hinders, judicial review." Patterson v. Commissioner, 846 F.3d 656, 662 (4th Cir. 2017). The court noted further that "[w]ithout documentation of the special technique, it is difficult to discern how the ALJ treated relevant and conflicting evidence," and that "[f]ailure to document application of the special-technique regulation constitutes error." *Id.*

C. STRESS

Although stress cannot itself be a qualifying disabling impairment, evidence of the effect of stress on a claimant's physical or mental condition can be very important. The effects of stress are considered most often in cases involving mental conditions or a combination of physical and mental conditions. Social Security Ruling SSR 85–15 (1985), which is discussed in the preceding section of this chapter on mental impairments, includes the following comments on stress relative to mental illness: "The reaction to the demands of work (stress) is highly individualized, and mental illness is characterized by adverse responses to seemingly trivial circumstances. The mentally impaired may cease to function effectively when facing such demands as getting to work regularly, having their performance supervised, and remaining in the workplace for a full day. A person may become panicked and develop palpitations, shortness of breath, or feel faint while riding in an elevator; another may experience terror and begin to hallucinate when approached by a stranger asking a question. Thus, the mentally impaired may have difficulty meeting the requirements of even so-called 'low-stress' jobs." *See also* SSR 85–16 (1985) (noting that reports from psychiatrists and other physicians, psychologists, and other mental health professionals "may also contain other observations and opinions or conclusions on such matters as the individual's ability to cope with stress, the ability to relate to other people, and the ability to function in a group or work situation.").

Ultimately, the issue is not simply the claimant's level of stress, but rather the effect that the stress has on a claimant's ability to function in a work setting. Weiler v. Shalala, 922 F. Supp. 689, 699–700, 50 Soc. Sec. Rep. Ser. 672 (D. Mass. 1996) (citing SSR 85–15 and SSR 85–16: "The ALJ's decision to focus on the amount of stress in a particular job rather than on Weiler's ability to handle stress was in error. Stress is not a characteristic of a particular job but instead 'reflects individual's subjective response to a particular situation.' ") (quoting Lancellotta v. Secretary of Health and Human Services, 806 F.2d 284, 285 (1st Cir.1986)). *But see* Vining v. Astrue, 720 F. Supp. 2d 126, 135 (D. Maine 2010) (applying SSR 85–15: "This court has deemed the requirement to take into account the effects of stress satisfied when an administrative law judge assesses the effect of a mental impairment on the ability to understand, carry out, and remember simple instructions; respond appropriately to supervision, co-workers, and customary work situations; and deal with changes in a routine work setting.").

Just as stress can affect persons in different ways, there are jobs with different levels of stress. A reaction to stress that does not prevent one from performing work that is non-stressful will not be disabling. *See, e.g.*, Schmidt v. Sullivan, 914 F.2d 117, 119, 31 Soc. Sec. Rep. Ser. 103 (7th Cir. 1990) ("Schmidt is an experienced executive with a college degree in business administration. As he is relatively little troubled by physical exertion, he can work in a variety of sedentary jobs, provided they are not stressful."). On the other hand, the effects of stress can be relevant in cases involving physical impairments alone. *See, e.g.*, Mulvenna v. Sullivan, 796 F. Supp. 325, 334, 38 Soc. Sec. Rep. Ser. 567 (N.D. Ill. 1992) ("It is worth observing at the outset that the combination of a weakened heart and high susceptibility to work-related stress may support a finding of disability.")

D. DRUG ADDICTION AND ALCOHOLISM (DAA)

The Social Security Act specifically prohibits a finding of disability based on alcoholism or drug addiction. It does so by providing—in the section defining disability—that a claimant "shall not be considered to be disabled for purposes of [obtaining disability benefits] if alcoholism or drug addiction would (but for this subparagraph) be a contributing factor material to the Commissioner's determination that the individual is disabled." 42 U.S.C. §§ 423(2)(C), 1382c(a)(3)(J).

Current policy regarding alcoholism and drug addiction dates back to 1996, when Congress enacted the Contract with America Advancement Act, Pub. L. No. 104–121 § 105 (1996). Prior to 1996, long-standing Social Security Administration policy provided that disability claims based on addiction to drugs or alcohol should be adjudicated in the same manner as claims based on any other impairment. Thus, both alcoholism and drug addiction were recognized as qualifying impairments, although at various times Congress and SSA imposed certain additional restrictions on awarding disability benefits to persons addicted to drugs or alcohol. This shift in policy reflected concerns that awarding benefits amounted to a sanctioning—and funding—of excessive drug and alcohol consumption.

1. THE EVALUATION PROCESS IN DAA CASES

Under current policy, SSA must first determine whether the claimant is disabled based on all the evidence in the record, including any evidence of alcoholism or addiction to drugs; then, if there is medical evidence that the claimant is addicted to alcohol or drugs, SSA must move on to determine whether the drug addiction or alcoholism was a material, contributing factor in making the disability decision. *See generally* 20 C.F.R. §§ 404.1535, 416.935. As stated specifically at 20 C.F.R. §§ 404.1535(a), 416.935(a): "If we find that you are disabled and have medical evidence of your drug addiction or alcoholism, we must determine whether your drug addiction or alcoholism is a contributing factor material to the determination of disability." *See also* Drapeau v. Massanari, 255 F.3d 1211, 1214–15, 74 Soc. Sec. Rep. Ser. 382 (10th Cir. 2001) ("The implementing regulations make clear that a finding of disability is a condition precedent to an application of § 423(d)(2)(C). 20 C.F.R. § 416.935(a). . . . The ALJ cannot begin to apply § 423(d)(2)(C) properly when, as here, he has not yet made a finding of disability.")

A finding of disability is, in effect, a "condition precedent" to applying the special rule on alcoholism and drug addiction. As a practical matter, this means that a claim must work its way through the full sequential evaluation process based on all of the claimant's circumstances, including any drug addiction or alcoholism, before the materiality of the drug addiction or alcoholism is considered as a disqualifying condition. Bustamante v. Massanari, 262 F.3d 949, 955, 75 Soc. Sec. Rep. Ser. 358 (9th Cir. 2001) ("an ALJ should not proceed with the analysis under §§ 404.1535 or 416.935 if he or she has not yet found the claimant to be disabled under the five-step inquiry.") Moreover, the full sequential evaluation process must be followed through to the end "without segregating out any effects that might be due to substance use disorders." Brueggemann v. Barnhart, 348 F.3d 689, 694, 92 Soc. Sec. Rep. Serv. 153 (8th Cir. 2003).

The key question, then, is whether the claimant—already found to be disabled based on the effects of all of his or her impairments—would still be found to be disabled if the disability determination were made on the non-addiction-related mental and physical impairments alone. If not, then alcoholism or drug addiction is considered a contributing factor material to the determination of disability and benefits will be denied. In making this determination, SSA evaluates the claimant's current physical and mental limitations upon which the finding of disability was based to determine which of those limitations would remain if the claimant stopped using drugs or alcohol. If the remaining limitations would not be disabling, the drug or alcoholism is a contributing factor material to the determination of disability and the claim must be denied; if the remaining limitations would be disabling, drug or alcohol addiction is not considered a contributing factor material to the determination of disability and benefits will be awarded notwithstanding the claimant's alcoholism or drug addiction. *See* 20 C.F.R. §§ 404.1535(b), 416.935(b). In cases involving mental impairments, the relationship between addiction and mental illness can be complex and difficult. *See, e. g.*, Kangail v. Barnhart, 454 F.3d 627, 629, 112 Soc. Sec. Rep. Serv. 513 (7th Cir. 2006) (noting that while bipolar disorder can precipitate substance abuse, "the fact that substance abuse aggravated [the claimant's] mental illness does not prove that the mental illness itself is not disabling.")

The Social Security Administration issued a comprehensive Ruling in 2013 on how cases involving drug addiction and alcoholism should be evaluated. The Ruling seeks to explain SSA policies on "how we consider whether 'drug addiction and alcoholism' (DAA) is a contributing factor material to our determination of disability in disability claims and continuing disability reviews." Of particular note is a six-step "DAA Evaluation Process" that describes how SSA decides whether it "must consider the issue of materiality and, if so, whether DAA is material to the determination of disability." *See* SSR 13–2p (2013), Question 5 (b).

2. ALLOCATION OF THE BURDEN OF PROOF IN DAA CASES

As noted previously in Chapter 5, the ultimate burden of proof on the question of disability rests with the claimant. While it is true that in applying the 5-step sequential evaluation process SSA must come forward with proof of jobs the claimant could perform after a finding at Step 4 that the claimant cannot perform their past relevant work, the claimant is responsible for providing the proof of impaired work capacity used at Step 5. Given the fact that claims involving alcoholism or drug addiction involve an evaluation of the materiality of the claimant's addiction only after a five-step finding of disability has been made, the question arises as to which party bears the burden of proof on this post-sequential evaluation process step. Claimant arguments that the drug and alcoholism rules essentially created a "sixth step" in the sequential evaluation process at which SSA must show that drug addiction or alcoholism was a contributing factor material to the disability determination have been rejected. Brown v. Apfel, 192 F.3d 492, 498, 64 Soc. Sec. Rep. Ser. 128 (5th Cir. 1999) (noting that claimants are in the best position to prove that they would still be disabled absent their drug or alcohol addiction, court concluded that the burden of proving that drug or alcohol addiction is not a contributing factor material to disability rests with the claimant.) This position was confirmed by SSA in a 2013 Ruling: "The claimant has the burden of proving disability throughout the sequential evaluation process. Our only burden is limited to producing evidence that work the claimant can do exists in the national economy at step 5 of the sequential evaluation process." SSR 13–2p (2013), Question 5(a).

However, the question of burden of proof becomes more complicated where the relative responsibility between addiction-related and non-addiction-related impairments for the claimant's inability to work cannot be allocated. Based in part on prior, sub-regulatory guidance from SSA, the court in Brueggemann v. Barnhart, 348 F.3d 689, 92 Soc. Sec. Rep. Serv. 153 (8th Cir. 2003) ruled that a finding of "not material" is appropriate when, after having made an initial determination that a claimant is disabled, it is not possible to separate mental restrictions and limitations imposed by the drug and alcohol addiction from other mental disorders shown by the evidence. The court thus concluded: "In colloquial terms, on the issue of the materiality of alcoholism, a tie goes to [the claimant]." 348 F.3d at 693. A subsequent Ruling, SSR 13–2p (2013), seems to be consistent with the "tie goes to the claimant" approach of the Eighth Circuit in *Brueggemann*. The Ruling provides: "[w]e will find that DAA is not material to the determination of disability and allow the claim if the record is fully developed and the evidence (including medical opinion evidence) does not establish that the claimant's physical impairment(s) would improve to the point of nondisability in the absence of DAA" and also "[w]e will find that DAA is not material to the determination of disability and allow the claim if the record is fully developed and the evidence does not establish that the claimant's co-occurring mental disorder(s) would improve to the point of nondisability in the absence of DAA."

3. REPRESENTATIVE PAYEES AND TREATMENT REQUIREMENTS IN DAA CASES

As explained in Chapter 7, under certain circumstances OASDI and SSI benefits are paid through a representative payee. The appointment of representative payees for persons receiving disability benefits in DAA cases because their drug addiction or alcoholism is not a contributing factor material to the determination that they are disabled, is a bit confusing. SSA regulations concerning the appointment of representative payees distinguish between SSI disability benefit recipients who are also addicted to drugs or alcohol (which expressly reference a need for representative payees in certain SSI DAA cases) and those receiving benefits under the OASDI program (which do not mention DAA). *Compare* 20 C.F.R. § 404.2010(a) (when SSA has information that an OASDI beneficiary is "legally incompetent or mentally incapable of managing benefit payments" or "physically incapable of managing or directing the management of his or her benefit payments") *with* 20 C.F.R. § 416.610(a)(3) (for SSI recipients, also when SSA has information that the beneficiary is "eligible for benefits solely on the basis of disability and drug addiction or alcoholism is a contributing factor material to the determination of disability"). While § 416.610(a)(3) has limited present application in view of the 1996 change in the law, removing eligibility for SSI benefits where drug or alcohol abuse is a contributing factor material to the determination of a claimant's disability, the SSI title of the Social Security Act provides: "the payment of such benefits shall be made to a representative payee if the Commissioner of Social Security determines that such payment would serve the interest of the [disabled] individual because the individual also has an alcoholism or drug addiction condition (as determined by the Commissioner) and the individual is incapable of managing such benefits." 42 U.S.C. § 1383(a)(2)(A)(ii)(II). Presumably, this provision is intended to apply to situations where a claimant's drug addiction or alcoholism is not found to be disqualifying as "a contributing factor material to disability" but is still found to undermine the claimant's ability to manage the benefits.

Claimants who qualify for disability benefits where alcohol or drugs are involved but were not a material factor in determining disability may be required to undergo treatment for their alcoholism or drug addiction. SSA regulations provide, with respect to all claims, that the failure to follow prescribed medical treatment can be grounds for denial of benefits if following the prescribed treatment can restore the claimant's ability to engage in substantial gainful activity. 20 C.F.R. § 404.1530, 416.930. The requirement to follow prescribed treatment is discussed generally in the next section of this chapter. (Other federal regulations still retain special treatment requirements that reference pre-1996 rules that allowed a finding of disability based on drug addiction or alcoholism. *See* 20 C.F.R. § 416.214(a) (requiring "appropriate treatment" for drug addiction or alcoholism); 20 C.F.R. § 416.1326(a) (referral to treatment facility and suspension of benefits for failure to "comply with the terms, conditions and requirements of treatment prescribed by the institution or facility.")).

Moreover, a claimant's record in following treatment for alcoholism or addiction to drugs can be a factor when assessing the claimant's credibility. But the connection between the claimant's treatment record and the credibility finding must have a firm factual basis. *See, e.g.*, Rey v. Astrue, 2010 WL 1222158 (C.D. Cal. 2010) (insufficient evidence to support the ALJ's discrediting of the claimant's testimony where he reduced alcohol consumption for health reasons and completed many treatment programs) (citing Fair v. Bowen, 885 F.2d 597, 603 (9th Cir. 1989); Bunnell v. Sullivan, 947 F.2d 341, 346 (9th Cir. 1991)). Credibility of claimant's and lay witness's testimony are covered generally in Chapter 9.

E. REMEDIABLE DISABILITY AND EFFECTS OF PRESCRIBED MEDICATION

Ordinarily, persons with disabilities are under some sort of medical treatment. A Social Security disability benefit claimant's treatment can have an impact on eligibility in two related ways. First, there is the possibility that a course of treatment could remove or reduce limitations resulting from the claimant's impairments and allow the claimant to work. Second, there is the question of the extent to which side effects of treatment can be the basis for a finding of disability. Issues raised by both of these questions are discussed in this Section.

In some circumstances, as discussed above with respect to alcoholism and drug addiction, undergoing treatment can effectively be a condition for eligibility. Such a requirement is not limited to drug addiction and alcoholism; the Listing of Impairments, for example, includes some listings that require proof of certain symptoms "despite treatment." *See, e.g.*, 20 C.F.R. Part 404 Subpart P, Appx. 1 (Listings) §§ 11.02, 11.03 (requiring proof that major motor seizures occur more frequently than once a month, or minor motor seizures occur more frequently than once per week, "in spite of at least 3 months of prescribed treatment.").

1. REMEDIABLE DISABILITY

Generally, claimants must follow treatment prescribed by their physicians in order to obtain benefits—if the treatment can restore their ability to perform substantial gainful activity. *See* 20 C.F.R. §§ 404.1530, 416.930. Benefits will be denied or terminated when a claimant fails to follow prescribed treatment without a good reason. 20 C.F.R. §§ 404.1530(b), 416.930(b). SSA recognizes, however, that there are acceptable reasons for failing to follow prescribed treatment. These include, but are not limited to, the following: prescribed treatment is "contrary to the established teaching and tenets of [the claimant's] religion"; the same surgery was previously performed unsuccessfully; or because of its magnitude, unusual nature, or other reason, the treatment is "very risky" for the claimant. 20 C.F.R. §§ 404.1530(c), 416.930(c); *see also* SSR 82–59, 1975–1982 Soc. Sec. Rep. Ser. 793 (1982) (noting that an individual does not have to present documentation to develop church teachings in Christian Science cases, because it is well established that the religion proscribes acceptance of medical treatment). Moreover, SSA will consider an individual's physical, mental, educational, and linguistic limitations (including any lack of facility with the English language) when determining if he or she has an acceptable reason for refusing treatment. 20 C.F.R. §§ 404.1530(c), 416.930(c).

Social Security Administration policy and procedures relative to the prescribed treatment requirement are detailed in SSR 18–3p (2018), which provides that there must be evidence that the claimant's own medical source prescribed treatment for the "medically determinable impairment(s) upon which the disability finding is based." Therefore, SSA will not require claimants to follow treatment prescribed by a consultative examiner, medical or psychological consultant, medical expert, or by "a medical source during an evaluation conducted solely to determine eligibility to any State or Federal benefit." *Id.*

SSR 18–3p also sets the process by which SSA determines whether an individual has failed to follow prescribed treatment. First, the treatment must, if followed, be expected to restore the person's ability to engage in substantial gainful activity (SGA). *See also* Gutierrez v. Colvin, 67 F.Supp.3d 1198, 1204, 218 Soc. Sec. Rep. Serv. 178 (D. Colo. 2014) ("A treatment that is ineffective (or worse yet, exacerbating) is no treatment at all, and a claimant cannot be faulted for failing to follow such a course of treatment."). If so, SSA will assess whether the person has "good cause" for not following that treatment. The Ruling then goes on to identify examples of good-cause reasons, including those based on religion, cost, prior history, and risk. Thus, if the reason is that the treatment goes against the tenets of the person's religion, the claimant "must identify the religion, provide evidence of the individual's membership in or affiliation to his or her religion, and provide evidence that the religion's teachings do not permit the individual to follow the prescribed treatment"; a claimant who cannot afford the prescribed treatment "must demonstrate why he or she does not have health insurance that pays for the prescribed treatment or why he or she failed to obtain treatment at [an available] free or subsidized healthcare provider." Consistent with the prior Rulings, SSR 18–3p provides that one cannot refuse surgery just because "success is not guaranteed or [the claimant] knows of someone else for whom the treatment was not successful."

In a separate Ruling, SSA has highlighted the efficacy of prescribed treatment in the evaluation of epilepsy. *See* SSR 87–6 (1987) (noting that "only a small percentage of epileptics" under appropriate treatment cannot engage in SGA; "Situations where the seizures are not under good control are usually due to the individual's noncompliance with the prescribed treatment rather than the ineffectiveness of the treatment itself.").

A failure to follow treatment results in ineligibility only if the treatment is "prescribed." *See* 20 C.F.R. §§ 404.1530, 416.930. Thus, treatment that is merely recommended or suggested need not be followed. Schena v. Secretary 635 F.2d 15, 19 (1st Cir. 1980) ("the denial of benefits because of Schena's alleged 'willful refusal to follow a recommended course of treatment' disregards the language of the regulation which specifically speaks in terms of the willful failure to follow 'prescribed' treatment. That various physicians suggested the operation does not necessarily mean that they prescribed it."). Moreover, the treatment must have been prescribed by a treating source; a prescription by a consultative physician does not meet this requirement. If any treating source of the claimant advises against treatment prescribed by another treating source, the claimant's failure to follow the treatment is justified. SSR 18–3p (2018) ("we will only determine if the individual has failed to follow prescribed treatment . . . if the individual's own medical source(s) prescribed the treatment."). This is also the case if the claimant chooses alternative treatment prescribed by a second treating source.

As noted above, a lack of financial resources can be a justifiable cause for failing to follow prescribed treatments if a claimant cannot afford the treatment. The claimant's financial circumstances and contacts with all possible free or subsidized treatment sources must be documented (when treatment is not reasonably available, a referral to the state vocational rehabilitation agency should be made). *See, e.g.*, Stennett v. Commissioner, 476 F.Supp.2d

665, 673 (E.D. Mich. 2007) (error to find condition remediable without inquiring into whether claimant could afford the treatment; treatment notes indicated that the claimant "was not attending physical therapy 'secondary to cost,' not because he had improved"). *See also* SSR 18–3p (2018) (listing circumstances where "an individual's failure to follow prescribed treatment will be generally accepted as 'justifiable' and, therefore, such 'failure' would not preclude a finding of 'disability' or that disability continues": "The individual is unable to afford prescribed treatment which he or she is willing to accept, but for which free community resources are unavailable[;]" if the person cannot afford the prescribed treatment, he or she "must demonstrate why he or she does not have health insurance that pays for the prescribed treatment or why he or she failed to obtain treatment at [an available] free or subsidized healthcare provider."). The rule on inability to afford treatment applies equally to treatments that, if followed, would reduce impairment severity to the point of no longer meeting listing criteria at Step 3 of the sequential evaluation process. *See, e.g.,* Gamble v. Chater, 68 F.3d 319, 322, 49 Soc. Sec. Rep. Serv. 241 (9th Cir. 1995) (listing for leg amputation required proof of the "[i]nability to use a prosthesis effectively, without obligatory assistive devices"; "The relevant question is not whether somewhere on the planet there exists a prosthesis that the claimant could use, if only he could afford the enormous price; rather, the question is whether the claimant, himself, can realistically obtain such a prosthesis. A claimant who cannot afford a prosthesis is, as a practical matter, unable to obtain one. There is no prosthesis for him to use effectively.").

The issue of failure to follow prescribed treatment can arise in situations where a doctor advises a claimant to lose weight or to stop smoking. Generally, the failure to do so, or to do so successfully, will not preclude eligibility. *See, e.g.*, Russ v. Barnhart, 363 F.Supp.2d 1345, 1347, 103 Soc. Sec. Rep. Serv. 614 (M.D. Fla. 2005) ("In cases involving obesity, '[a] physician's recommendation to lose weight does not necessarily constitute a prescribed course of treatment, nor does a claimant's failure to accomplish the recommended change constitute a refusal to undertake such treatment.' ")(quoting McCall v. Bowen, 846 F.2d 1317, 1319 (11th Cir.1988)).

Finally, a claimant's history in following prescribed treatment aimed at alleviating disabling symptom, such as pain, can be taken into account—one way or another—when evaluating a claimant's subjective symptom testimony. As set out in SSR 16–3p (2016): "Persistent attempts to obtain relief of symptoms, such as increasing dosages and changing medications, trying a variety of treatments, referrals to specialists, or changing treatment sources may be an indication that an individual's symptoms are a source of distress and may show that they are intense and persistent. In contrast, if the frequency or extent of the treatment sought by an individual is not comparable with the degree of the individual's subjective complaints, or if the individual fails to follow prescribed treatment that might improve symptoms, we may find the alleged intensity and persistence of an individual's symptoms are inconsistent with the overall evidence of record." *See also* Myles v. Astrue, 582 F.3d 672, 677, 147 Soc. Sec. Rep. Serv. 48 (7th Cir. 2009) ("ALJ was required to consider explanations for instances where Myles did not keep up with her treatment, and he did not do so"). Issues of claimant credibility and the credibility of lay witnesses are discussed generally in Chapter 9.

2. DISABILITY DUE TO EFFECTS OF PRESCRIBED MEDICATION

Social Security regulations do not speak generally to the evaluation of side effects; however, the regulations reflect SSA's policy to consider all of an individual's symptoms, including pain. 20 C.F.R. §§ 404.1529(a), 416.929(a). As noted earlier in this chapter, those regulations acknowledge that subjective symptoms can demonstrate that an impairment is more severe than can be shown by objective medical evidence alone and that SSA will evaluate any other information that an individual submits about his or her symptoms. *See* 20 C.F.R. §§ 404.1529(c)(3), 416.929(c)(3). Among the factors that are considered as potentially relevant to an assessment of an individual's symptoms, such as pain, include the type, dosage, effectiveness, and side effects of any medication taken to alleviate those symptoms. 20 C.F.R. §§ 404.1529(c)(3)(iv), 416.929(c)(3)(iv).

Strictly speaking, disability cannot be based on the effects of prescribed medication alone. There must also be an underlying physical or mental impairment for which the drug treatment has been prescribed. Thus, this is better understood as a combination-of-impairments issue, involving a primary impairment for which medications have been prescribed and a secondary set of limitations due to the side effects of the medications.

As with all any impairment, the burden of proof is on the claimant to show that there are disabling side effects caused by a particular drug. The side effects of medication should be taken into account at all steps of the sequential evaluation process, including for certain listings in the Listing of Impairments. *See, e.g.*, 20 C.F.R. Part 404 Subpart P, Appx. 1 (Listings) § 11.00(A) (epilepsy listings; "Where adequate seizure control is obtained only with unusually large doses, the possibility of impairment resulting from the side effects of this medication must also be assessed."). *See also* Kennedy v. Heckler, 602 F. Supp. 709, 712, 8 Soc. Sec. Rep. Serv. 807 (W.D.N.C. 1985) ("the ALJ failed to take into account the . . . disabling effects of taking from ten to forty mg. of stellazine [sic] a day. [The claimant's] 'stability' is clearly attributable to her heavy medication and artificially stabilized environment") (citing listing for mental impairments). Side effects of medication must be considered as well in determining whether a claimant retains the ability to perform past relevant work, or any other work in the national economy. *See, e.g.*, Stewart v. Secretary, 714 F.2d 287, 288–290 (3d Cir. 1983) (claimant "testified that he took three or four percodan tablets a day as well as valium" and that these pain medications "made him feel 'drugged'" and "made it difficult for him to concentrate and impaired his memory"; ALJ erred by "fail[ing] to provide any explanation for his implicit rejection of [the claimant's] testimony regarding the effects of the medication"); McDevitt v. Commissioner, 241 Fed. Appx. 615, 616 (11th Cir. July 18, 2007) ("While the ALJ found McDevitt's testimony 'somewhat exaggerated,' the ALJ made no finding, as to credibility or otherwise, regarding McDevitt's claim that his medications caused severe concentration problems and made him drowsy. Since the ALJ failed to make a finding as to this claim, the ALJ's determination that McDevitt could perform the duties of a telemarketer was not based on substantial evidence in the record.").

CHAPTER 7

CALCULATION AND PAYMENT OF BENEFITS

The method for determining the amount of Old Age, Survivors, and Disability Insurance (OASDI) and Supplemental Security Income (SSI) benefit payments are fundamentally different because OASDI is a social insurance program while SSI is a public assistance program. Social insurance payments are tied, more or less, to the amount of workers' earnings subject to payroll taxes, while public assistance payments are tied to a fixed standard of financial need. Thus, OASDI benefit payments are calculated by using a formula that includes the number of years wage earners worked and the amount their earnings. SSI payments are set at the amount required for the individual to meet according to a federal standard of need. These two different methods for calculating benefit payment amounts are discussed in the next two sections of this chapter.

There are a number of other provisions that affect the amount of benefit payments, particularly with respect to the OASDI program. Although a detailed review of all of the factors that go into benefit computations is beyond the scope of this book, two related rules for reducing benefit payments deserve special attention: the treatment of certain other benefits received by the beneficiary, and the calculation of OASDI benefit payments to multiple beneficiaries on the basis of a single wage earner's earnings record. These rules are discussed immediately following the sections on OASDI and SSI benefit computations. The chapter concludes with a discussion of adjustments for overpayments and underpayments, rules governing the suspension of benefits, and payments made to representative payees.

A. OASDI INSURANCE FORMULA

Consistent with its purposes as a contribution-based social insurance program, the amount of benefits that an OASDI beneficiary is entitled to receive will be based, to a certain extent, on the earnings record of the claimant—or of the wage earner on the basis of whose earnings record a dependent's or survivor's claim is based. As described in detail in Chapters 2 and 3, a wage earner (or the wage earner on whose earnings record benefits are claimed) must have worked and paid Social Security taxes in a sufficient amount over a specified period of time in order to be "insured" under the program and for the wage earner (or the person seeking benefits based on the wage earner's earnings record) to be eligible to receive benefits. The base amount of benefits paid to insured wage earners is determined by applying various calculations to the data from their earnings record to arrive at their "Primary Insurance Amount."

1. PRIMARY INSURANCE AMOUNT (PIA)

The amount of monthly OASDI benefits paid to a beneficiary is based on the relevant wage earner's

Primary Insurance Amount (PIA), which is, in turn, based on the wage earner's average indexed monthly earnings (AIME). *See* 20 C.F.R. §§ 404.204, 210. (Other methods were used earlier for persons who turned 62 before 1979 or who did most of their eligible work prior to 1951.) AIMEs are calculated by indexing earnings to adjust for the upward trend in wages over the years. *See generally* 20 C.F.R. § 404.210; *see also* 20 C.F.R. § 404.211. Wage earners' earnings for years creditable for Social Security purposes are indexed by comparing those earnings in each year with the average earnings in that year, and then adjusting the earnings to reflect average increases in earnings in the relevant time period. *See* 20 C.F.R. § 404.211(d). Each year in which the wage earner had sufficient earnings to qualify for "insured status" is used, except that up to five of those years with lower earnings can be deducted to arrive at the required number of "benefit computation years." 20 C.F.R. § 404.211(e). The AIME is then calculated by adding together the indexed earnings in the benefit computation years; dividing that sum by the number of months in those years; and rounding down to the next dollar. 20 C.F.R. § 404.211(f). For an example of indexing a worker's earnings see 20 C.F.R. § 404.211(d).

SSA then uses a formula to convert wage earners' AIME to their PIA, which becomes the base amount of a wage earner's monthly benefit. This formula revolves around the use of certain "bend points," which operate by paying × percent of a first prescribed amount of the AIME, y percent of a next prescribed amount of the AIME, and so on. The practical reality of these bend points is to favor wage earners with lower AIME amounts, as can be seen by looking at the percentage of the AIME at each bend point that is included in the wage earner's PIA. The bend point amounts are adjusted each year. For example, in the year 2021, the formula adds together 90% of the AIME equal to or less than $996, 32% above $856 and up to $6002, and only 15% over $6002. As a result, the higher a wage earner's AIME, the less the percentage of that amount is included in the wage earner's PIA and thus in the amount of monthly benefits the wage earner actually receives. *See generally* 20 C.F.R. § 404.212.

2. EARLY- AND DELAYED-RETIREMENT BENEFITS

Social Security old age benefits are reduced when the beneficiary begins receiving them before full retirement age. Typically, the amount of reduced benefits represents the amount that the beneficiary would have received at full retirement age less a percentage that reflects the number of months prior to full retirement age at which the beneficiary began receiving benefits. *See* 20 C.F.R. §§ 404.312, 410. Thus, there is a reduction of 5/9 of 1% for each of the first 36 months of early retirement and 5/12 of 1% for each month in excess of 36. 20 C.F.R. § 404.410(a). In other words, persons who retire three years before full retirement age receives 20% (36 months × 5/9 of 1%) less per month than they would have received if benefits began only at full retirement age. For every month over 36 months in which wage earners retires early, they receive an additional 5/12 of 1% reduction for each additional month of early retirement. Therefore, wage earners who retire four years before full retirement—the earliest retirement date for persons with the current full retirement age of 66—receive 25 percent (36 months × 5/9 of 1% plus 12 months × 5/12 of 1%) less per month than they would receive if they had retired at full retirement age.

The Social Security Act also includes the option of delaying retirement up to the age of 70 and thereby receive a larger benefit amount, either by continuing to work beyond full retirement age or by simply waiting to receive benefits. *See generally* 20 C.F.R. § 404.313. The amount of delayed-retirement benefits is calculated by increasing the amount paid on one's PIA. For individuals born after January 1, 1943, the rate of increase is 2/3 of 1% per month, or up to 8% per year. 20 C.F.R. § 404.313(b)(2).

3. DEPENDENT BENEFITS

When a dependent of an insured wage earner—usually a spouse or a child—receives benefits under the wage earner's account, the benefits formula begins with the insured wage earner's Primary Insurance Amount (PIA). Then, depending on the type of benefit involved, the basic benefit amount can be a percentage of—or the full amount of—the wage earner's PIA. In the case of child's benefits, for example, the amount is 75% of the wage earner's PIA if the wage earner has died and 50% if retired or disabled (42 U.S.C. § 402(d)(2); 20 C.F.R. § 404.353); in the case of widow(er)'s benefits, the basic amount is 100% of the insured wage earner's PIA, unless the wage earner had been receiving old age benefits that were reduced because he or she began receiving those benefits before reaching full retirement age. 42 U.S.C. § 402(e)(2)(A), (f)(2)(A); 20 C.F.R. § 404.338. Finally, the benefit amount actually paid may be reduced for a number of other reasons. The two most important are the payment of secondary benefits to other persons on the same wage earner's account—the so-called family maximum—and the receipt of certain other benefits, both of which are discussed later in this chapter.

B. SSI STANDARD OF NEED

The Supplemental Security Income (SSI) program is designed to provide elderly, blind, and disabled people a certain minimum level of income. As discussed in Chapter 2, this policy is reflected in the financial requirements for eligibility. Unlike OASDI benefits, SSI benefit amounts are not based on earnings since SSI is not a contribution-based social insurance program. SSI benefits are available only to persons who are disabled, blind, or elderly and have limited resources and limited income. If an SSI applicant or beneficiary has income low enough to qualify for eligibility, then that income will be taken into consideration when calculating the amount of benefit payments. (The SSI financial eligibility rules also take into account a claimant's resources. However, unlike the income rules, once a claimant meets the resource requirements for eligibility those rules have no effect on the amount of benefits paid—except to the extent that income produced from certain allowed resources can be considered income.)

SSI benefit calculations begin with a national standard of need based on an initial monthly benefit rate set by Congress when the program began in 1974 plus various cost-of-living increases passed by Congress since then (including an automatic cost-of-living increase currently in place). The 2021 benefit amount for individuals is $794 per month; the amount for an eligible couple is $1,191 per month. States may supplement the federal program with additional payments, at their option. *See* 20 C.F.R. § 416.110(f) (requiring also that states supplement SSI benefits for persons who had received old age or disability benefits in 1973 under pre-SSI federal-state programs to insure that they receive at least as much as they did under the discontinued federal-state programs).

A beneficiary with no other income will receive the full amount of the standard of need. For beneficiaries with other sources of income, the base amount is reduced dollar-for-dollar by the amount of any income received and not otherwise excluded as countable income under essentially the same income rules that are used to determine eligibility. The most common exclusion is the first $20 per month of other Social Security benefits. (The SSI income exclusion rules are discussed in detail in Chapter 2)

C. MULTIPLE BENEFITS; FAMILY MAXIMUM

Persons eligible for OASDI or SSI benefits often are eligible for other benefits under the Social Security Act or through other types of benefit programs. To the extent that any such benefits are considered income by the applicable federal regulations, they will be counted as appropriate in determining the amount of benefits. There are, in addition, special income rules that apply to the treatment of certain types of other benefits.

One set of special rules applies when claimants are eligible for benefits on the basis of both their own and someone else's earnings, typically a spouse or parent. This occurs, for example, where someone is entitled to old age or disability benefits as an insured wage earner and is also entitled to secondary benefits as a spouse or child. In such cases, the secondary benefit is reduced by the amount of the primary benefit, but not below zero, so that the total amount of benefits will be the greater amount of the two. 20 C.F.R. § 404.407(a). Children eligible for benefits on more than one wage earner's account receive the benefits payable through the account with the largest Primary Insurance Amount. 20 C.F.R. § 404.407(d). The basic approach of these rules is to leave the beneficiaries with at least the amount of the highest paying benefits to which they are entitled.

There are also rules as to how receipt of certain non-Social Security benefits can affect the amount of OASDI benefits. For example, a wage earner's Social Security benefits are reduced when the wage earner receives payments under a worker's compensation law as well, and that reduction is also passed on to children receiving benefits under the wage earner's account. The formula for this "workers' compensation offset" is set out at 20 C.F.R. § 404.408(c); *see also id.*

§ 404.408(h)(2), Example 2 (essentially reducing the amount of disability benefits so that the total amount of the two benefit payments will not exceed 80% of the beneficiary's pre-injury earnings, using one of three methods specified in the statute). Also, certain dependent benefits are reduced if the beneficiary is receiving a government pension not covered by the Social Security Act. *See* 20 C.F.R. § 404.408a.

Finally, there are special rules where several persons are eligible for and receiving Social Security benefits based on a single wage earner's earnings record. Because the number of potential claimants on a single wage earner's earnings may be quite large, the Social Security Act sets a maximum amount of benefits payable in any month on any account. This amount, known as the "family maximum," is determined using the insured wage earner's Primary Insurance Amount (PIA). There are a number of different ways to calculate the family maximum depending on the year that the wage earner died, turned 62, or became disabled—all of which set the amount somewhere between approximately 150 to approximately 175 percent of the wage earner's PIA. *See generally* 42 U.S.C. § 403(a); 20 C.F.R. § 404.403. The basic rule is to reduce proportionately all benefits other than those of the primary wage earner so that the total amount paid to all beneficiaries does not exceed the family maximum. 20 C.F.R. § 404.404. Benefit payments to divorced spouses, including surviving divorced spouses, are determined outside of the family maximum rule, presumably because these persons are considered outside of the wage earner's family. Thus, those benefits are calculated without regard to other benefits based on the insured deceased former spouse's account. 42 U.S.C. § 403(a)(3)(C).

SSI benefits usually are reduced dollar-for-dollar to account for any other benefit payments. However, as noted earlier, the first $20 per month of other Social Security benefits are not counted, resulting in a $20 net gain for SSI recipients receiving other Social Security benefits as well. Payments of retroactive monthly Social Security benefits are treated as unearned income, but the amount is calculated as if the retroactive benefits were received on a regular, monthly basis. *See* 42 U.S.C. § 1320a–6; 20 C.F.R. § 416.1123(d). The idea is to prevent potential windfalls to an individual who may qualify for both OASDI and SSI benefits. In effect, the retroactive benefits are reduced by an amount equal to the amount of SSI payments that would not have been paid if the Social Security benefits had been paid when regularly due, rather than retroactively. 20 C.F.R. § 416.1123(d)(1). Since the amount of the reduction is calculated based on what would have been the impact of the receipt of the Social Security benefits, if a balance is owed after the reduction is made that balance will not count as unearned income for SSI purposes in a subsequent month in which it is received.

D. PAYMENT OF BENEFITS

OASDI benefits are payable beginning with the first month covered by an application in which the claimant meets all of the requirements for entitlement. 20 C.F.R. § 404.316(a). An application for old-age benefits can be effective for up to 6 months prior to the date it was filed; applications for disability benefits can be effective for up to 12 months prior to the date they were filed. These same rules apply to claims by dependent spouses and dependent children. *See, e.g.*, 20 C.F.R. § 404.621.

There is, however, a five-month waiting period for disability benefits, which means that claimants are eligible to receive disability benefit payments only after the first five months of disability. *See* 42 U.S.C.A. §§ 423(a)(1), 423(c)(2); 20 C.F.R. § 404.315(a)(4). The waiting period begins with the first full month in which the claimant is both disabled and insured for disability; it cannot begin, however, earlier than the seventeenth month before the claimant filed for benefits, no matter how long the claimant may have been disabled before then. 42 U.S.C.A. § 423(c)(2)(B); 20 C.F.R. § 404.315(a)(4). While this allows the effect of the waiting period to be cancelled for persons meeting the waiting period requirements up to five months preceding the date they first become eligible to receive payment, it precludes earlier periods of qualifying disability from avoiding the effect of the waiting period. It does not apply, however, to persons who were previously entitled to disability benefits or to a period of disability any time within five years of the month they again became disabled. 20 C.F.R. § 404.315(a)(4). Nor does it apply to persons with amyotrophic lateral sclerosis (ALS), or "Lou Gehrig's disease," who applied for disability benefits on or after December 23, 2020. *See* ALS Disability

Insurance Access Act of 2019, Public Law No: 116–250, 134 Stat. 1128 (December 22, 2020).

Unlike OASDI, Supplemental Security Income (SSI) benefits are payable only from the first day of the month following the date the application was filed or eligibility was first established, whichever is later. 20 C.F.R. § 416.501. On the other hand, there is no waiting period for SSI benefits.

When first found eligible for benefits, most claimants receive a lump sum payment of "past-due" benefits covering the period from the first month of eligibility to the month when the first regular payment is made. If past-due benefits for SSI recipients under the age of 18 are greater than six times the monthly benefit amount, the funds must be placed in a dedicated account and spent only for limited purposes. Expenses that may be paid with these funds include certain medical, personal, and educational needs of the child. *See* 20 C.F.R. §§ 416.546, 416.640(e).

E. OVERPAYMENTS AND UNDERPAYMENTS

Federal regulations provide for the adjustment of OASDI and SSI benefit payments if a recipient receives more or less than the amount due under applicable law. *See generally* 42 U.S.C. § 404(a)(1); 20 C.F.R. §§ 404.502, 503. When a recipient receives more than the correct amount due for any given period, it is called an overpayment; when less than the correct amount of benefits is received, including when no payment is made at all, it is called an underpayment.

In the absence of a waiver (discussed below), SSA can recover overpayments by withholding all or part of a recipient's monthly or past-due benefits. *See generally* 20 C.F.R. §§ 404.535, 416.573. The entire amount of current benefit payments may be withheld if the recipient "willfully misrepresented or concealed material information" concerning the overpayment. 20 C.F.R. §§ 404.535(a), (b)(2)(ii), 416.573(a), 573(b)(3)(ii). Otherwise, monthly overpayment repayment is limited to 10 percent from monthly benefits. 20 C.F.R. §§ 404.535(b)(1), 416.573(b)(1).

As for paying an underpayment, if the recipient is still living SSA will pay the amount due either through a separate lump sum payment or by increasing the recipient's monthly payment. 20 C.F.R. §§ 404.503(a), 416.542(a). If an underpaid OASDI recipient is dead, SSA will make payments to their dependents. 42 U.S.C.A. § 404(d); 20 C.F.R. § 404.503(b)–(e). If an SSI recipient is dead, underpaid surviving spouses will be paid only if they were living with the underpaid recipient and eligible for SSI. 20 C.F.R. § 416.542(b).

1. WAIVER OF OVERPAYMENT RECOVERY AND RIGHT TO APPEAL

An overpayment of an OASDI benefit can be waived if the recipient was "without fault" in obtaining the overpayment and if recovery would either defeat the purpose of the Social Security Act or be "against equity and good conscience." 42 U.S.C.

§ 404(b)("there shall be no adjustment of payments to, or recovery by the United States from, any person who is without fault if such adjustment or recovery would defeat the purpose of this subchapter or would be against equity and good conscience."). *See also* 20 C.F.R. § 404.506. Whether a recipient was at fault depends on whether the overpayment resulted from an incorrect statement the recipient knew or should have known to be incorrect, failed to furnish information that the recipient knew or should have known to be material, or, with respect to a payment already received, if the recipient knew or could have been expected to know that accepting the payment was incorrect. 20 C.F.R. § 404.507. *See also* 20 C.F.R. § 404.510(a) (setting out an extensive, nonexclusive list of situations where an individual will be considered to be "without fault"). Fault is assessed with respect to the recipient only, not with respect to others who may have known better. *See, e.g.*, Coulston v. Apfel, 224 F.3d 897, 899, 71 Soc. Sec. Rep. Serv. 35 (8th Cir. 2000) (recipient's ex-wife and a friend knew of or should have suspected the error; "This may well be true, but it is irrelevant. The Administration's regulations state that a claimant is at fault if he knew or should have known the overpayment was incorrect. The Administration's regulations also state that the determination of fault is only made as to the overpaid individual or any other person from whom the Administration seeks to recover.") (citing 20 C.F.R. § 404.507).

Recouping an OASDI overpayment will be considered to defeat the purpose of the Act if it would "deprive a person of income required for ordinary and necessary living expenses," which "depends upon whether the person has an income or financial resources sufficient for more than ordinary and necessary needs, or is dependent upon all of his current benefits for such needs," including fixed living expenses, medical expenses, and expenses for others the person is legally responsible for supporting." 20 C.F.R. § 404.508(a). Waiver of an SSI overpayment is also available if the recipient was without fault and recovery would defeat the purpose of the Act, be against equity and good conscience, or "impede the efficient or effective administration" of the program because of the small amount involved. 42 U.S.C. § 1383(b)(1)(B). *See also* 20 C.F.R. § 416.550.

SSA is required to send notice to an overpaid recipient (and anyone else from whom it intends to recover benefits or whose benefits it intends to adjust) informing them of their right to request a waiver of the recovery or adjustment. 20 C.F.R. §§ 404.502a, 416.558(a). Although the Social Act does not require that SSA hold a hearing to determine whether an overpayment has occurred or if a recipient is entitled to a waiver of recovery, the Supreme Court has held that when a recipient requests a waiver, an oral hearing is required before any recoupment can take place. Califano v. Yamasaki, 442 U.S. 682 (1979).

Where a beneficiary has been both overpaid and underpaid before neither the overpayment nor the underpayment has been accounted for, SSA adjusts future benefit payments in order to resolve the underpayment and the overpayment at the same time. In effect, the agency "nets" the overpayment and underpayment amounts by calculating the difference between an underpayment and an overpayment and treating the netted amount either as an adjusted overpayment or an adjusted underpayment, as the case may be. *See* 20 C.F.R. §§ 404.504, 416.538(a). The Supreme Court upheld the "netting" system in Sullivan v. Everhart, 494 U.S. 83 (1990).

F. SUSPENSION OF BENEFITS

The Social Security Administration may, under certain circumstances, temporarily suspend benefits awarded under both the OASDI and the SSI program. This may occur in the SSI program when a beneficiary's "countable income" or "countable resources" exceed the standards for financial need. *See* 20 C.F.R. §§ 416.1323(a), 416.1324(a)(1). SSI benefits may also be suspended if eligibility was conditioned on the beneficiary disposing of specified resources and failed to do so. 20 C.F.R. § 416.1324(a)(2). Benefits can be suspended under both programs if a beneficiary fails to provide certain information, including medical information relevant to determining whether a recipient of disability benefits is still disabled. *See* 20 C.F.R. §§ 404.1596(b)(2)(i), 416.1322.

SSI benefits will also be suspended when a beneficiary is confined to prison or most other public institutions, subject to certain limited exceptions. 20 C.F.R. §§ 416.1325, 416.211 (listing exceptions).

OASDI benefits will be suspended as well when a beneficiary is confined to prison, but not when confined to other types of public institutions unless, with respect to a criminal offense, confined by court order after having been found guilty but insane, not guilty by reason of insanity, or incompetent to stand trial—or if confined on the basis of "a similar verdict or finding with respect to such an offense based on similar factors (such as a mental disease, a mental defect, or mental incompetence)." 42 U.S.C. § 402(x)(1)(A)(ii). *See* Artz v. Barnhart, 330 F.3d 170, 88 Soc. Sec. Rep. Serv. 1 (3d Cir. 2003) (suspension of benefits for recipient involuntarily committed to a state psychiatric hospital upheld as confinement "in connection with not-guilty-by-reason-of-insanity verdict").

G. REPRESENTATIVE PAYEES

Representative payees are persons or organizations selected by the Social Security Administration to receive payments on behalf of a recipient of OASDI or SSI benefits. *See generally* 42 U.S.C.A. §§ 405(j), 1383(a)(2)(A)(ii). SSA reserves the right to certify benefit payments to a representative payee if "the interests of the beneficiary would be better served" by doing so due to the beneficiary's mental or physical condition, or their young age. 20 C.F.R. §§ 404.2001(a), 416.601(a). Although this may include a beneficiary otherwise considered to be legally competent, *see* 20 C.F.R. §§ 404.2001(a), 416.601(a), for the most part representative payees are used where the beneficiary is either "legally incompetent or mentally incapable of managing benefit payments" or is "physically incapable of managing or directing the management of his or her benefit payments." *See* 20 C.F.R. §§ 404.2010(a), 416.610(a); *see also id.* §§ 404.2010(a), 416.610(a) (special rules for beneficiaries under the age of 18). As noted in Chapter 6, until 1996 alcoholism could itself be a qualifying disabling condition, but now someone addicted to drugs or alcohol can be eligible only if the addiction was not material to the determination of disability. Current SSI regulations still state that representative payees will be certified where the beneficiary is "eligible for benefits solely on the basis of disability and drug addiction or alcoholism is a contributing factor material to the determination of disability," 20 C.F.R. § 416.610(a)(3), but presumably in practice that rule means that a representative payee may be appointed where an otherwise eligible recipient has an addiction that was not material to the determination of their disability.

The highest priority is given to legal guardians or spouses for beneficiaries who are at least 18 years old, and to the natural or adoptive parents or guardians for beneficiaries under the age of 18. *See* 20 C.F.R. §§ 404.2021(a)(1), 404.2021(c)(1), 416.621(a)(1), 416.621(c)(1). Federal, state, and certain private agencies can become representative payees for recipients receiving certain services, including foster care and institutional care, and can use the funds they receive to pay for that care. 20 C.F.R. §§ 404.2040(b), 416.640(b). *See also* 20 C.F.R. §§ 404.2035, 416.635 (listing qualified individuals and organizations that can serve as representative payees and be compensated for that service). Representative payees should be persons or organizations that "best serve the interest of the beneficiary," which, for individuals, should include consideration of the relationship between the beneficiary and the possible payee, the amount of interest the payee shows in the beneficiary, and any legal authority that the payee may have relative to the beneficiary—such as being the beneficiary's custodian. 20 C.F.R. §§ 404.2020, 416.620.

As of 2020, beneficiaries can designate a preferred represented payee in advance. 20 C.F.R. §§ 404.2018, 416.618. SSA will consider appointing such "advance designees" before considering any other potential representative payee. 20 C.F.R. §§ 404.2021, 416.921.

The regulations set out examples of the proper use of funds on behalf of a beneficiary, such as for their current maintenance, institutional care, support of legal dependents, and claims of creditors. 20 C.F.R. §§ 404.2040, 416.640. There are also a number of regulations aimed specifically at institutional representative payees. These include rules on notifying beneficiaries when SSA intends to appoint a representative payee, giving the beneficiary the opportunity to appeal the proposed appointment. *See* 20 C.F.R. §§ 404.2030, 416.630.

Finally, SSA regulations require criminal background checks on potential representative payees every 5 years and also prohibit persons who have been convicted of certain crimes from serving. 20 C.F.R. §§ 404.2026, 404.2022, 416.626, 416.622.

While the regulations identify specifically certain of those crimes, including human trafficking, false imprisonment, kidnapping, rape or sexual assault, fraud to obtain government benefits, theft of government funds or property, and abuse or neglect, 20 C.F.R. §§ 404.2022(f), 416.622(f), they also provide for an exception "if the nature of the conviction is such that selection of the applicant poses no risk to the beneficiary and the exception is in the beneficiary's best interest." 20 C.F.R. §§ 404.2022(b), 416.622(b).

CHAPTER 8

SOCIAL SECURITY PRACTICE

As with other areas of law practice, Social Security practice involves both substantive law—the various provisions of the Social Security Act, Social Security Administration rules and regulations interpreting and implementing the Act, and federal court case law as presented and discussed in previous chapters of this book—and rules of procedure. In the case of Social Security practice, the procedural rules are influenced to a large extent by the sheer volume of cases that pass through the system, especially at the administrative level. This chapter covers the basic structure for processing claims for Old Age, Survivors, and Disability Insurance (OASDI) and Supplemental Security Income (SSI) benefits, including all levels of administrative decision making and appeals. It also covers briefly judicial review and various provisions for attorney's fees.

For the most part, Social Security practice is concentrated at the administrative appeals process. And the vast majority of cases handled by lawyers involve claims for disability benefits. Selected issues of administrative advocacy that are particularly important when handling a Social Security disability benefits case are covered in more detail in Chapter 9.

A. ADMINISTRATIVE DECISIONMAKING PROCESS

Social Security claims pass through one of the largest administrative decision-making systems in the world. Millions of claims are filed every year and hundreds of thousands of claims are contested through three of levels of administrative review. The current Social Security decision-making process is complex not only because of the large numbers of claims and appeals, but also because the vast majority of disputed claims involve the determination of disability. Deciding whether any one claimant is unable to engage in "substantial gainful activity" in light of not only his or her physical and mental impairments, but also while taking into account any effects of age, education, and prior work experience, can be difficult; making fair and accurate disability determinations for millions of claims (and in hundreds of thousands of appeals) is a daunting task. Some of this work is reflected in the statutory disability standard and the various regulations that interpret that standard. As explained in Chapter 5, the "sequential evaluation process" and its components, including the Listing of Impairments and the Medical-Vocational Guidelines, provide important structure for reaching a decision. The setting in which it all takes place—and which influences greatly the quality of decisions on claims for benefits—is the administrative process.

There are four levels of administrative decision-making for Social Security claims—the initial decision plus up to three stages of administrative review—and most claims must pass through each before a decision is subject to judicial review. The process begins at the local Social Security Administration district office, but the all-important disability decisions are then contracted out to state-run agencies. SSA, together with the relevant state agency for claims for disability benefits, makes the initial decision and, in case of appeal, performs the first level of review known as reconsideration. The next two levels of administrative appeal are handled also by SSA, but through two separate appeal units: the Office of Hearing Operations (OHO) and the Office of Appellate Operations (OAO), known together formerly as the Office of Disability Adjudication and Review (ODAR). OHO is responsible for de novo administrative hearings conducted by independent administrative law judges; OAO includes the Appeals Council, which reviews administrative hearing decisions on appeal or on its own initiative and can, in limited circumstances, conduct the initial administrative hearing. Each of these four parts of the Social Security administrative process—the initial decision, reconsideration, administrative hearings, and Appeals Council review—are discussed in some detail in the next two sections of this chapter.

Much has been written about the problems associated with Social Security claim processing and appeals, and SSA has attempted over the years to meet various criticisms by proposing—but usually failing to implement—broad systemic reform. One prominent example was an experiment with eliminating reconsideration altogether, which continued in different offices and various forms for decades only to be abandoned in 2018. *See* 83 Fed. Reg. 63965 (December 12, 2018).

B. APPLICATION AND INITIAL DECISION

An application for Old Age, Survivors, and Disability Insurance (OASDI) or Supplemental Security Income (SSI) benefits must be filed with the Social Security Administration. If an applicant has any doubt as to which program would be appropriate, or if eligibility may be established for both, applications for both types of benefits may be filed. Most applications are filed at a local SSA office. *See* 20 C.F.R. §§ 404.614, 416.325. Applications for OASDI benefits usually are considered filed on the date received; however, the postmark date will be used if the date received "would result in the loss or lessening of rights." 20 C.F.R. § 404.614(b)(2). The same rule is used for SSI, if use of the later date would result in "a loss of benefits." 20 C.F.R. § 416.325(b)(1). SSA also allows applications for OASDI benefits to be filed online via the SSA website. 20 C.F.R. § 422.505(a). Applications for SSI benefits can be filed online as well, but only when applying for both Disability Insurance Benefits and SSI at the same time (known as a "concurrent" application).

Most SSA offices have "specialists" who deal with claims for OASDI benefits and different specialists who deal with claims for SSI. These specialists assist the claimant with the application process. The initial application form includes detailed questions relevant to program eligibility and the claimant is expected to provide full information to support his or her claim.

Not surprisingly, the greatest amount of information requested is for disability claims. A special disability report form requests information used to determine the nature of the claimant's physical and mental impairments, the date of onset of the alleged disability, and whether the claimant performed any work after the alleged date of onset. It includes space for claimants to list their medical problems and to explain how the impairments affect their ability to perform work and to participate in daily activities. It also requests information about the claimant's medical records, including any medical tests performed in the past year; the name, address, and telephone number of any doctor or other medical source seen by the claimant; the reasons for the visits; and the type of treatment received. There is also an online version of the disability report form that tracks the paper version of the form. Additional medical and school records can be submitted online as well through an "Electronic Records Express" service on the SSA website. Congress imposed new penalties in 1999 for persons who knowingly make a false or misleading statement or who omit a material fact for use in determining eligibility for benefits. The penalties, which apply to all statements made on or after December 14, 1999, are nonpayment for six months for the first incident, 12 months for the second, and 24 months for any others. *See* 42 U.S.C. § 1320a–8a; 20 C.F.R. §§ 404.459, 416.1340.

Only a few claims for disability benefits—those that can be resolved at Step 1 of the sequential evaluation process—are decided at the local office. This is because Step 1 denials are based on the claimants' performance of substantial gainful activity during the period for which they are seeking benefits. As such, these claims can be determined based on relatively simple and objective vocational evidence without having to assess any alleged physical or mental impairments. All other claims—those that require an assessment of medical evidence—are forwarded for further evaluation to the local state agency charged with the specific responsibility for making disability determinations. *See* 20 C.F.R. §§ 404.1503(a), 416.903(a).

When a claim is received by the state agency, it is assigned to a disability examiner who works together with a member of the medical staff, known as a medical consultant, to determine whether the claimant is disabled, the date the disability began, and, in termination cases, the date the disability ended. After reviewing the file, the examiner decides whether additional medical records are needed and, if so, from which medical sources additional records should be requested. SSA regulations provide that before making a disability determination it will develop a "complete medical history" and "make every reasonable effort" to help claimants obtain relevant evidence from their medical sources. 20 C.F.R. §§ 404.1512(b), 416.912(b). For claims that may involve a mental impairment, the agency must make "every reasonable effort . . . to ensure that a qualified psychiatrist or psychologist has completed the medical portion of the case review and any applicable residual functional capacity assessment." 20 C.F.R. §§ 404.1617(c), 416.1017(c). While claimants are responsible for providing sufficient evidence to prove that they are disabled, SSA can pay for additional existing evidence that the claimant cannot obtain. 20 C.F.R. §§ 404.1514, 416.914. Moreover, if the agency's disability examiner is not able to obtain enough current medical information from the claimant's medical sources, SSA will arrange and pay for a consultative examination. *See* 20 C.F.R. §§ 404.1517, 416.917. Special rules on the weight given to the reports of consultative examinations, particularly when they conflict with reports from a claimant's treating physician, are discussed in detail in Chapter 9.

Once the disability examiner has enough medical information, the examiner—together with a state agency medical consultant—evaluates the claimant's condition according to SSA's sequential evaluation process for determining disability. (The sequential evaluation process is covered in detail in Chapter 5.) Disability examiners usually make the preliminary evaluation at the second and third steps of the process, which require a decision as to whether the claimant has a "severe" impairment and, if so, whether the criteria in the Listing of Impairments have been met or equaled. For claims that may turn on whether the criteria in the Listing have been met, the examiners must consult with the medical consultant on the issue of medical equivalence. *See* SSR 17–2 (2017). If the claim is not granted based on the Listing of Impairments, the examiner works up the last two steps of the sequential evaluation process—on the claimants' ability to perform past work or other work in light of their age, education and work experience—in conjunction with the medical consultant and, in some cases, with a vocational expert. Medical consultants are charged with determining claimants' residual functional capacity (RFC); that is, whether they are able to perform sedentary, light, or medium work. 20 C.F.R. §§ 404.1546, 416.946. The final disability decision is made by the examiner and the consultant together, unless there is no medical evidence in the record—because the agency was unable to obtain any—and the claimant refused to attend a consultative examination without good cause, or, as discussed below, if the claim qualifies for a "Quick Disability Determination." 20 C.F.R. §§ 404.1615(c), 416.1015(c). *See also* 20 C.F.R. §§ 404.1518, 416.918 (setting out the consequences of failure to appear at a consultative examination).

For many years, there were no guidelines for purchasing consultative examinations and the extent to which they were ordered varied widely. In 1991, SSA published detailed regulations that outline when it will, and will not, purchase a consultative examination. Basically, the regulations provide that SSA will purchase a consultative examination "when the evidence as a whole is not sufficient to support a decision" on the claimant's disability, such as when an examination could "secure needed medical evidence, such as clinical findings, laboratory tests, a diagnosis, or prognosis." 20 C.F.R. §§ 404.1519a(b), 416.919a(b). Generally, consultative examinations will not be purchased where non-medical evidence indicates that the claimant would not be eligible for disability benefits over the period at issue. *See* 20 C.F.R. §§ 404.1519b, 416.919b.

Although disability decisions are made by state agencies, the final eligibility decision is always made at the local Social Security district office. Technically, the agency's disability decision is a recommended decision. *See* 20 C.F.R. §§ 404.1503(d), 416.903(d). The reality, however, is that the agency's recommended decision is followed in virtually all cases. But SSA does have the authority to review any decision that an individual is under a disability, either before or after any action is taken on the claim. 42 U.S.C. § 421(c)(1).

Initial disability decisions that SSA does not review are implemented as recommended by the state agency; those that are reviewed are either approved for implementation or returned to the agency for a new decision. Claims are then processed at the local SSA office, including the development of any additional nonmedical requirements, especially for SSI claims, and the awarding of auxiliary benefits to dependents, when required. If the decision is to deny the claim, the notice will explain to the claimant why the claim was denied. The claimant is also notified that a request for reconsideration must be filed within 60 days of the denial. The administrative appeals process is discussed in detail below.

SSA began implementing a special process in 2006 for certain types of claims where it appears that an initial finding of disability can be made within a short period of time. Nationwide implementation of these "Quick Disability Determinations" (QDD) began in early 2008. Claims are selected for a QDD if the file indicates that there is a "high degree of probability" that the claimant is disabled and where the evidence necessary to establish disability can "be easily and quickly verified." *See generally* 20 C.F.R. §§ 404.1619, 416.1019. Under the 2006 rules, the time limit for making a quick decision was twenty days; the twenty-day limit was removed when QDDs were extended nationwide in 2007, on the theory that most QDD decisions would be made within that time period even without a specific requirement and that the advantage of continuing the process beyond twenty days in rare cases outweighed any benefit of holding to a rigid limit. If a claim goes through the QDD procedure but cannot be approved, it continues on through the regular disability determination process. 20 C.F.R. §§ 404.1619(c), 416.1019(c). Around the same time, SSA instituted a process for approving "compassionate allowances" for claimants with medical conditions that "invariably qualify under the Listing of Impairments . . . based on minimal, but sufficient, objective medical evidence." *See* 20 C.F.R. §§ 404.1602, 416.1002. The initial list of 50 conditions included amyotrophic lateral sclerosis (ALS or "Lou Gehrig disease") and various types of cancers; SSA has since added around 200 new conditions including early onset Alzheimer's disease, heart transplant graft failure, and juvenile onset Huntington Disease. The current complete list can be found on the SSA website.

Until 2011, one could re-file a claim for benefits while the earlier claim was on appeal; that is, file a second claim after an earlier claim for the same benefit and benefit period had been denied. If the claimant's condition had worsened significantly in the meantime, the second claim could be granted before the first claim was heard on appeal. However, SSA changed its policy so that one can no longer have two claims for the same type of benefits pending before the agency at the same time. SSR 11–1p (2011). In effect, a claimant now must choose between filing a new claim and pursuing an administrative appeal. The Ruling provides, however, that one can still report new medical conditions, or a worsening of existing medical conditions, in which case SSA will forward that information to the office handling the pending appeal. Claimants also commonly file new applications after their cases have proceeded beyond the administrative levels and are on judicial review in federal court.

C. ADMINISTRATIVE APPEALS: OVERVIEW

As noted earlier, there are three levels of administrative appeal from benefit decisions by the Social Security Administration: reconsideration, administrative hearing, and Appeals Council review. Generally, a claimant must pass through all three levels of appeal before an adverse decision can be reviewed in court. Although they all take place within SSA, each has its own distinctive features. Each of the three levels will be discussed in this section. Judicial review is discussed in the next section.

The following chart provides an overview of the progression of disability claims through the initial decision and administrative appeals process, with data from Fiscal Year 2020:

Table 3.25 – Fiscal Year 2020 Disability Decision Data[1, 2]

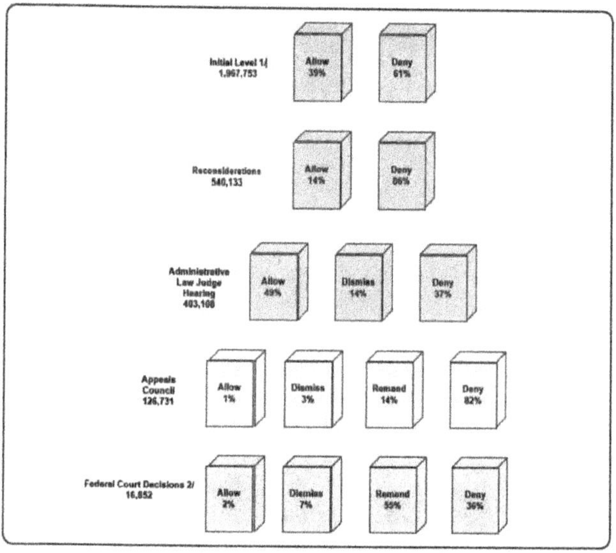

*Source: Social Security Administration,
FY 2022 Budget Justification at 162.

Decisions that cannot be appealed may nonetheless be reopened. 20 C.F.R. §§ 404.987, 416.1487. Decisions can be reopened based on one of three sets of criteria: within one year of the date of the decision involved, "for any reason"; within four years for OASDI benefits or within two years for SSI benefits, upon a showing of "good cause"; and at any time, if the decision "was obtained by fraud or similar fault" or under certain other specific, limited circumstances. *See generally* 20 C.F.R. §§ 404.988, 416.1488. Grounds for finding good cause include the production of "new and material" evidence, where the computation of benefits was due to "clerical error, or if the evidence on which a decision was made "clearly shows" the decision was in error. 20 C.F.R. §§ 404.989(a), 416.1489(a). However, good cause will not be found "if the only reason for reopening is a change of legal interpretation or administrative ruling upon which the determination or decision was made." 20 C.F.R. §§ 404.989(b), 416.1489(b). While the latter rule ordinarily prevents reopening when a policy or legal precedent that SSA applied in adjudicating cases changed as a result of subsequent court decisions, so long as the law or policy was correct and reasonable when made, SSA issued a Ruling that distinguishes the situation where SSA made a determination or decision by applying a federal or state law that the Supreme Court subsequently determined to be unconstitutional. In such circumstances "the application of that law would not have been correct and reasonable when made." SSR 17–1p (2017).

There was some doubt a number of years ago whether SSA could initiate reopening of claims according to the same criteria as claimants. A few courts held that only claimants could request reopening, or that SSA's ability to do so was severely limited. However, current regulations make it clear that SSA may reopen claims on its own initiatives according to the same criteria as those applicable to requests by claimants. *See* 20 C.F.R. §§ 404.987(b), 416.1487(b).

1. TIME LIMITS FOR FILING AN ADMINISTRATIVE APPEAL

The time limit for seeking review at each of the three levels of administrative appeal is the same: within 60 days following receipt of notice of the prior administrative action. *See* 20 C.F.R. §§ 404.909, 416.1409 (reconsideration); 20 C.F.R. §§ 404.933, 416.1433 (administrative hearings); 20 C.F.R. §§ 404.968, 416.1468 (Appeals Council review). The rules for extensions of time and for counting the 60-day time period are also the same for all levels of administrative appeal. (The regulations cited below address requests for reconsideration; however, the substance applies equally to requests for administrative hearings and Appeals Council review.)

The 60-day time limit begins on the day after the notice of the action appealed from was received. 20 C.F.R. §§ 404.909(a)(1), 416.1409(a). SSA assumes that notices are received five days after the date of mailing shown on the notice; therefore, as a practical matter an appeal must be filed within 65 days after the decision was mailed, not counting the day of mailing. The five-day period is, however, only a presumption and can be rebutted with statements claiming non-receipt. *See* 20 C.F.R. §§ 404.901, 416.1401 ("Date you receive notice means 5 days after the date on the notice, unless you show us that you did not receive it within the 5-day period.").

Moreover, a dated copy of a notice is not itself sufficient proof that the notice was mailed properly. *See* Hobt v. Commissioner, 175 Fed. Appx. 709, 710 2006 WL 988282 (6th Cir. 2006) ("a presumption of receipt is inappropriate where there is no evidence that the notice was ever mailed") (citing McKentry v. Secretary, 655 F.2d 721, 724 (6th Cir. 1981). On the other hand, most courts insist that claimants cannot simply state that they did not receive the notice within five days. *See e.g.*, Rouse v. Harris, 482 F. Supp. 766, 769 (D.N.J.1980) (requiring "a more concrete showing that the [claimant] or her attorney actually did not receive the Secretary's notice within five days of the date of mailing").

Although requests for an administrative appeal must be timely, under certain circumstances SSA will grant an extension of time to file. The appellant must show "good cause" as to why the deadline was missed, examples of which are set out in a nonexclusive list in the regulations. *See* 20 C.F.R. §§ 404.911, 416.1411. In considering whether a claimant had "good cause" for an extension, SSA will take into account whether the claimant had "any physical, mental, educational, or linguistic limitations" which prevented the claimant from filing a timely request or from understanding or knowing about the need to file a timely request for review. 20 C.F.R. §§ 404.911(a)(4), 416.1411(a)(4). These rules give the relevant person at SSA a great deal of discretion, in part because—as discussed later in this chapter—there is only very limited judicial review of a decision to deny a request for an extension.

2. APPEALS FROM TERMINATION OF BENEFITS

Generally, decisions to terminate benefits are appealed in the same way as appeals from any other SSA decision. As noted in Chapter 4, there are separate standards for terminating benefits on the ground that a recipient is no longer disabled and, as noted later in this chapter, there is a special limited hearing at reconsideration if disability benefits were terminated on medical grounds. In addition, persons whose SSI benefits are terminated and those whose OASDI disability benefits were terminated on medical grounds can have their benefit payments continued pending an appeal—if they file a request for an appeal within 10 days. 20 C.F.R. §§ 404.1597a(f), 416.1336(b). Payment of SSI benefits pending appeal is a constitutional right for need-based programs since the Supreme Court's decision in Goldberg v. Kelly, 397 U.S. 254 (1970) (involving the former Aid to Families with Dependent Children (AFDC) program). The Court declined to extend that right to social insurance programs in Mathews v. Eldridge, 424 U.S. 319 (1976); however, Congress extended the same rights to OASDI disability benefit recipients whose benefits were terminated on medical grounds a few years later. *See* 42 U.S.C. § 423(g).

D. RECONSIDERATION

The first step in appealing an adverse decision by SSA—with respect to an application for benefits or any other decision made by the agency—is to request a "reconsideration" of the decision. 20 C.F.R. §§ 404.907, 416.1407. A request for reconsideration must be filed with the local Social Security office within 60 days of receiving a notice of decision, unless the time to appeal has been extended for good cause. 20 C.F.R. §§ 404.909, 416.1409.

Reconsideration is an internal re-examination of all the evidence in the file at the time of the appealed-from decision, together with any subsequently submitted additional evidence. In an appeal from a disability decision, reconsideration takes place under the same procedures at the same state agency where the initial decision was made; however, the reconsideration decision is made by examiners and consultants who did not take part in the initial determination. Thus, if an initial denial was based on a finding of medical ineligibility, a different two-person team at the agency will examine the claimant's medical condition at the reconsideration stage. This means that at this first level of administrative review, the review is still on paper only; there is no face-to-face meeting with the decision maker. However, in termination cases where a beneficiary is found to be no longer disabled for medical reasons, the beneficiary can request a face-to-face "disability hearing" as part of the reconsideration process. Disability hearings are discussed in more detail below.

Only a small percentage of decisions are reversed at reconsideration, and all reconsideration reversals are reviewed at the appropriate regional SSA office. Most reversals are based on new medical evidence;

sometimes, however, claims that were denied because the duration requirement was not met are reversed on reconsideration simply because of the passage of time. A reversal may also result because of a clearer demonstration or further progression of the claimant's disability.

As noted earlier, there is one notable situation in which reconsideration is not limited to review of a paper record. In 1983, Congress amended the Social Security Act to require special reconsideration procedures for all claims where SSA terminated benefits upon a finding of nondisability, but only if the decision was based on medical factors. *See* 42 U.S.C. §§ 405(b)(2), 1383(a)(7)(A). Thus, where disability benefits are terminated because the claimant's impairment ceased, did not exist, or is no longer disabling, reconsideration includes a "disability hearing." 20 C.F.R. §§ 404.914, 416.1414. *See generally* 20 C.F.R. §§ 404.916, 416.1416. Disability hearings are held by disability hearing officers, who are experienced disability examiners who were not involved in the initial determination of the claim. 20 C.F.R. §§ 404.915, 416.1415. The scope of the disability hearing is limited to the initial or revised determination based on medical factors that the claimant is not disabled. All other issues must be reviewed in accordance with the reconsideration procedures described above.

E. ADMINISTRATIVE HEARING

The next level of appeal is an administrative hearing before an administrative law judge (ALJ).

Administrative hearings and Appeals Council review, discussed below, are administered by the Office of Hearing Operations (OHO), one of the largest administrative judicial systems in the world. OHO has ten regional offices, 168 hearing offices, five national hearing centers, and two national case assistance centers. Currently, it has approximately 1,500 ALJs and 7,000 support staff that issue more than 650,000 hearing and appeal decisions each year. The administrative hearing stage has been heavily criticized for substantial backlog and delays. Critics argue that such delays impose significant burdens on individuals in immediate need of benefits, thereby undermining a core purpose of the Social Security program and raising questions about its efficiency. Another persistent criticism of the administrative hearing stage and the disability determination process more generally is that ALJs and other decision makers often make determinations based on incomplete evidentiary records.

Two major factors contribute to the incomplete record problem. First, medical conditions may change during the many years it takes claimants to go through the various stages of the administrative process. As a result, medical records which were accurate at the time of the initial determination may no longer be accurate at later stages in the process. Second, decision makers are neither properly trained nor given sufficient resources to compile the detailed medical information needed to make a disability determination. SSA added a new attorney advisor position in the mid-90s to address the increased workload at the hearing level and expedite the processing of pending cases without infringing on a claimant's right to a hearing before an ALJ. Currently, attorney advisors are authorized to conduct prehearing proceedings under most circumstances and to issue decisions wholly favorable to the claimant. They may request additional evidence, including medical evidence, and, if necessary, hold a conference. If an attorney advisor is unable to issue a fully favorable decision, the case is returned without additional delay for an ALJ hearing. *See generally* 20 C.F.R. §§ 404.942, 416.1442.

A claimant has 60 days from the date of receipt of a reconsideration notice to request an administrative hearing, unless the time limit is extended for good cause. 20 C.F.R. §§ 404.933(b)–(c), 416.1433(b)–(c). Hearing requests may be filed electronically or in writing. 20 C.F.R. § 422.203(b). However, electronic filing is mandatory if an attorney requests direct payment of attorney's fees. 20 C.F.R. §§ 404.1713, 416.1513; *See also* SSR 19–3p (2019). If the claimant requests a hearing, one will be held unless the ALJ decides to issue a fully favorable decision without a hearing, or to remand for further administrative action because the ALJ believes that a revised decision will be favorable to the claimant. 20 C.F.R. §§ 404.948(c), 416.1448(c). The ALJ may also dismiss the appeal on certain specified grounds. 20 C.F.R. §§ 404.957, 416.1457.

The administrative hearing record begins with the evidence compiled during the initial decision and at reconsideration, which is forwarded to the Office of

Hearing Operations. The ALJ, working together with OHO staff, then reviews and develops the record independently without assuming, in a case involving disability benefits, that the state agency obtained all of the information available at the time it made its decisions. They decide what additional evidence is necessary, if any, and whether a vocational expert or medical expert should be called to appear at the hearing. OHO staff can obtain existing medical reports from treating sources or hospitals and can order consultative examinations. The case may also be referred for a prehearing case review. *See* 20 C.F.R. §§ 404.941, 416.1441.

Once the claimant's file has been completed, the case is set for hearing unless the claimant chooses not to appear or the ALJ decides to issue a favorable decision without a hearing or to remand the claim for further evaluation at the state agency level. 20 C.F.R. §§ 404.948, 416.1448. At the hearing itself, claimants, on their own or through their representatives, can present any testimony and additional documentary evidence they wish. 20 C.F.R. §§ 404.950, 416.1450. Except for disability hearings at the reconsideration level where benefits were terminated on medical grounds, the ALJ is the only decision maker in the entire administrative appeals process that sees the claimant in person.

The hearing is informal and non-adversarial. (As explained in more detail in Chapter 9, SSA is not represented at these hearings and, as a result, ALJs are expected to participate more actively in questioning witnesses than are trial judges.)

Additionally, the rules of evidence do not apply to these hearings. Typically, the administrative law judge will ask a series of questions and then, if the claimant is represented, the claimant's representative will continue the questioning. The hearing is the first opportunity to take sworn testimony from outside witnesses and is typically the first stage at which the claimant obtains representation. Following the hearing, the ALJ must issue a formal written decision that includes a recitation of the evidence considered, findings of facts, and detailed reasons for the decision. 20 C.F.R. §§ 404.953, 416.1453. An administrative hearing decision is final unless a request for review is filed with the Appeals Council within 60 days. (The roles of the administrative law judge and the claimant's representative at Social Security administrative hearings are discussed in more detail in Chapter 9).

SSA sets the date, time, and place for hearings through Regional Centralized Scheduling Units. Under current regulations, SSA will schedule claimants to appear in person or by videoconference, or, in limited circumstances, by telephone. 20 C.F.R. §§ 404.929, 416.1429. The decision as to whether the claimant will appear in person or by videoconference will take into consideration the relative efficiency of teleconferencing vs. an in-person appearance, as well as "any facts in [the claimant's] particular case that provide a good reason to schedule [the claimant's] appearance by video teleconferencing or in person." 20 C.F.R. §§ 404.936(c)(1), 416.1436(c)(1). Claimants can object to appearing by teleconference within 30 days after receipt of notice and the ALJ will then schedule an in-person hearing. 20 C.F.R. §§ 404.936(d), 416.1436(d). SSA also controls whether to schedule its witnesses by videoconference or telephone, including a medical or vocational expert. 20 C.F.R. §§ 404.936(c)(4), 416.1436(c)(4). SSA's criteria for witness appearances by videoconference or telephone are the same as for a party; however, the claimant only has a qualified right to object to the manner in which SSA witnesses appear and the ALJs in their discretion, may overrule such objections in writing or at the hearing. *See* 20 C.F.R. §§ 404.936(c)(2), 416.1436(c)(2).

Claimants can also object to the time and place of the hearing within 30 days, subject to a finding of good cause by the administrative law judge assigned to the claim. Among the good cause criteria are circumstances that make travel to the hearing site impossible, or other circumstances affecting the claimant's ability to present their claim such as the need for additional time to obtain representation or the unavailability to a witness with evidence that cannot be obtained otherwise. 20 C.F.R. §§ 404.936(f), 416.1436(f).

F. APPEALS COUNCIL REVIEW

A claimant who is dissatisfied with the decision of the administrative law judge following an administrative hearing has one final opportunity for administrative review within the Social Security Administration: review of the hearing decision by the Appeals Council. *See* 20 C.F.R. §§ 404.967, 416.1467. The Appeals Council is an independent, quasi-judicial body within SSA with exclusive jurisdiction to decide appeals from ALJ decisions. The Appeals Council was designed to oversee the administrative appeals process, promote national consistency in ALJ hearing decisions, and ensure that the Commissioner's records are adequate for judicial review. Currently, it consists of 71 Administrative Appeals Judges, approximately 45 Appeals Officers, and several hundred support personnel.

A request for review by the Appeals Council must be filed within 60 days of receipt of the hearing decision, unless the time limit is extended for good cause. 20 C.F.R. §§ 404.968, 416.1468. Claimants and representatives can request Appeals Council review electronically and those requests will be routed automatically to the correct Appeals Council office. Requests for review can also still be filed by mail with hard-copy forms. The Appeals Council can grant or deny the request for review; if the petition for review is granted, the Council will either issue a decision or remand the case for further administrative action. Social Security regulations list four grounds for review: an abuse of discretion by the administrative law judge; an error of law in the administrative hearing decision; the decision is not supported by substantial evidence; and the decision presents "broad policy or procedural issues that may affect the general public interest." *See* 20 C.F.R. §§ 404.970(a), 416.1470(a). In practice, the Appeals Council rarely grants review. If review is granted, the claimant may request an oral argument; however, in most cases a decision or remand order is issued at the same time the Council grants review. The Council can also dismiss an appeal if not timely filed or under other limited circumstances.

The Appeals Council does not see the claimant but merely reviews the record. A claimant may submit new evidence to the Appeals Council together with a request for review, which will be considered by the Council together with the record established at the hearing. However, the new evidence must be "material," relate to the time period relevant to the pending application, which means before the date of the administrative hearing decision, and there must also be "a reasonable probability that the additional evidence would change the outcome of the decision." 20 C.F.R. §§ 404.970(a)(5), 416.1470(a)(5).

In addition to claimant-initiated review of an adverse ALJ decision, the Appeals Council can review the decision of an administrative law judge on its own motion, through both random and selective sampling. *See generally* 20 C.F.R. §§ 404.969, 416.1469. When the Appeals Council reviews a favorable administrative hearing decision on its own motion, the claimant is entitled interim benefits during the review process if a final decision on the review is not issued within 110 days. 20 C.F.R. §§ 404.969(d), 416.1467(d).

A decision by the Appeals Council, either to deny a request for review or, following the granting of a request for review, to affirm, modify, or reverse the hearing decision, is a final decision by SSA, subject to judicial review. The circuit courts of appeal are more broadly divided on the question whether new evidence submitted to the Appeals Council is part of the record subject to judicial review, when the Appeals Council denies the request for review. *Compare* Lesterhuis v. Colvin, 805 F.3d 83, 87, 223 Soc. Sec. Rep. Serv. 24 (2d Cir. 2015) (new and material evidence submitted by claimant to the Appeals Council is part of the record for judicial review when the Appeals Council denied review); Meyer v. Astrue, 662 F.3d 700, 704–07, 173 Soc. Sec. Rep. Serv. 381 (4th Cir. 2011) (same); Hardman v. Colvin, 820 F.3d 142, 150–51, 230 Soc. Sec. Rep 40 (5th Cir. 2016) (same); Brewes v. Comm'r of Soc. Sec. Admin., 682 F.3d 1157, 1161–64, 180 Soc. Sec. Rep. Serv. 46 (9th Cir. 2012)(same); Krauser v. Astrue, 638 F.3d 1324, 1328–29, 166 Soc. Sec. Rep. Serv. 20 (10th Cir. 2011) (same); Bergmann v. Apfel, 207 F.3d 1065, 1068, 68 Soc. Sec. Rep. Serv. 223 (8th Cir. 2000)(same; "[i]n practice, this requires the court to decide how the ALJ would have weighed the new evidence had it existed at the time of the initial hearing"); Ingram v. Comm's Soc. Sec. Admin., 496 F.3d 1253, 1261–66, 123 Soc. Sec. Rep. Serv. 21 (11th Cir. 2007) (claimant must challenge "both the decision of the [ALJ] to deny benefits and the decision of the Appeals Council to deny review" for court to consider the new evidence as part of the record) *with* Mills v. Apfel, 244 F.3d 1, 4–7, 73 Soc. Sec. Rep. Serv. 1 (1st Cir. 2001) ("we agree with the Commissioner's view that we may review the ALJ decision solely on the evidence presented to the ALJ."); Matthews v. Apfel, 239 F.3d 589, 593–94, 72 Soc. Sec. Rep. Serv. 400 (3d Cir. 2001) (same); Cotton v. Sullivan, 2 F.3d 692, 696, 42 Soc. Sec. Rep. Serv. 116 (6th Cir. 1993) (court may only consider the new evidence if the

Appeals Council granted review or for a sentence six remand if good cause is shown for failing to submit the evidence to the ALJ); Eads v. Sec. of Dept. of Health and Human Servs., 983 F.3d 816–18, 39 Soc. Sec. Rep. Serv. 696 (7th Cir. 1993) (same). If the Appeals Council remands the case for further action by an ALJ, there is no final decision and the administrative process continues.

In addition to cases seeking review of an ALJ decision as the next step in the process, the Appeals Council deals with cases in two other situations. First, the Appeals Council hears claims where a civil action has been filed in federal district court and the government attorney asks the Council to conduct a supplemental review. This may happen when the attorney believes the case is indefensible in court, even if it was correctly denied initially. In such cases, the attorney may recommend that the case be remanded to SSA to pay the claim, further develop the evidentiary record, or flesh out the written rationale for denial. Second, the Appeals Council hears cases after the district judge has issued a final decision or has remanded the case to the SSA with orders to conduct a new hearing or adduce new evidence. If the district court's orders are clear, the case may go directly back to the ALJ. If not, the Appeals Council may supplement the court's remand order with additional guidance before sending the case to an ALJ. After the new hearing on court remand, the ALJ's decision become the Commissioner's final decision subject to further court appeal, unless the Appeals Council assumes jurisdiction of the case based either on the claimant's written exceptions to the ALJ's decision filed within 30 days or based on the Council's authority exercised within 60 days after the ALJ's decision, even where no objections are filed. *See* 20 C.F.R. §§ 404.984, 416.1484. Because the Council rarely exercises jurisdiction after post-court remand ALJ hearings in the absence of written objections, claimants may elect to bypass the Appeals Council after most post-court remand ALJ hearings.

Over the years, there have been a number of calls to eliminate the Appeals Council or to reduce its role to discretionary review. Much of the criticism comes from the fact that—with the passage of time and the ability to consider new evidence—the Appeals Council often reviews a substantially different record than that which was before the ALJ. Another common criticism is that requiring Appeals Council action before judicial review in all cases lengthens the process unnecessarily for the vast majority of claims that are denied review. As seen on the Disability Decision Data chart earlier in this chapter, the Appeals Council level accounts for very few changes in result (1% reversal, 14% remand). Others point to the long delays at the Appeals Council with current processing times in excess of a full year. On the other hand, proponents of the Appeals Council argue that it serves a valuable function in screening and resolving cases before they reach the district court, thereby protecting district courts from excessive litigation and conserving judicial resources. They also contend that the Appeals Council acts as a centralized final reviewing authority to create a uniform agency position. Despite continuing criticism, the Appeals Council remains in operation today essentially as it has throughout its history.

1. SCOPE OF APPEALS COUNCIL REVIEW

When a claimant seeks Appeals Council review of an administrative hearing decision, the entire claim is subject to review. This is certainly the case where the claimant requests review generally from an unfavorable decision. Full review of the ALJ's entire decision by the Appeals Council is appropriate also where the claimant has requested review only on certain issues or parts of that decision, at least so long as the claimant was notified that a request for review of a partially favorable decision could be subject to full-scale review. See, e.g., Williams v. Sullivan, 970 F.2d 1178, 1182, 38 Soc. Sec. Rep. Serv. 220 (3d Cir. 1992)("the Appeals Council need not limit its review to the issue appealed, but may review a claimant's entire case provided it gives sufficient notice that appeals will be subject to full review.")

G. JUDICIAL REVIEW

The Social Security Act provides specifically for judicial review of adverse benefit determinations on Social Security claims in the federal district courts. Federal court appeals of Social Security administrative decisions follow, in most respects, the usual rules for judicial review of administrative action. On the other hand, there are some serious jurisdictional questions with respect to other types of cases that a Social Security claimant may want to file in federal court. The basic jurisdictional rules for individual claims and some of these other jurisdictional issues are covered later in this section, followed by a discussion of the scope and standard of review.

1. USE OF MAGISTRATE JUDGES

Magistrate judges are term-limited Article I federal trial judges appointed by life-tenured Article III federal district court judges. *See generally* 28 U.S.C. § 631. Magistrate judges play an increasingly important role in Social Security cases, as in many judicial districts Social Security appeals are referred routinely to magistrate judges to prepare a report and recommendation to the court. In addition, parties can consent to have a magistrate judge act as a district judge in a particular case.

When a district judge assigns a case to a magistrate judge, the magistrate judge conducts a hearing and prepares proposed findings of fact and a recommended decision. The parties then have fourteen days to ask the district judge to review the magistrate judge's findings and recommendations under Rule 72(b) of the Federal Rules of Civil Procedure. District judges review the cases de novo and may accept, reject, or modify the magistrate judge's report in whole or in part. *See* 28 U.S.C. § 636(b)(1). If the plaintiff does not object to the magistrate judge's report in that allotted time period, the district judge still has discretion to review the report. *See* Thomas v. Arn, 474 U.S. 140, 154 (1985) (noting, on the other hand, that a strict waiver rule on further appellate review from the Article I magistrate's report does not violate Article III or the Due Process Clause, at least when proper notice is provided about the failure to object within the time limit.) In practice, in the absence of timely objections the district court's adoption of the magistrate report without de novo review is the likely result and will usually be sustained as a waiver of plaintiff's objections to that report. *See, e.g.*, Smalls v. Sec. of Health and Human Services, 892 F.2d 15, 16 (2d Cir. 1989) (failure to object to a magistrate's report operates as a waiver of any further judicial review of the magistrate's decision; however, a pro se claimant's failure to object will not be deemed a waiver unless clear notice of the consequences of failure to object is provided in the magistrate's report). In some circuits, appellate review may still be available even if the plaintiff failed to object to the magistrate's report and the district court did not review the report de novo. *See, e.g.*, Welch v. Heckler, 808 F.2d 264, 266–67 (3d Cir. 1985). But even in those circuits, if notice of waiver is provided by the magistrate report the circuit court is more likely to sustain the waiver or apply a more limited (plain/manifest error) standard of appellate review. *See* Nara v. Frank, 488 F.3d 187, 193–97 (3d Cir. 2007); *see also* Popcock v. Astrue, 373 Fed. Appx. 903, 904 (11th Cir. 2010) ("When there are no objections to a magistrate judge's report and recommendation, we review the findings of fact only for plain error or manifest injustice, but we still review de novo the report's legal conclusions.").

When a magistrate judge hears a case with the consent of the parties, the magistrate judge's decision is the final decision of the district court. 28 U.S.C. § 636(c). For this reason, the parties' consent must be express and in writing. McGinnis v. Shalala, 2 F.3d 548, 551 (5th Cir. 1993) ("A magistrate judge may act in the capacity of a federal district court under 28 U.S.C. § 636(c) only upon the express, written consent of both parties. . . . [C]onsent to trial by magistrate judge must be express; we have 'refused to "infer this statutorily required consent from the conduct of the parties." ' ") (citations omitted).

2. JURISDICTION

The Social Security Act addresses directly the matter of federal court jurisdiction over Social Security cases. Thus, 42 U.S.C. § 405(g) provides, in part:

> Any individual, after any final decision of the Commissioner of Social Security made after a hearing to which he was a party, irrespective of the amount in controversy, may obtain a review of such decision by a civil action commenced within sixty days after the mailing to him of notice of such decision or within such further time as the Commissioner of Social Security may allow. Such action shall be brought in the district court of the United States for the judicial district in which the plaintiff resides, or has his principal place of business, or, if he does not reside or have his principal place of business within any such judicial district, in the United States District Court for the District of Columbia. . . . The court shall have power to

> enter, upon the pleadings and transcript of the record, a judgment affirming, modifying, or reversing the decision of the Commissioner of Social Security, with or without remanding the cause for a rehearing.

The Act also authorizes district courts to remand cases to SSA for further action, including taking new evidence, but only if "there is new evidence which is material and that there is good cause for the failure to incorporate such evidence into the record in a prior proceeding." *Id.* Together with this broad grant of jurisdiction to review decisions on individual claims for benefits after an administrative hearing has been held, the Act explicitly precludes other bases for federal court jurisdiction:

> The findings and decision of the Commissioner of Social Security after a hearing shall be binding upon all individuals who were parties to such hearing. No findings of fact or decision of the Commissioner of Social Security shall be reviewed by any person, tribunal, or governmental agency except as herein provided. No action against the United States, the Commissioner of Social Security, or any officer or employee thereof shall be brought under section 1331 or 1346 of Title 28 to recover on any claim arising under this subchapter.

42 U.S.C. § 405(h). The Act thus provides a clear jurisdictional basis for federal district court review of any ordinary individual disability claim where the issue is eligibility under applicable laws and regulations. It is equally clear that ordinary

individual claims can be appealed to federal court only after all administrative remedies have been exhausted. As noted earlier, usually this is accomplished by first seeking a hearing before an administrative law judge and then appealing the decision, if it is unfavorable, to the Appeals Council. According to SSA regulations, if the Appeals Council grants review of a claim the decision of the Appeals Council is the SSA's final decision; if the Appeals Council denies the request for review, the ALJ's decision becomes the final decision. *See* 20 C.F.R. §§ 404.900(a)(4)–(5), 404.955, 404.981, 422.210(a). If a claimant fails to request review from the Appeals Council in such cases, there is no final decision and the claimant is not entitled to judicial review.

Once the exhaustion requirement has been satisfied, an appeal must be filed within 60 days of the Appeal Council decision—whether on the merits or denying a request for review. This 60-day filing deadline is considered to be a waivable statute of limitations, as opposed to a jurisdictional requirement; accordingly, SSA will grant an extension of time to file an appeal upon a showing of good cause. *See* 20 C.F.R. §§ 404.982, 416.1482.

a. Exhaustion of Administrative Remedies

While, as explained above, exhaustion of administrative remedies is required in ordinary individual Social Security appeals, exhaustion may or may not be required in other types of court cases involving Social Security benefits. The Supreme Court has found that the exhaustion requirement has two components, one of which is jurisdictional and non-waivable and the other waivable. *See* Mathews v. Eldridge, 424 U.S. 319, 328 (1976). The Non-waivable component, known as the presentment requirement, is that the claimant present a claim for benefits to the Social Security Administration. It can be satisfied by having an application for benefits denied by the agency, or having one's benefits proposed for termination and submitting a questionnaire asserting continued disability; it does not require presentation at the various subsequent stages of the administrative process such as the ALJ hearing or Appeals Council. *See* City of New York v. Heckler, 742 F.2d 729, 735–36 (1984), aff'd, sub nom., Bowen v. City of New York, 476 U.S. 476 (1986) (summarizing Supreme Court's statutory SSA "presentment" nonwaivable exhaustion requirement caselaw); *see also* Mathews v. Eldridge, 424 U.S. 319, 329 (1976); Matthews v. Diaz, 426 U.S. 67, 72 (1976). The waivable component requires that the claimant pursue the claim through each stage of the administrative process. Mathews v. Eldridge, 424 U.S. 319, 328 (1975).

Situations may arise where, for some reason, the waivable exhaustion requirement has not been or cannot be met. Both the agency and the courts can waive this requirement in certain circumstances, notwithstanding the Act's removal of general federal question jurisdiction pursuant to 28 U.S.C. § 1331 in Social Security cases. *See* Weinberg v. Salfi, 422 U.S. 749, 756–62 (1975) (discussing 42 U.S.C. § 405(h)). These circumstances include where exhaustion of a claim through all of the various administrative stages would be futile because the agency is not empowered or lacks jurisdiction to decide the issues or grant the relief sought. Weinberger v. Salfi, 422 U.S. at 765–67. Another situation is where a claimant's interest in having a particular issue resolved promptly is great and the challenge is entirely collateral to a substantive claim of entitlement. *See* Mathews v. Eldridge, 424 U.S. at 330. These exceptions often arise in class action challenges to the legality or constitutionality of agency policies or systemic practices.

b. Issue Exhaustion

The Supreme Court has twice rejected the assertion that federal courts should require "issue exhaustion" in Social Security cases, in addition to exhaustion of administrative remedies. First, the Court rejected the requirement that issues be raised at the Appeals Council as prerequisite to judicial review of those same issues in federal court. *See* Sims v. Apfel, 530 U.S. 103 (2000). In rejecting the application of issue exhaustion in this context, the Court in *Sims* relied on the absence of a statute or regulation requiring exhaustion of issues, as in other administrative systems; the lack of prudential justification for common law or judicially imposed issue exhaustion due to the uniquely informal, non-adversarial and inquisitorial nature of Social Security administrative proceedings; and the absence of sufficient notice or warning of an issue exhaustion requirement in the agency's forms and notices about the Appeals Council stage. Second, the Court also rejected the agency's invocation of issue exhaustion in cases involving Appointments Clause challenges to administrative law judges that were not first asserted at the hearing stage. *See* Carr v. Saul, 141 S. Ct. 1352 (2021).

In *Carr*, the Court reaffirmed the general incompatibility of issue exhaustion with SSA's uniquely informal, non-adversarial and inquisitorial administrative proceedings, including at the hearing stage, but also relied on the futility of raising Appointment Clause and presumably other structural or legal issues at the hearing stage when the ALJs and the agency lack authority to remedy or properly address these issues if raised. The Court left open the question whether there might be a basis for ALJ hearing level issue exhaustion in more "routine objections to individual benefit determinations" since resolution of that issue was not necessary for the Court's judgment. Three members of the court indicated that they would also reject application of common law ALJ hearing level issue exhaustion in all SSA cases. 141 S. Ct. at 1362–63. (Thomas, J., joined by Gorsuch and Barrett, JJ. concurring in part and concurring in the judgment). In any event, most legal issues appropriate for judicial review do not arise until after the ALJ decision. However, the effort to raise "new and material evidence" on judicial review that was not asserted in the agency proceedings will remain governed by the restrictive "good cause" requirement in the sixth sentence of 42 U.S.C. § 405(g), as described above and below.

c. Review of Decisions Made Without a Hearing

Another type of case that presents jurisdictional issues is where there were no administrative remedies to exhaust. Certain administrative decisions have the effect of denying a claim but are made without an opportunity for a hearing. The most important of these are refusals to reopen an application and dismissals of appeals, usually on grounds that the appeal was not filed on time or that the claim was barred by administrative res judicata. The Supreme Court held in Califano v. Sanders, 430 U.S. 99, 108, 97 S. Ct. 980, 986 (1977), that federal courts have no jurisdiction to review SSA decisions not to reopen prior applications for benefits because such decisions are not made following a hearing. The rationale of *Sanders* has been extended regularly to preclude judicial review where claims were dismissed because administrative review was not requested within applicable time limits and an extension of time to file was not granted. The Court recognized in *Sanders*, however, that a constitutional challenge to decisions not to reopen claims may be subject to different exhaustion requirements, thereby laying the groundwork for a recognized exception to the jurisdictional bar in reopening and dismissal cases where the claimant raises a colorable constitutional issue. 430 U.S. at 109.

Most successful arguments invoking the *Sanders* exception appear to be based on due process issues arising from a claimant's mental incapacity. *See, e.g.*, Udd v. Massanari, 245 F.3d 1096 (9th Cir. 2001) ("where a claimant alleges that a prior determination should be reopened because he suffered from a mental impairment and was not represented by counsel at the time of the denial of benefits, he has asserted a colorable constitutional claim"). SSA also recognizes that claimants with no one legally responsible for prosecuting a claim on their behalf who later present evidence that mental incapacity prevented them from requesting timely review of an administrative action "will have established mental incapacity for the purpose of establishing good cause when the evidence establishes that he or she lacked the mental capacity to understand the procedures for requesting review." SSR 91–5p (1991). The Ruling specifies that the following four factors must be considered: (1) inability to read or write; (2) lack of facility with the English language; (3) limited education; and (4) any mental or physical condition which limits claimants' ability to do things for themselves. In all cases, "[t]he adjudicator will resolve any reasonable doubt in favor of the claimant."

The Supreme Court has also ruled that an Appeals Council dismissal on timeliness grounds after a claimant has had an ALJ hearing on the merits qualifies as a "final decision made after a hearing" for purposes of allowing judicial review under 42 U.S.C. § 405(g). Smith v. Berryhill, 139 S. Ct. 1765, 1773–80 (2019). The Court noted that if the reviewing court disagrees with the procedural ground for the Appeals Council dismissal, the court should ordinarily remand the case to allow the agency to address the substantive issues in the first place, recognizing that while the court would have jurisdiction to reach the merits, such a general rule comports with basic administrative law principles and is consistent with the Court's Social Security exhaustion precedents. *Id.* at 1778–80.

3. SCOPE OF JUDICIAL REVIEW

The scope of judicial review in Social Security appeals is limited. Federal court review is based exclusively on the record developed at the administrative hearing or before the Appeals Council; new evidence in support of the claim cannot be introduced at the district court. As noted above, if a claimant comes across "new and material evidence" after the administrative process is complete and can show "good cause" for failing to submit it earlier, the evidence can be presented to the court as a basis for remand. *See generally* 42 U.S.C. § 405(g). If the court agrees to remand the case, the new evidence is developed at the administrative level and any further judicial review will be based on the new administrative record.

The scope of review is essentially the same in the courts of appeal. However, the courts of appeal may refuse to consider, or may limit its review of, an issue that was not raised at the district court. *See, e.g.*, Young v. Secretary, 925 F.2d 146, 149 (6th Cir. 1990) (Social Security claimant "cannot raise an issue before the court of appeals that was not raised before the district court"). On the other hand, some courts have held that a strict "waiver" rule for arguments not raised in the district court may be inconsistent with the circuit courts' independent responsibility to carefully scrutinize the record to ensure that Social Security decisions are supported by substantial evidence. *See* Wallace v. Secretary of Health and Human Services, 722 F.2d 1150, 1153 n.3 (3d Cir. 1983) ("the proposition that issues should not be heard for the first time on appeal is not jurisdictional in nature. Thus, even assuming that the non-exertional impairments point was not raised below, this court is able to exercise its 'responsibility to scrutinize the entire record and to reverse or remand if the Secretary's decision is not supported by substantial evidence.' "). *See also* Castillo v. Barnhart, 325 F.3d 550, 553, 87 Soc. Sec. Rep. Serv. 10 (5th Cir. 2003) ("[T]his court ordinarily does not review issues raised for the first time on appeal. In exceptional circumstances, however, the court "may, in the interests of justice, review an issue that was not raised in the district court.") (citing Kinash v. Callahan, 129 F.3d 736, 739 n. 10, 54 Soc. Sec. Rep. Ser. 491 (5th Cir. 1997)).

4. STANDARD OF REVIEW

The question on an appeal of a claim for Social Security benefits is whether the Social Security Administration's decision comports with relevant legal standards and whether there is sufficient evidence to support the decision. Questions of law are reviewed *de novo* by the reviewing court, while questions of fact are reviewed under the "substantial evidence" standard. *See* 42 U.S.C. § 405(g) ("The findings of the Commissioner of Social Security as to any fact, if supported by substantial evidence, shall be conclusive"). As the Supreme Court said in Richardson v. Perales, 402 U.S. 389, 401, 91 S. Ct. 1420 (1971) (quoting Consolidated Edison Co. v. NLRB, 305 U.S. 197, 229 (1938)), the statutory standard of "substantial evidence" set out in § 405(g) means "more than a mere scintilla. It means such relevant evidence as a reasonable mind might accept as adequate to support a conclusion." *See also* 20 C.F.R. §§ 404.901, 416.1401 ("Substantial evidence means such relevant evidence as a reasonable mind might accept as adequate to support a conclusion."). The Court has also suggested that whatever the meaning of "substantial" in other contexts, "the threshold for such evidentiary sufficiency is not high." Biestek v. Berryhill, 139 S. Ct. 1148, 1154 (2019). However, courts strive for judicial review under the substantial evidence standard to be "deferential without being so obsequious as to be meaningless." Brown v. Apfel, 192 F.3d 492, 496 (5th Cir. 1999) (citation omitted). For the most part, a finding of fact is not considered supported by substantial evidence where it is contrary to uncontradicted evidence or based on evidence that is slight in relation to much stronger contrary evidence. As one court put it: "A single piece of evidence will not satisfy the substantiality test if the [Commissioner] ignores, or fails to resolve, a conflict created by countervailing evidence. Nor is evidence substantial if it is overwhelmed by other evidence—particularly certain types of evidence (e.g., that offered by treating physicians)—or if it really constitutes not evidence but mere conclusion." Kent v. Schweiker, 710 F.2d 110, 114 (3d Cir. 1983).

In effect, proper application of the substantial evidence standard requires that reviewing judges not draw independent factual conclusions from the evidence. Instead, they should ask whether a reasonable mind could infer facts found by the ALJ (or the Appeals Council) from the evidence; if so, then those facts must be taken as true for purposes of determining whether the decision is supported by substantial evidence in the record as a whole. Even if a court finds that a preponderance of the evidence favors the claimant and therefore would have ruled otherwise in the first instance, administrative findings should be accepted when supported by substantial evidence.

a. Substantial Evidence Rule in Practice

The substantial evidence rule has important implications in key areas of Social Security practice, including credibility determinations, vocational findings, and determinations of pain. Generally, it is applied strictly; however, there are many qualifications to the general rule which, together with guidelines on the weight to be given different types of medical evidence discussed in Chapter 9, leave claimants room to argue that SSA's findings of fact should be disregarded as not supported by substantial evidence. Although courts should not substitute their judgment for that of the Social Security Administration, courts must keep in mind the overall beneficent purposes of the Social Security Act. Moreover, "this very narrow ambit of judicial review does not release [the courts] from [their] responsibility to scrutinize the record in its entirety to determine whether substantial evidence does support [SSA's] findings." Millet v. Schweiker, 662 F.2d 1199, 1201 (5th Cir. 1981).

On the other hand, it is clear that a reviewing court need not give special deference to conclusions of law reached by an administrative law judge or the Appeals Council. Moreover, the facts in the record must have been evaluated by SSA in light of the correct legal standards in order for its findings to be protected by the substantial evidence test. Therefore, when the proper legal standard is not used, the Administration's decision will be set aside even though the findings are supported by substantial evidence.

b. Required Findings and Reasoning

In order for courts to be able to apply the substantial evidence standard to administrative decisions, the administrative decision must include sufficient findings, reasoning, and articulation to permit meaningful judicial review. Courts should not be compelled to engage in speculation about the reasons for particular findings or for crediting or rejecting particular sources of evidence, and those findings should be clear, analytical, and not merely boilerplate or conclusory. *See, e.g.*, Blakes ex rel. Wolfe v. Barnhart, 331 F.3d 565, 569, 88 Soc. Sec. Rep. Serv. 217 (7th Cir. 2003) ("We require the ALJ to build an accurate and logical bridge from the evidence to her conclusions so that we may afford the claimant meaningful review of the SSA's ultimate findings."); Ortiz v. Shalala, 856 F. Supp. 243, 248–

49, 45 Soc. Sec. Rep. Serv. 214 (E.D. Pa. 1994) (ALJ must indicate the evidence rejected and explain reasons for rejecting relevant evidence). This can be particularly important where the issue is an ALJ's finding on evaluation of a claimant's credibility. *See, e.g.*, Brown-Hunter v. Colvin, 806 F.3d 487, 489, 223 Soc. Sec. Rep. Serv. 368 (9th Cir. 2015) ("To ensure that our review of the ALJ's credibility determination is meaningful, and that the claimant's testimony is not rejected arbitrarily, we require the ALJ to specify which testimony she finds not credible, and then provide clear and convincing reasons, supported by evidence in the record, to support that credibility determination."). Thus, failure to provide adequate findings or reasoning is itself a basis for setting aside the administrative decision on judicial review. *See, e.g.*, Cotter v. Harris, 650 F.2d 481, 482 (3d Cir. 1981), denying reh'g on, 642 F.2d 700 (3d Cir. 1981) (requiring ALJs to "indicate that s/he has considered all the evidence, both for and against the claim, and provide some explanation of why s/he has rejected probative evidence which would have suggested a contrary disposition" while noting that specifying the information courts need to conduct judicial review "contributes to enhanced understanding between the ALJs and the court and thereby facilitates the final resolution of applications for disability benefits.").

SSA regulations, revised substantially in 2017 in order to clarify articulation and reasoning requirements for evaluating medical evidence, provide that supportability and consistency are the most important factors when evaluating medical opinions and findings—and that the application of those factors must be explained. 20 C.F.R. §§ 404.1520c, 416.920c; *see generally* 82 Fed. Reg. 5844 (January 18, 2017). *See also* Johnson v. Saul, 2021 WL 1625149 at *2 (N.D. Ind. 2021) ("The most important factors are supportability and consistency, and an ALJ is required to explain how he considered these factors in determining the persuasiveness of a medical opinion. Failure to properly consider, and explain consideration of an opinion, warrants remand.") (citing 20 C.F.R. § 404.1520c(b)(2); other citations omitted). Other factors which "will be considered" and about which adjudicators "may but are not required to explain" are the medical source's "treatment relationship" with the claimant, including the length, frequency, purpose and extent of the treating relationship, and whether the source has an examining (as opposed to a non-examining) relationship with the claimant; specialization; and "other factors," such as whether the source has familiarity with other evidence in the claim or understands the SSA disability program's policies and evidentiary requirements. 20 C.F.R. §§ 404.1520c(b)–(c), 416.920c(b)–(c). Adjudicators are also "not required to articulate how [they] considered evidence from nonmedical sources using [the above factors]." 20 C.F.R. §§ 404.1520c(d), 416.920c(d). Finally, SSA adjudicators "will not provide any analysis in their determination or decision about a decision made by any other governmental agency or a nongovernmental entity about whether [claimants] are disabled, blind, employable, or entitled to any benefits." 20 C.F.R. §§ 404.1504, 416.904. The application of these rules is discussed further in

Chapter 9 in the context of measuring the weight and sufficiency of medical evidence, both in general and with respect to evidence from a claimant's treating physician.

The requirement of adequate administrative findings and reasoning also implicates a "foundational principle of administrative law that a court may uphold agency action only on the grounds that the agency invoked when it took the action." Michigan v. EPA, 576 U.S. 743, 758 (2015) (citing SEC v. Chenery Corp., 318 U.S. 80, 87 (1943)). This principle, frequently referred to as the *Chenery* doctrine based on its origin case and often invoked in Social Security judicial review decisions, precludes SSA from attempting to correct manifest inadequacies in the ALJ's findings and reasoning by supplying more supportable findings and reasoning on appeal in the government's briefs, and then asserting "harmless error." As the Seventh Circuit explained in a case where SSA's brief and oral argument "seem[ed] determined to dissolve the Chenery doctrine in an acid of harmless error," the responsibility for articulating legally reasoned grounds for the decision has been delegated by Congress to—and rests with—the SSA, not the Department of Justice. Spiva v. Astrue, 628 F.3d 346, 353 (7th Cir. 2010) ("The Chenery doctrine 'provides an assurance that the object of the court's review is the product of a body or official to whom Congress delegated authority. That constraint in turn polices the conditions for judicial deference to agency action.'") (quoting Kevin M. Stack, *The*

Constitutional Foundations of Chenery, 116 Yale L.J. 952, 1021 (2007)).

5. THE COURTS' REMEDIAL AUTHORITY

a. Sentence Four and Sentence Six Remands

As noted earlier, the Social Security Act specifically authorizes district courts to remand Social Security cases for further administrative proceedings. With respect to remands, 42 U.S.C. § 405(g) provides:

> The court shall have power to enter, upon the pleadings and transcript of the record, a judgment affirming, modifying, or reversing the decision of the Commissioner of Social Security, with or without remanding the cause for a rehearing. . . . The court may, on motion of the Commissioner of Social Security made for good cause shown before the Commissioner files the Commissioner's answer, remand the case to the Commissioner of Social Security for further action by the Commissioner of Social Security, and it may at any time order additional evidence to be taken before the Commissioner of Social Security, but only upon a showing that there is new evidence which is material and that there is good cause for the failure to incorporate such evidence into the record in a prior proceeding; and the Commissioner of Social Security shall, after the case is remanded, and after hearing such additional evidence if so ordered, modify or affirm the Commissioner's findings of fact or the

> Commissioner's decision, or both, and shall file with the court any such additional and modified findings of fact and decision, and a transcript of the additional record and testimony upon which the Commissioner's action in modifying or affirming was based. Such additional or modified findings of fact and decision shall be reviewable only to the extent provided for review of the original findings of fact and decision.

The remands authorized by the first part of Section 405(g) quoted above—those ordered following a judgment either affirming, modifying, or reversing the administrative decision—are known as "sentence four" remands, so-named because that authority appears in the fourth sentence of Section 405(g). Typically, these are cases where a remand is ordered following a ruling on the merits affirming, modifying, or reversing the decision of an administrative law judge (or a lower court). Remands authorized by the second part of Section 405(g) quoted above—where the court simply orders additional evidence to be taken without reaching a judgment on the merits—are known as "sentence six" remands, as that authority appears in the sixth sentence of Section 405(g). Courts can order sentence six remands either on SSA's motion before it files an answer, upon a showing of good cause, or upon a showing that there is material new evidence and the moving party had good cause for failing to submit that evidence during the administrative appeal process.

Common situations where sentence four remands are ordered include cases where the administrative decision was based on an incorrect application of the law and a new assessment is required under the correct legal standard, and those where the ALJ or the Appeals Council failed to consider key evidence or failed to make required findings or supply adequate reasoning. A sentence four remand does not necessarily mandate a full *de novo* hearing in all cases but may be limited to application of certain legal issues or redetermination of certain factual issues as directed by the court. However, where a court remands the administrative decision due to inadequate reasoning, findings, or articulation by the ALJ, the remand order may not simply direct the ALJ to supply the missing findings or reasoning but must also provide notice and the opportunity for the claimant to be heard and develop the record on the inadequately reasoned issue. *See* Thomas v. Comm'r of Soc. Sec., 625 F.3d 798, 800 (3d Cir. 2010). That is because the purpose of a remand when the ALJ has issued a decision which is "beyond meaningful judicial review" due to inadequate reasoning or findings on an important issue is "not to require a formulaic process that must be adhered to on remand, but rather to ensure that the parties have an opportunity to be heard on the remanded issue and prevent post hoc rationalization by administrative law judges." 625 F.3d at 801.

Cases where the court finds that new evidence needs to be developed can be remanded under sentence four or sentence six, depending on whether the court also affirms, modifies, or reverses the appealed-from administrative decision. Basically, remands that do not address the administrative decision's correctness but simply call for the evaluation of identifiable new and material additional evidence which could not have been submitted in the prior proceedings fall under sentence six; those where additional evidence is required due to an error of law or a determination that a decision is not supported by substantial evidence fall under sentence four. While SSA may use sentence six to seek a remand in advance of the court's decision, if challenged it generally must show why the case should not proceed to judgment—in effect, requiring SSA to demonstrate that it is not just trying to avoid litigating a poorly handled claim and extending greater relief to the claimant. Sentence six remands requested by claimants are limited by the requirements that new evidence be material and that there was good cause for failing to submit that evidence into the administrative record. *See* 20 C.F.R. §§ 404.970(a)(5), 404.970(b), 416.1470(a)(5), 416.1470(b).

In a sentence six remand, the district court retains jurisdiction until SSA files a modification or affirmation of the prior agency determination with the district court, along with a transcript of the additional record and testimony upon which the new administrative action on remand is based. The district court then enters judgment after SSA has made this required filing. In a sentence four remand, the remand order terminates the action and divests the court of jurisdiction. *See* Shalala v. Schaefer, 509 U.S. 292, 297–98 (1993). Accordingly, remand orders under sentence four are immediately appealable and claimants can seek greater relief than that provided in the remand order by the district court; on the other hand, remands under sentence six remain under the district court's jurisdiction and may not be appealed. Forney v. Apfel, 524 U.S. 266 (1988).

It is possible for a court to enter a remand order under both sentence four and sentence six. For example, where an ALJ committed the substantive legal error of failing to develop the record on behalf of a *pro se* claimant (a sentence four remand basis) and where that same claimant also presented the district court with new, material evidence for which there was good cause for the inability to procure and present such evidence in the administrative proceedings (a sentence six remand ground), the remand order addressing both of those concerns would be a "dual basis" remand order. *See, e.g.*, Jackson v. Chater, 99 F.3d 1086, 1089–98 (11th Cir. 1996). In such a "dual section" or dual basis remand, the district court retains jurisdiction over the action due to the inclusion of a sentence six ground in the remand order.

Special Appeals Council rules apply when a case is remanded by the court to SSA for further proceedings. In effect, the Appeals Council may either reconsider the case itself or send it back to OHO for further action by an administrative law judge. *See* 20 C.F.R. §§ 404.983, 416.1483. If sent to OHO, the ALJ may consider any issues regardless of whether they were raised in the initial administrative proceedings. *Id.* The procedures that are followed when the Appeals Council takes the case are set out in 20 C.F.R. §§ 404.984, 416.1484.

The courts of appeal are divided on a remedial question involving the interaction of sentence four and sentence six when the agency has not met its Step 5 burden of proving other work the claimant can perform: whether sentence six's "good cause" language limits remands for further proceedings potentially sought by SSA in cases involving substantive sentence four errors under those circumstances, or instead, more properly supports complete reversals and immediate benefit awards without further proceedings under sentence four since the agency has not met its burden of proof. *Compare* Balsamo v. Chater, 142 F.3d 75, 82 (2d Cir. 1998) (claimant showed on appeal that he could not perform his past relevant work and yet SSA had not met its burden of producing evidence of other jobs in the economy to which he could adjust; judgment vacated "with directions to remand the case to the Commissioner for the calculation of benefits, subject to the district court's disposition, according to the foregoing standards fixed by § 405(g), of any motion by the Commissioner for a remand to the ALJ for the consideration of additional evidence."); Woody v. Sec. of Health and Human Serv., 859 F.2d 1156, 1163, 23 Soc. Sec. Rep. Serv. 370 (3d Cir. 1988) (ALJ "developed nothing to rebut [claimant's] well-developed *prima facie* case . . .Under these circumstances, we conclude that this is an appropriate case for the exercise of our prerogative to direct an award of benefits.") *and* Field v. Chater, 920 F. Supp. 240, 244–45 (D. Me. 1995) ("where the claimant has made out a prima facie case for benefits and the Commissioner's vocational expert does not present the required evidence of the claimant's ability to perform work that exists in the national economy, the appropriate relief is an award of benefits absent some good cause for the evidentiary gap.") *with* Seavey v. Barnhart, 276 F.3d 1, 11 (1st Cir. 2001) ("[T]he rule we adopt is that ordinarily the court can order the agency to provide the relief it denied only in the unusual case in which the underlying facts and law are such that the agency has no discretion to act in any manner other than to award or to deny benefits. . . . Conversely, if an essential factual issue has not been resolved, as here, and there is no clear entitlement to benefits, the court must remand for further proceedings [and SSA should not be viewed as a "party" against whom a default is ordered simply for failing to meet a proof burden since ALJ hearings are non-adversarial] . . . . Sentence six and its good cause limitation come into play only [for new evidence that might change the result] . . . Unlike sentence six, sentence four does not contain any statutory limits on the ability to supplement the record on remand").

Because sentence four remand orders, as opposed to those under sentence six, are deemed final orders, the Supreme Court has authorized appeals from sentence four district court remand orders seeking greater relief than that provided in the order, such as a full reversal and remand solely to calculate benefits. *See* Forney v. Apfel, 524 U.S. 266 (1998). The distinction between remands ordered under sentence four or under sentence six can be critical to an attorney's ability to receive fees under the Equal Access to Justice Act (EAJA). The EAJA aspects of sentence four and sentence six remands are covered at the end of this chapter.

b. Sentence Six Remands and Successful New Applications

As noted earlier, claimants can file new applications for benefits after having fully adjudicated a prior application unsuccessfully through all four stages of administrative review. In such cases, claimants often seek to introduce successful agency decisions on the new application as "new and material evidence" justifying a remand of the earlier decision pursuant to sentence six of 42 U.S.C. § 405(g). While ordinary application of administrative res judicata principles would prevent a finding of disability up through the date of the hearing decision on a prior application, the onset date of the new application may be in close temporal proximity to the prior hearing decision date—as close as one day in some cases. The courts of appeal are divided on the question whether and when a new decision awarding benefits with a disability onset date in close proximity to the date of a previous decision denying benefits justifies a sentence six remand of the prior decision for consideration of the new decision and the evidence supporting the benefit award in that new decision. *Compare* Luna v. Astrue, 623 F.3d 1032 (9th Cir. 2010) (when SSA grants a second application within very close proximity to the date of a previous denial decision, the new decision itself presents a reasonable possibility that the two decisions are irreconcilable and reflects new and material evidence justifying a remand on the prior application for a new hearing pursuant to sentence six) *with* Allen v. Comm'r of Soc. Sec., 561 F.3d 646 (6th Cir. 2009) (demanding a higher threshold for demonstrating a reasonable possibility of a changed determination justifying a sentence six remand in this context, reasoning that while new and material evidence supporting a subsequent favorable decision may justify a sentence six remand, the "mere existence" of the decision was not itself sufficient.)

c. Remedies for Unreasonable Delay: Interim Benefits

SSA's four-stage administrative process described above is highly delay-prone and time-consuming, especially at the ALJ hearing stage. When ordering a remand, courts sometimes order interim benefits to claimants, or impose time limits after which interim benefits will be triggered, to address excessive delays. The most common situation giving rise to such relief is where significant delay is attributable to identifiable agency fault or neglect, such as lost, misplaced, or incomplete casefiles or hearing transcripts. Courts differ, however, as to whether and when an award of interim benefits is appropriate. *Compare* Dandeneau v. Heckler, 607 F. Supp. 583, 584, 9 Soc. Sec. Rep. Serv. 785 (D. Me. 1985) (interim benefits awarded where remand required due to 139 "inaudibles" in a 22-page transcript of administrative hearing) *and* Davila v. Shalala, 848 F. Supp. 1141, 1144, 44 Soc. Sec. Rep. Serv. 355 (S.D. N.Y. 1994) (ordered payment pending the reconstruction of the administrative record, reasoning that "[w]here a government agency fails to act with all deliberate speed in performing its duties or correcting its own failure to maintain its own records, the private party should not be placed at a cruel disadvantage because of the resulting delay.") *with* Mullen v. Secretary, 878 F. Supp. 682, 684–86, 47 Soc. Sec. Rep. Serv. 312 (D. Del. 1995) (refusing to grant interim benefits despite inaudible hearings tapes, noting that U.S. Constitution, Art. I, § 9, cl. 7 provides that "No money shall be drawn from the Treasury, but in Consequence of Appropriations made by Law").

Some courts have found authority to authorize judicial remedies for unreasonable agency delay in either the Social Security Act, 42 U.S.C. § 405(b)(1) ("the Commissioner shall give . . . reasonable notice and opportunity for a hearing"), the Administrative Procedure Act, 5 U.S.C. § 706(1) ("The reviewing court shall compel agency action . . . unreasonably delayed") and 5 U.S.C. § 555(b) ("With due regard for the convenience and necessity of the parties or their representatives and within a reasonable time, each agency shall proceed to conclude a matter presented to it."), and/or the Due Process Clause. *See, e.g.*, White v. Mathews, 434 F. Supp. 1252 (D. Conn. 1976) (relying on Social Security Act, APA, and the Due Process Clause to support time limits and interim benefits remedies for excessive SSA delays). However, the Supreme Court placed significant restrictions on the imposition of class-based or across-the-board time limits and automatic awards of interim benefits to class members when time limits are not met due to systemic delays in Heckler v. Day, 467 U.S. 104 (1984). Noting congressional concerns "that mandatory deadlines would subordinate quality to timeliness," the Court concluded that "it would be an unwarranted judicial intrusion into this pervasively regulated area for federal courts to issue injunctions imposing deadlines with respect to future disability claims." 467 U.S. at 111–19. Nevertheless, the Court explicitly declined in *Day* to preclude judges in individual cases from awarding the payment of interim benefits and setting time limits to remedy excessive delays in individual cases: "We make clear that nothing in this opinion precludes the proper use of injunctive relief to remedy individual violations of § 405(b)." 467 U.S. at 119 n.33. Since *Day*, the lower courts are divided on the courts' authority to award interim benefits due to excessive delays on remands in individual cases where claimants are initial applicants for benefits as opposed to beneficiaries challenging the termination of their benefits. *See generally* Hoffman v. Apfel, 122 F. Supp. 2d 1001, 1013–16, (N.D. Iowa. 2000) (reviewing court of appeals and district court decisions; listing and applying factors to consider when awarding interim benefits); *compare* Rivera v. Apfel, 99 F. Supp. 2d 358 (S.D.N.Y. 2000) (awarding interim benefits to applicant for benefits) *with* Mullen v. Secretary of Health and Human Servs., 878 F. Supp. 682 (D.Del.1995) (no authority to award interim benefits to applicant based on excessive delays).

H. ATTORNEY'S FEES

There are two main sources of attorney's fees in Social Security cases. Most awards by far are paid by the claimant, usually out of past-due benefits. Another source of fees is the Equal Access to Justice Act (EAJA), a federal fee-shifting statute. Both are discussed below. For the most part, attorney's fees for OASDI and SSI claims are governed by the same or similar rules. Many of the same rules apply also to non-attorney representatives. The status of non-attorney representatives at the Social Security Administration is covered in Chapter 9.

1. FEE FROM THE CLAIMANT

Attorney's fees paid out of the claimant's benefits are regulated by statute and regulations. *See generally* 42 U.S.C. § 406(a)–(b); 20 C.F.R. §§ 404.1720, 1725, 1728, 1730 (OASDI); 42 U.S.C. § 1383(d)(2); 20 C.F.R. §§ 416.1520, 416.1525, 1528, 1530 (SSI). Fees for claims resolved within SSA are authorized at the administrative level where the final decision is reached. Thus, administrative law judges approve fees in cases where a favorable hearing decision was issued, and the Appeals Council authorizes fees in cases decided finally only by the Appeals Council. The representative must file a request for fees in writing, which must include a list of services performed, the amount of the fee, and any expenses incurred. 20 C.F.R. §§ 404.1725(a), 416.1525(a). SSA considers a number of factors when evaluating a representative's request for fees, including the type and amount of services performed, the difficulty of the case (including the skill required of the representative), and the results achieved. *See* 20 C.F.R. §§ 404.1725(b)(1), 416.1525(b)(1). Although the amount of benefits received is taken into consideration, it does not control the amount of fee authorized. 20 C.F.R. §§ 404.1725(b)(2), 416.1525(b)(2).

Separate from its role in authorizing the amount of fees, which are not subject to a statutory limit and can be awarded even if no past-due benefits have accrued, SSA will withhold up to 25 percent of past-due benefits for direct payment to claimant representatives for agency-level representation. This applies to all attorneys and some non-attorney representatives for both OASDI and SSI. *See* 20 C.F.R. §§ 404.1720(b), 416.1520(b). Starting in 1999, Congress imposed a "user fee" on representatives whose fees are paid by SSA out of withheld past-due benefits. The rate is 6.3% with a cap that is adjusted periodically to account for inflation, set most recently in 2021 at $98. *See* 42 U.S.C. § 406(d); 20 C.F.R. §§ 404.1720(d), 416.1520(d).

In order to encourage attorneys to handle Social Security cases where little or no past-due benefits can be withheld, SSA has approved the use of agreements by which claimants agree to deposit funds into a trust or escrow account that can be used to pay attorney's fees. The funds can be used only to pay fees approved by SSA and any funds in excess of the amount authorized must be refunded to the claimant. SSR 82–39 (1982).

A claimant and his or her representative can also agree on the amount of the fee, which will be awarded automatically so long as the agreement was filed with SSA before the claim was approved. 42 U.S.C. §§ 406(a)(2)(A)(i), 1383(d)(2)(A). The amount of an agreed fee is limited to 25% of past-due benefits or $6000, whichever is less. 42 U.S.C. §§ 406(a)(2)(A)(ii), 1383(d)(2)(A); *see* 74 Fed. Reg. 6080 (January 29, 2009) ("increasing the maximum dollar amount limit for fee agreements approved under [these sections] to $6,000") (effective June 29, 2009). These rules on agreed-upon fees apply to non-attorney representatives as well.

Finally, courts can award fees for representation in judicial proceedings. The Social Security Act limits the amount of an attorney's fee in cases where the claimant prevailed in court to 25 percent of past-due benefits. 42 U.S.C. §§ 406(b), 1383(d)(2)(A). In addition, as noted earlier, an award up to this amount can be withheld from past-due benefits for direct payment to the attorney. The 25 percent limitation on court-awarded fees is intended as a maximum, not an amount to be awarded routinely. In awarding a fee, courts will look to many factors similar to those SSA considers when setting a fee for administrative representation, including the difficulty of the case, the amount of time involved, the level of skill required, and the result achieved. The Supreme Court addressed the question of how courts should determine the amount of fees in Gisbrecht v. Barnhart, 535 U.S. 789 (2002). The Court rejected a lodestar approach based on hours spent and an hourly rate, noting that 42 U.S.C. § 406(b) "calls for court review of such arrangements as an independent check, to assure that they yield reasonable results in particular cases." 535 U.S. at 807. As a result, courts exercise independence when setting these fees. *Compare* Crawford v. Astrue, 586 F.3d 1142 (9th Cir.

2009)(examining the implications of compensating for risk in contingency litigation and the practical ability of Social Security attorneys to make a living handling these cases, the need to assure fairness to claimants and to protect claimants whose interests may be adverse to their attorneys, and potential windfalls to attorneys who may not have properly or reasonably earned the fee award and whose actions may have promoted delay to increase amount of back benefit; ultimately approving award reflecting up to $902 per hour); *with* Jeter v. Astrue, 622 F.3d 371 (5th Cir. 2010) (eschewing the need to force "our lower courts into applying an arbitrary, formulaic set of factors of our own making" and considering factors in addition to the lodestar rate, such as risk of loss in the representation, experience of the attorney, percentage of the past-due benefits the fee constitutes, value of the case to a claimant, degree of difficulty; rejecting requested fee as an attorney "windfall" which would have reflected rate of $846 per hour).

In Culbertson v. Berryhill, 139 S. Ct. 517 (2019), the Supreme Court held that the 25% cap applies only to fees for representation in court and not to aggregate fees awarded for both court and agency representation. The practical impact of the decision is that lawyers in certain circumstances can receive up to a 50% contingency fee from past claimant benefits where the successful representation required work both in court and before the agency. However, SSA is only required to withhold the 25% of past benefits for direct payment to representatives from agency representation, thereby averting the sometime awkward fee collection process from clients on that amount, and only "may" withhold more for direct payment for representation before the courts. 139 S. Ct. at 523.

2. FEES UNDER THE EQUAL ACCESS TO JUSTICE ACT

The Equal Access to Justice Act (EAJA), 28 U.S.C. § 2412, is a fee-shifting statute that authorizes an award of attorney's fees against government agencies—including the Social Security Administration—unless the government's position was "substantially justified" or there are special circumstances that would make the award unjust. EAJA fees are awarded, however, only if the claimant is the "prevailing party" on a contested issue. They are not limited to 25 percent of past-due benefits, as are fees paid out of a claimant's award; they can be awarded in any amount, as long as the total fee is reasonable. However, if the EAJA fee amounts to more than 25% of the claimant's past-due benefits SSA will not authorize an additional fee under 42 U.S.C. § 406(b). On the other hand, if the EAJA fee is less than 25% of the claimant's past-due benefits, then § 406(b) allows the difference, up to the 25%, to be paid out of past-due benefits.

The EAJA is limited to cases where the government is a party to the proceeding, and therefore does not apply to non-adversary administrative proceedings before the Social Security Administration. There had been a great deal of debate among courts concerning the applicability of the Act to an attorney's administrative work when a claimant files an appeal in federal court and obtains a court order remanding the claim for further administrative proceedings. As discussed earlier in this chapter, there are two different types of remands authorized in 42 U.S.C. § 405(g): "sentence four" remands, in conjunction with a judgment affirming, modifying, or reversing SSA's decision; and "sentence six" remands, which merely send the matter back to SSA for collection of additional evidence. In Shalala v. Schaefer, 509 U.S. 292 (1993), the Supreme Court limited the authorization of EAJA fees for administrative work following a remand to "sentence six" remands; that is, EAJA fees are available for work at the agency level only when done following a remand ordered for the purpose of considering additional evidence. In "sentence-four" cases, attorney's fees are available, if allowed, only for the lawyer's work in federal court that resulted in the remand order. Pursuant to *Schaefer*, EAJA fees are available for court work immediately after the sentence four remand order because such orders are deemed final and immediately appealable. On the other hand, fees based on sentence six remand orders, which are non-final orders since the court retains jurisdiction of the case pending the remand for the taking of new evidence, do not accrue until remand proceedings awarding benefits to the claimant are completed.

A common issue in EAJA fee disputes is determining whether SSA's position opposing the claimant was substantially justified. While the term "substantially justified" does not lend itself to a precise definition, the courts and Congress have set out several guidelines. As the Supreme Court stated in an early EAJA case, "as between the two commonly used connotations of the word 'substantially,' the one most naturally conveyed by ['substantially justified'] is not 'justified to a high degree,' but rather 'justified in substance or in the main'—that is, justified to a degree that could satisfy a reasonable person. * * *. . . To be 'substantially justified' means, of course, more than merely undeserving of sanctions for frivolousness; that is assuredly not the standard for Government litigation of which a reasonable person would approve." Pierce v. Underwood, 487 U.S. 552, 565, 108 S. Ct. 2541 (1988). *See also* 487 U.S. at 566 n.2 ("our analysis does not convert the term 'substantially justified' into 'reasonably justified.' . . . [A] position can be justified even though it is not correct, and we believe that it can be substantially (i.e., for the most part) justified if a reasonable person could think it correct, that is, if it has a reasonable basis in law and fact").

An even more prevalent question arising in EAJA disputes in Social Security cases is the reasonableness of hours claimed. SSA frequently asserts the categorical proposition that no more than forty hours is ever reasonable for prosecuting a Social Security claimant's federal court appeal. The Ninth Circuit has rejected reliance on such an arbitrary suggested hourly limit in assessing reasonableness *See* Costa v. Commissioner, 690 F.3d 1132, 1136, 183 Soc. Sec. Rep. Serv. 1 (9th Cir. 2012) ("While district courts may consider [that twenty to forty hours is the range most often requested and granted] in determining the reasonableness of a specific fee request, courts cannot drastically reduce awards simply because the attorney has requested compensation for more than forty hours or make reductions with a target number in mind. Instead, district courts must explain why the amount of time requested for a particular task is too high.").

Another common issue in EAJA litigation with Social Security appeals is the determination of the hourly rate. EAJA's principal provision on costs and fees provides in relevant part that "attorney fees shall not be awarded in excess of $125 per hour unless the court determines that an increase in the cost of living or a special factor, such as the limited availability of qualified attorneys for the proceedings involved, justifies a higher fee." 28 U.S.C. § 2412(d)(1)(D)(2)(A)(ii). Since there have been significant increases in the cost of living from when the $125 rate was set in 1996, prevailing parties almost always attempt to demonstrate that the $125 per hour base rate should be enhanced to reflect cost of living increases since the EAJA's re-enactment in 1996. This determination almost always entails two components: 1) cost of living adjustments (COLA) since 1996, usually shown through U.S. Department of Labor Consumer Price Index monthly reports; and 2) proof that the attorney's market rate is equal to or greater than the maximum EAJA rate of $125 per hour enhanced by the appropriate COLA.

The second component of the determination is complicated in Social Security cases by the fact that the Social Security Act's own fee provision, which authorizes attorney's fees amounting up to 25% of the claimant's retroactive benefits recovered through the representation, makes it a federal crime for an attorney to charge fees from the claimant in any different, greater manner—such as based on a retainer at an hourly rate or charging a non-contingent fee to the claimant. *See* 42 U.S.C. § 406(b)(2) ("Any attorney who charges, demands, receives, or collects for services rendered in connection with proceedings . . . any amount in excess of that allowed by the court thereunder shall be guilty of a misdemeanor and upon conviction thereof shall be subject to a fine of not more than $500, or imprisonment for not more than one year, or both."). Therefore, unlike most attorneys, those who specialize in Social Security representation do not have an established market rate for their Social Security work or the ability for the market to reveal what a claimant would be willing to pay per hour for Social Security representation. Many attorneys use their market rates in other types of cases or the market rates used by attorneys of similar experience and skill to demonstrate the COLA. *See, e.g.*, Sprinkle v. Colvin, 777 F.3d 421, 423, 212 Soc. Sec. Rep. Serv. 19 (7th Cir. 2015)("An EAJA claimant seeking a cost-of-living adjustment to the attorney fee rate need not offer either (1) proof of the effects of inflation on the particular attorney's practice or (2) proof that no competent attorney could be found for less than the requested rate. Instead, an EAJA claimant may rely on a general and readily available measure of inflation such as the Consumer Price Index, as well as proof that the requested rate does not exceed the prevailing market rate in the community for similar services by lawyers of comparable skill and experience. An affidavit from a single attorney testifying to the prevailing market rate in the community may suffice to meet that burden.").

The question of to whom the fee accrues—plaintiff or counsel—can affect the ability to allow offsets for federal debt. The Supreme Court has determined that the EAJA attorney's fee is payable to the claimant, not counsel, and therefore is subject to an administrative offset to satisfy any pre-existing debts owed by the claimant to the federal government. Astrue v. Ratliff, 560 U.S. 586, 130 S. Ct. 2521, 153 Soc. Sec. Rep. Serv. 352 (2010). Typically, lawyers execute assignments of EAJA fee awards in their retainer agreements with their clients which enables the courts to award these fees directly to counsel in the event there are no pre-existing client debts owed to the government. *See, e.g.*, Bilak v. Colvin, 73 F.Supp. 3d 481, 488 and n.3 (D.N.J. 2014) (awarding $34,207.02 in EAJA fees directly to counsel in a social security case pursuant to an assignment filed with the court).

Courts have also had to address the relationship between EAJA fees and fees available under the Social Security Act, 42 U.S.C. § 406(b). In Astrue v. Ratliff, *supra*, the Supreme Court explained that the 1985 amendments to the EAJA address the fact that Social Security claimants may be eligible to receive fee awards under both the SSA and EAJA, and clarified the procedure that attorneys and their clients must follow to prevent the windfall of an unauthorized double recovery of fees for the same work. Thus, § 406(b) provides that no violation of law occurs "if, where the claimant's attorney receives fees for the same work under both [the Social Security Act] and [the EAJA], the claimant's attorney refunds to the claimant the amount of the smaller fee." Astrue v. Ratliff, 560 U.S. at 595. It has been called "obvious malpractice" not to seek EAJA fees when also recovering § 406(b) fees because the § 406(b) fees come from the client's past-due benefits and the EAJA fees, coming from the United States Treasury, would avoid the loss of a portion of their client's past-due benefits. Coup v. Heckler, 706 F. Supp. 405, 407 (E.D.Pa.1989). Accordingly, in some jurisdictions, attorneys must give prior notice to their Social Security clients if they are not filing for EAJA fees and explain why (i.e., the belief the Commissioner's position in denying benefits was clearly substantially justified thereby precluding EAJA fee eligibility) and facilitate the right to object to counsel's failure to file for EAJA fees. Failure to provide such notice can be a basis for denying all § 406(b) fees to counsel. *See* Bordes v. Astrue, 2011 WL 1740179, at *1–2 (D.N.J. 2011) ("If counsel chooses to proceed under § 406 alone, counsel shall give notice to the client (i) advising the client of his or her right to object either in person or by letter to the amount of the fee requested; and (ii) advising the client that counsel has chosen to make application under § 406(b) rather than the EAJA and explaining the reasons for that decision. Such notice shall be filed with the Clerk.")

(quoting In re Standing Order in Social Security Cases, Misc. 85–465 (D.N.J. December 27, 1985)).

CHAPTER 9

ADMINISTRATIVE ADVOCACY

This chapter is intended to present key aspects of substantive law and administrative procedure in the context of Social Security practice. Disability claims make up the bulk of any Social Security practice and disability issues dominate judicial cases and decisions in social security law. As explained in Chapters 5, 6, and 8, the critical contested disability issues in Social Security cases are developed and resolved for the most part during the administrative process—from initial claim processing through up to three levels of administrative appeal. Although benefit decisions by the Social Security Administration are subject to judicial review, for most cases that can occur only after the administrative appeals process has been exhausted—and even then, the scope of review is limited by the "substantial evidence" rule.

Administrative advocacy is, therefore, a critical part of Social Security practice. As with other areas of law practice, there is no substitute for experience. Nonetheless, an introduction to certain practical aspects of administrative advocacy may be helpful. Accordingly, this chapter covers selected topics of administrative advocacy central to a Social Security practice, including the role of key actors in the administrative process, the sources of Social Security law, and various standards and rules governing proof of eligibility.

A. LAWYERS AND REPRESENTATIVES

Social Security claimants are entitled to be represented at all stages of the administrative process. 20 C.F.R. §§ 404.1700, 416.1500; 42 U.S.C. § 406(a). Although there is no constitutional right to appointed counsel, claimants have a constitutional right to bring a lawyer to a Social Security hearing. Mathews v. Eldridge, 424 U.S. 319, 339, 96 S. Ct. 893 (1976). Claimants can be represented by an attorney or by a non-attorney "authorized representative." *See generally* 20 C.F.R. §§ 404.1705, 416.1505. An attorney must be in good standing and must not have been disqualified or suspended from acting as a representative in dealings with the Social Security Administration. 20 C.F.R. §§ 404.1705(a), 416.1505(a). A non-attorney authorized representative must be "generally known to have a good character and reputation," "capable of giving valuable help" in connection with the claim, and neither disqualified or suspended from acting as a representative before SSA nor prohibited by law from acting as a representative. 20 C.F.R. §§ 404.1705(b), 416.1505(b).

These special rules, particularly those authorizing non-attorney representatives, apply only to administrative appeals. Only licensed attorneys can handle cases appealed to the federal courts, although some courts have held that non-attorney parents can handle their child's Social Security appeals in federal court. *See, e.g.*, Harris v. Apfel, 209 F.3d 413, 417, 68 Soc. Sec. Rep. Serv. 437 (5th Cir. 2000) ("We are persuaded that prohibiting non-attorney parents from proceeding pro se in appeals from administrative SSI decisions, on behalf of a minor child, would jeopardize seriously the child's statutory right to judicial review"). Most courts restrict this authority, however, to situations where the parents have "a sufficient interest in the case" to warrant the responsibility. *Compare* Machadio v. Apfel, 276 F.3d 103, 107, 77 Soc. Sec. Rep. Serv. 559 (2d Cir. 2002) (non-attorney parent serving as representative payee for his child's SSI benefits; "Where a district court, after appropriate inquiry into the particular circumstances of the matter at hand, determines that a non-attorney parent who brings an SSI appeal on behalf his or her children has a sufficient interest in the case and meets basic standards of competence, we hold that in such cases a non-attorney parent may bring an action on behalf of his or her child without representation by an attorney.") *with* Sabbia v. Commissioner, 669 F.Supp.2d 914, 917, 150 Soc. Sec. Rep. Serv. 553 (N.D. Ill. 2009) (distinguishing cases where custodial parents financially responsible for their children sought to handle appeal; "because the parents had a personal stake in the outcome of their children's actions, they could be trusted to represent their children's interests. That rationale is clearly inapplicable here, since both Dominic Jr. and Nicole are adults.") (citations omitted).

Once appointed, the representative can have access to all information otherwise available only to the claimant, can submit evidence and advocate on behalf of the claimant, and is entitled to receive notice of all SSA action on the claim. 20 C.F.R. §§ 404.1710(a), 404.1715, 416.1510(a), 416.1515.

Correspondence sent from SSA to an authorized representative has the same force and effect as if it had been sent directly to the claimant. 20 C.F.R. §§ 404.1715, 416.1515. Moreover, for the purpose of computing timeliness to file appeals in light of the short, 60-day filing period for notices of appeal, the period runs from receipt by the appointed representative, even where the claimant received notice earlier. Roberts v. Shalala, 848 F. Supp. 1008, 1015, 44 Soc. Sec. Rep. Serv. 310 (M.D. Ga. 1994)("In those cases in which a representative has been designated by a claimant according to the regulations, this court would begin the sixty day period for filing an appeal from the date of notification of the representative, whether it be the presumed date of notification or the actual date established by reasonable evidence."). *See also* Boley v. Colvin, 761 F.3d 803 (7th Cir. 2014) (finding jurisdiction to review an ALJ's order dismissing an untimely request for a hearing and remanding to determine if the failure to notify the claimant's counsel (in addition to the claimant) of the reconsideration decision establishes good cause for the late hearing request filing); AR 16–1(7) (acquiescing to and agreeing to apply Boley in the Seventh Circuit, but otherwise reasserting SSA's national position that a dismissal is not a final decision subject to judicial review). (As noted in Chapter 8, Smith v. Berryhill, 139 S. Ct. 1765 (2019) upheld jurisdiction to review dismissal of an Appeals Council request for review, ruling that a dismissal after an ALJ hearing is a "final decision . . . made after a hearing" subject to review under 42 U.S.C. § 405(g)).

Claimants may waive their right to be represented at a hearing. However, the claimant must be competent to waive the right. *See, e.g.*, Earp v. Commissioner, 168 F.Supp.2d 628, 634, 76 Soc. Sec. Rep. Serv. 483 (E.D. Tex. 2001) ("Since there is conflicting evidence in this record regarding whether Plaintiff is mentally retarded, the Court must find that she has not properly waived her right to counsel."). Simply asking if a claimant had been represented before and would like to proceed without counsel may not be sufficient to establish a knowing and competent waiver. Lewis v. Barnhart, 201 F. Supp. 2d 918, 939, 81 Soc. Sec. Rep. Serv. 83 (N.D. Ind. 2002) (waiver invalid; "The fact that Lewis had been represented by counsel in another setting does not mean that he understood the benefits of counsel in the context of a social security disability administrative hearing."). Moreover, many courts have held that a waiver is not effective at an administrative hearing unless the ALJ advises the claimant of the possibility of either obtaining free counsel or working out a contingency fee arrangement with a private lawyer. *See, e.g.*, Wilks v. Apfel, 113 F. Supp. 2d 30, 34, 71 Soc. Sec. Rep. Serv. 74 (D.D.C. 2000) ("The ALJ did not adequately inform plaintiff about his right to counsel, specifically what that right entailed."); Frank v. Chater, 924 F. Supp. 416, 421–26, 50 Soc. Sec. Rep. Serv. 790 (E.D.N.Y. 1996) (written notices to claimant did not advise him of the benefits of counsel or of the possibility of free legal services or a contingency fee arrangement). As set out by the Seventh Circuit in Binion v. Shalala, 13 F.3d 243, 245, 43 Soc. Sec. Rep. Serv. 289 (7th Cir. 1994): "To ensure a valid waiver of counsel, we require the ALJ to explain to the pro se claimant (1) the manner in which an attorney can aid in the proceedings, (2) the possibility of free counsel or a contingency arrangement, and (3) the limitation on attorney fees to 25 percent of past due benefits and required court approval of the fees." Consistent with this view, SSA regulations provide that where a claimant is not represented by an attorney it will include in its notice of any adverse decision information about options for obtaining an attorney, including from a legal services organization. 20 C.F.R. §§ 404.1706, 416.1506.

1. STANDARDS OF CONDUCT FOR REPRESENTATIVES

The Social Security Administration has issued comprehensive standards for the conduct of claimant representatives. *See generally* 20 C.F.R. §§ 404.1740, 416.1540. The standards require representatives to obtain promptly any evidence that the claimant wants to present, including any material medical evidence, as well as evidence requested by SSA. 20 C.F.R. §§ 404.1740(b)(1)–(2), 416.1540(b)(1)–(2). In addition, both claimants and their representatives are required to "inform [SSA] about or submit all [known] evidence" that relates to the disability claim, whether favorable or unfavorable. 20 C.F.R. §§ 404.1512(a), 416. 912(a). As SSA explained when this requirement was first published: "This duty is ongoing and requires you to disclose any additional related evidence about which you become aware. This duty applies at each level of the administrative review process, including the Appeals Council level if the evidence relates to the period on or before the date of the administrative law judge hearing decision." 80 Fed. Reg. 14828–01 (March 20, 2015).

The regulations include exemptions for attorney/representative client-privileged materials or for work product materials related to the claimant's representative's "analysis of the claim." 20 C.F.R. §§ 404.1513(b)(1), 416.913(b)(1). Significantly, the agency may sanction representatives with suspensions or disqualifications from representing claimants before the agency for failing to carry out the affirmative duties established in these regulations. 20 C.F.R. §§ 404.1745(b), 416.1545(b). In addition, under the Social Security Protection Act of 2004, the agency can impose civil monetary penalties against claimants and representative alike for failing to disclose "material facts" which fall under the above provisions. *See* 42 U.S.C. § 1320a–8(a). Finally, under other provisions of the Social Security Act, the agency "shall disregard evidence if there is reason to believe that fraud or similar fault was involved in the providing of that evidence." 42 U.S.C. §§ 405(u), 1631(e)(7). "Similar fault" is involved if "an incorrect or incomplete statement that is material to the determination is knowingly made" or "information that is material to the determination is knowingly concealed." *Id. See also* SSR 16–2p (2016) (describing ways in which a "similar fault" finding may, or may not, have significant evidentiary consequences beyond the tainted evidence in question); SSR 16–1p

(2016) (describing process for redetermination of eligibility where an initial application was predicated on fraud or similar fault).

SSA has long required that claimants' representatives must further the "efficient, fair and orderly conduct of the administrative decisionmaking process" by providing competent representation and acting with reasonable diligence and promptness. *See* 20 C.F.R. §§ 404.1740(b)(3), 416.1540(b)(3). They are bound not to "threaten, coerce, intimidate, deceive or knowingly mislead a claimant" or to make false statements, unreasonably delay proceedings, divulge information without the claimant's permission, or engage in other various unprofessional or illegal behavior. 20 C.F.R. §§ 404.1740(c), 416.1540(c). Broadly speaking, current standards require representatives to "provide competent assistance to the claimant and recognize [the agency's] authority to lawfully administer the [claims] process." 20 C.F.R. §§ 404.1740(a)(1), 416.1540(a)(1). Representatives must also "be forthright in their dealings with [SSA] and with the claimant and must comport themselves with due regard for the nonadversarial nature of the proceedings." 20 C.F.R. §§ 404.1740(a)(2), 416.1540(a)(2). The regulations also prohibit "[c]ommunicating with agency staff or adjudicators outside the normal course of business or other prescribed procedures in an attempt to inappropriately influence the processing or outcome of a claim(s)." 20 C.F.R. §§ 404.1740(b)(3), 416.1540(c)(7)(ii)(C).

The Social Security Administration issued regulations at the end of 2016, effective in 2017, entitled "Ensuring Program Uniformity at the Hearing and Appeals Council Levels of the Administrative Review Process." 81 Fed. Reg. 90987 (December 16, 2016). Among other provisions, the new regulations set out a "5-day rule" modifying the period when claimants (and their representatives) must submit or inform SSA about written evidence. 20 C.F.R. §§ 404.935(a), 416.1435(a). The 5-day rule, which counts only business days, contains certain exceptions, including: where SSA misled the claimant; if the claimant's failure to submit or inform SSA of the evidence was due to a physical, mental, educational, or linguistic limitation; or some "other unusual, unexpected, or unavoidable circumstance beyond your control prevented you from informing us about or submitting the evidence earlier." 20 C.F.R. §§ 404.935(b), 416.1435(b). The new regulations also lengthen the time frame for notifying claimants of a hearing date from at least 60 days to at least 75 days. 20 C.F.R. §§ 404.938(a), 416.1438(a). The following year, SSA issued SSR 17–4p (2017) that further defined the scope of its new regulations and imposed obligations on claimants and their representatives beyond the plain language requirements of the regulations. With respect to the new 5-day rule, the Ruling provides that claimants "must provide information specific enough to identify the evidence (source, location, and dates of treatment) and show that the evidence relates to the individual's medical condition, work activity, job history, medical treatment, or other issues relevant to whether or not the individual is disabled or blind."

SSR 17–4p also sets out certain expectations of claimant representatives regarding their obligation to submit evidence. Thus SSA expects them "to submit or inform us about written evidence as soon as they obtain or become aware of it [and] should not wait until 5 business days before the hearing to submit or inform us about written evidence unless they have compelling reasons for the delay," noting that "it is only acceptable for a representative to inform us about evidence without submitting it if the representative shows that, despite good faith efforts, he or she could not obtain the evidence." The Ruling also delineates new avenues for imposing discipline and sanctions against representatives, such as failing to submit in a timely manner evidence they had informed the agency about, including waiting until the late date under the 5-day rule, and where "clients of a particular representative have a pattern of informing us about written evidence instead of making good-faith efforts to obtain and timely submit the evidence."

Since 2004, persons who have been disbarred or suspended from practice in any court or disqualified from participating in any federal program or from appearing before any federal agency can be refused (or disqualified from) the right to appear before SSA. *See* Social Security Protection Act of 2004, § 205, Pub. L. No. 108–203; 42 U.S.C.A. § 406(a). SSA has issued implementing regulations on disqualification and reinstatement of claimant representatives. *See generally* 20 C.F.R. §§ 404.1745, 404.1770, 416.1545, 416.1570. Specifically, the regulations distinguish between situations where the person was disbarred or disqualified by reason of misconduct, in which case disqualification or suspension from appearing before SSA is mandatory, and where such action was taken for "solely administrative reasons," in which case the person will not be prohibited from appearing before SSA. 20 C.F.R. §§ 404.1770(a)(2), 416.1570(a)(2). The regulations also set out standards for reinstatement. 20 C.F.R. §§ 404.1799, 416.1599.

A representative may challenge a disqualification or suspension by appealing to the Appeals Council. 20 C.F.R. §§ 404.1770(b)(1), 416.1570(b)(1). However, judicial review is not readily available. As noted in Chapter 8, federal court jurisdiction is limited where the administrative decision appealed from was other than a claim for benefits. *See* Stanley v. Astrue, 298 Fed. App'x 537, 2008 WL 4394251 (8th Cir. 2008) (denying jurisdiction under 42 U.S.C. § 405(g) and the Administrative Procedures Act (APA) where attorney challenged SSA's decision to suspend him from representing claimants because he collected and retained a fee in excess of the SSA-authorized fee.).

B. SOURCES OF LAW AND LEGAL EFFECT

1. SSA SUB-REGULATORY GUIDANCE: SOCIAL SECURITY RULINGS; HEARINGS, APPEALS AND LITIGATION LAW MANUAL (HALLEX); AND PROGRAM OPERATIONS MANUAL SYSTEMS (POMS)

The Social Security Act, most of which is codified at 42 U.S.C. § 401 et seq., is, of course, binding law. Similarly, regulations promulgated by the Social Security Administration, most of which are codified at 20 C.F.R. Parts 404 and 416, are binding and have the effect of law. Moreover, courts must defer to regulatory interpretations of silent or ambiguous provisions of the Social Security Act if the agency's interpretation is merely "reasonable." Barnhart v. Thomas, 540 U.S. 20, 25–26 (2003) (applying so-called "Chevron deference," as set out in Chevron U.S.A., Inc. v. NRDC, Inc., 467 U.S. 837, 843 (1984), to Social Security regulations); *see also* U.S. v. Mead Corp., 533 U.S. 218, 227 (2001) ("When Congress has 'explicitly left a gap for an agency to fill, there is an express delegation of authority to the agency to elucidate a specific provision of the statute by regulation,' and any ensuing regulation is binding in the courts unless procedurally defective, arbitrary or capricious in substance, or manifestly contrary to the statute.") (citation omitted).

In addition to the Social Security Act and the various regulations promulgated by the Social Security Administration, there are a number of other important published sources of Social Security law.

Three of these are described in this section: Social Security Rulings (including a sub-category of Acquiescence Rulings), which apply across the administrative process; Program Operations Manual System (often referred to as POMS), which is used at the local office level; and the Hearings, Appeals, and Litigation Law Manual (HALLEX), a special manual used principally at the ALJ hearing and Appeals Council stages of the administrative process.

Social Security Rulings are policy statements or interpretations of the Social Security Act and implementing regulations issued by SSA. "These rulings represent precedent final opinions and orders and statements of policy and interpretations that [SSA has] adopted" and "are binding on all components of the Social Security Administration." 20 C.F.R. § 402.35(b)(1). *See also* Heckler v. Edwards, 465 U.S. 870, 873 n.3 (1984) (" 'Once published, a ruling is binding on all components of the Social Security Administration. . . . Rulings do not have the force and effect of the law or regulations but are to be relied upon as precedents in determining other cases where the facts are basically the same.' ") (quoting Preface to Social Security Rulings at iii (cum. ed. 1981)).

Courts provide some deference, or at least respect, to Social Security Rulings. *See generally* Coskery v. Berryhill, 892 F.3d 1, 5 n.3 (1st Cir. 2018) ("There appears to be some disagreement among the courts of appeals as to what level of deference SSRs are entitled.") (Comparing Wilson v. Comm'r of Soc. Sec., 378 F.3d 541, 549 (6th Cir. 2004), which applied a "plainly erroneous or inconsistent with the regulation" level of deference set forth in Auer v. Robbins, 519 U.S. 452, 461, 117 S. Ct. 905, 137 L.Ed.2d 79 (1997), with Lauer v. Bowen, 818 F.2d 636, 640 n.8 (7th Cir. 1987), which applied a "respect" level of deference set forth in Skidmore v. Swift & Co., 323 U.S. 134, 65 S. Ct. 161, 89 L.Ed. 124 (1944)). Most courts find that they are entitled to respect or some deference because they constitute an agency's interpretations of its own regulations and the statute that it administers. As a result, courts often follow Social Security Rulings unless they are "plainly erroneous" or "inconsistent" with the Social Security Act. *See, e.g.*, Andrade v. Secretary, 985 F.2d 1045, 1051, 40 Soc. Sec. Rep. Serv. 117 (10th Cir. 1993). The Ninth Circuit has explained the status of Social Security Rulings within SSA and in federal court review as follows: "The Commissioner issues Social Security Rulings to clarify the Act's implementing regulations and the agency's policies. SSRs are binding on all components of the SSA. SSRs do not have the force of law. However, because they represent the Commissioner's interpretation of the agency's regulations, we give them some deference. We will not defer to SSRs if they are inconsistent with the statute or regulations." Holohan v. Massanari, 246 F.3d 1195, 1211 n. 1, 73 Soc. Sec. Rep. Serv. 243 (9th Cir. 2001) (internal citations omitted). *See also* Myers v. Apfel, 238 F.3d 617, 620, 72 Soc. Sec. Rep. Serv. 427 (5th Cir. 2001) ("The Social Security Administration's rulings are not binding on this court, but they may be consulted when the statute at issue provides little guidance.").

Where authoritative or official Social Security rules interpret "genuine" ambiguities in SSA regulations, they may be entitled to a stronger form of deference set out by the Supreme Court in Auer v. Robbins, 519 U.S. 452 (1997). *See* Kisor v. Wilkie, 139 S. Ct. 2400 (2019) (declining to overrule "*Auer*" deference doctrine but recognizing and reinforcing limits on its use). Thus, courts have occasionally applied *Auer* deference to SSRs in Social Security cases. *See, e.g.*, Sewall v. Comm'r of SSA, 2020 WL 1289554, *15 n.7 (D. Colo. March 18, 2020) (applying *Auer* deference to SSR 00–4p, post-*Kisor*).

SSA publishes its standard operating procedures and policies in the Program Operations Manual System (POMS). POMS is a multi-volume manual used for the processing and adjudication of all Social Security claims at SSA district and field offices and at state agencies charged with making disability determinations. POMS is intended to fill in the substantive and procedural gaps of the Social Security Act and implementing regulations as they are applied on the ground. POMS has been reworked and reorganized repeatedly in the past and is updated frequently through various types of instructions, some of which apply only on a regional basis. Originally, POMS was published in a series of difficult-to-manage volumes; however, since 2002 a "public version" identical to the version used by SSA employees (but without certain codes and sensitive instructions) is available on the SSA website.

The Supreme Court addressed the legal effect of POMS in Schweiker v. Hansen, 450 U.S. 785 (1981).

Noting that it is not a regulation but rather "a 13-volume handbook for internal use by thousands of SSA employees," the Court stated directly that "[i]t has no legal force, and it does not bind the SSA." 450 U.S. at 789. Later cases have cited *Hansen* for the proposition that POMS is not binding upon the agency; however, other courts have held that POMS does have some persuasive force. *See, e.g.*, Bubnis v. Apfel, 150 F.3d 177, 181, 57 Soc. Sec. Rep. Serv. 547 (2d Cir. 1998) (dispute involving worker's compensation offset; "Because these guidelines represent the Commissioner's interpretation of the statutory mandate, they deserve substantial deference, and will not be disturbed as long as they are reasonable and consistent with the statute."); Davis v. Secretary, 867 F.2d 336, 340, 24 Soc. Sec. Rep. Serv. 495 (6th Cir. 1989) ("Although the POMS is a policy and procedure manual that employees of the [Social Security Administration] use in evaluating Social Security claims and does not have the force and effect of law, it is nevertheless persuasive"); Kennedy v. Colvin, 738 F.3d 1172, 1177–78 (9th Cir. 2013) ("We have held that "POMS may be 'entitled to respect' under Skidmore v. Swift & Co., 323 U.S. 134, 65 S. Ct. 161, 89 L. Ed. 124 (1944), to the extent it provides a persuasive interpretation of an ambiguous regulation, but it 'does not impose judicially enforceable duties on either this court or the ALJ.' ").

Hearings, Appeals, and Litigation Law Manual (HALLEX) is an internal guidance manual that includes authoritative policy statements from the Appeals Council and also "defines procedures for carrying out policy and provides guidance for processing and adjudicating claims at the Hearing, Appeals Council and Civil Action levels." HALLEX I-1-001. Courts have interpreted HALLEX similarly to POMS. *See, e.g.*, Moore v. Apfel, 216 F.3d 864, 869 (5th Cir. 2000) ("HALLEX does not have the force and effect of law, it is not binding on the Commissioner and we will not review allegations of noncompliance with the manual."); Power v. Barnhart, 292 F. 781, 786, 81 Soc. Sec. Rep. Serv. 230 (D.C. Cir. 2002) (HALLEX, POMS, and internal memoranda of the Associate Commissioner "lack the administrative formality or other attributes that would justify substantial judicial deference under *Chevron* and hence . . . would at best qualify for the more limited form of deference ["respect"] accorded under *Skidmore*.") (citations omitted). However, one of those same courts has held that "while HALLEX does not carry the authority of law, . . . 'where the rights of individuals are affected, an agency must follow its own procedures, even where the internal procedures are more rigorous than otherwise would be required,' " and "[i]f prejudice results from a violation, the result cannot stand." Morgan v. Colvin, 803 F.3d 773, 777, 222 Soc. Sec. Rep. Serv. 471 (5th Cir. 2015) (quoting Newton v. Apfel, 209 F.3d 448, 459 (5th Cir.2000); finding prejudice from violation of HALLEX rule requiring subsequent ALJs to hold a new hearing).

2. EFFECT OF PRECEDENTIAL COURT OF APPEALS DECISIONS AND SSA ACQUIESCENCE RULINGS

There are twelve United States circuit courts of appeals deciding appeals from district court affirmances of SSA decisions denying or terminating SSA benefits. Each of these twelve courts of appeal is independent of each other and a decision of one is not binding in any other circuit. Yet, the Social Security Administration is a federal agency with a national mandate. Its regulations, rulings and policies apply in all parts of the nation. Accordingly, through a practice known as "non-acquiescence," SSA resisted for many years adhering to decisions of the courts of appeal when those decisions conflict with or deviate from SSA nationwide policy, even within the circuits from which those decisions arose. SSA confronted a spate of challenges in the 1980s to its non-acquiescence policy including challenges to de jure, formal, non-acquiescence based on the agency's issuance and application of formal "non-acquiescence" Social Security Rulings. *See, e.g.*, Lopez v. Heckler, 787 F.2d 1432, 1438 (9th Cir. 1983).

The Social Security Administration issued new regulations outlining a transparent "acquiescence" policy in 1990. Under those regulations, still in effect, when the agency expressly and formally determines that circuit court decisions are inconsistent with Administration policy, SSA follows those circuit court decisions at all levels of the administrative process and judicial review within the particular circuit, unless it decides to seek further judicial review of that decision or to re-litigate the relevant issue in another case. This action is formalized in an "Acquiescence Ruling," which explains how SSA will apply the particular rule in the relevant circuit. *See* 20 C.F.R. §§ 404.985, 416.1485. However, SSA may still "informally non-acquiesce" in circuit court precedent by simply failing to issue an Acquiescence Ruling on conflicting or varying circuit precedent. Some courts have continued to reject "informal non-acquiescence," where demonstrated, on a case-by-case basis. *See, e.g.*, Hutchison v. Chater, 99 F.3d 286, 287–88 (8th Cir. 1996) ("regardless of whether the Commissioner formally announces her acquiescence, however, she is still bound by the law of this Circuit and does not have the discretion to decide whether to adhere to it."); Laird v. Stidwell, 969 F. Supp. 1167, 1195–1200 (N.D. Iowa 1997) (finding continued non-acquiescence; "it is clear that the Commissioner's policy of nonacquiescence is indeed purposeful. There may, in fact, be a legitimate, rational, nondiscriminatory reason the Commissioner chooses to embark on this policy of ignoring Eighth Circuit decisions. The defendants have not, however, offered an explanation for this policy in any of their numerous filings."). In turn, SSA has continued to re-affirm its directive to adjudicators to disregard all circuit court precedent not embodied in SSA Acquiescence Rulings. *See* 63 Fed. Reg. 24927, 24930–31 (May 6, 1998) ("SSA adjudicators are to follow SSA's nationwide rules until the Commissioner determines that a circuit court holding is in conflict with our national rules and publishes an AR [acquiescence ruling] instructing adjudicators on how the decision is to be followed within the applicable circuit."); SSR 96–1p (1996) (same); SSR 13–2p, § 15.c (2013) (same).

C. PROOF OF ELIGIBILITY

Social Security claimants have the burden of establishing eligibility for benefits. The claimant is thus responsible for obtaining the evidence necessary to prove eligibility and for providing that evidence, including necessary documents, to SSA. 20 C.F.R. § 404.704; *see also* 20 C.F.R. § 416.200. This is particularly true with regard to the most difficult and most often contested issue in such cases: whether the claimant is disabled according to the applicable disability standard. The Social Security Act states specifically that a claimant "shall not be considered to be under a disability unless he furnishes such medical and other evidence of the existence thereof as the [Social Security Administration] may require." 42 U.S.C. § 423(d)(5)(A). *See also* 20 C.F.R. §§ 404.1512(a), 416.912(a) ("In general, [claimants] have to prove to [the Social Security Administration] that [they] are blind or disabled."). SSA regulations also inform claimants that it "will consider only impairments you say you have or about which we receive evidence." 20 C.F.R. §§ 404.1512(a), 416.912(a). If requested, a claimant must also provide information about their age, education and training, work experience, daily activities, efforts to work, and any other factors showing how the claimant's impairment affects ability to work. 20 C.F.R. §§ 404.1512(a), 416.912(a). If a claimant does not give SSA the necessary information, SSA will make a decision based on the information available. 20 C.F.R. §§ 404.1516, 416.916. Claimants are not excused from giving evidence because they have "religious or personal reasons against medical examinations, tests, or treatment." *Id.* At the same time, SSA must make "every reasonable effort" to help the claimant obtain medical reports, 20 C.F.R. §§ 404.1512(b), 416.912(b), and, as discussed further later in this chapter, in some cases the SSA may pay for a consultative examination.

Courts often list four sources of evidence for proving disability: objective medical facts; diagnoses or opinions of medical experts based on those facts; subjective statements of symptoms of disability, such as pain or fatigue, from the claimant or other lay witnesses; and information about the claimant's age, education, and prior work experience. *See, e.g.*, Perez v. Barnhart, 415 F.3d 457, 462, 105 Soc. Sec. Rep. Serv. 399, 2005 WL 1540802 (5th Cir. 2005) ("In determining whether substantial evidence of disability exists, this court weighs four factors: (1) objective medical evidence; (2) diagnoses and opinions; (3) the claimant's subjective evidence of pain and disability; and (4) the claimant's age, education, and work history."). One or more of these sources, or perhaps other evidence such as the opinion of a vocational expert about the claimant's vocational ability and the availability of jobs, may be necessary in a particular case. The evidence required depends on where in SSA's "sequential evaluation process" for determining disability the disability decision is made. The sequential evaluation process is covered in Chapter 5.

While claimants bear the burden of proof, the burden is satisfied by a simple preponderance of the evidence. *See* Mandziej v. Chater, 944 F. Supp. 121, 129, 52 Soc. Sec. Rep. Serv. 267 (D.N.H. 1996) ("The Act places a heavy initial burden on the plaintiff to establish the existence of a disabling impairment. . . . Nevertheless, the plaintiff is not required to establish a doubt-free claim; the initial burden is satisfied by the usual civil standard, a 'preponderance of the evidence.' "). SSA codified this long-standing practice in 2009 "to clarify that we apply the preponderance of the evidence standard when we make determinations and decisions at all levels of our administrative review process." 73 Fed. Reg. 76940–41 (December 18, 2008). *See also* 20 C.F.R. §§ 404.902, 416.1402 (initial determinations); 20 C.F.R. §§ 404.920, 416.1420 (reconsideration); 20 C.F.R. §§ 404.953(a), 416.1453(a) (administrative hearings). The preponderance of the evidence standard is defined at 20 C.F.R. §§ 404.901, 416.1401 as "such relevant evidence that as a whole shows that the existence of the fact to be proven is more likely than not."

There are no more detailed guidelines on the amount of evidence necessary to establish eligibility for benefits. The claimant must show that the relevant necessary findings are more likely than not, but the context in which decisions for Social Security benefits are made can have an influence. Thus, one court noted that although the claimant has the burden of proving disability, "due regard for the beneficent purposes of the legislation requires that a more tolerant standard be used . . . than . . . where the adversary system prevails." Hess v. Secretary, 497 F.2d 837, 840 (3d Cir. 1974). On the other hand, the claimant's burden has been described as "heavy" and "bordering on the unrealistic." Johnson v. Harris, 612 F.2d 993, 997 (5th Cir. 1980). *See also* Bazile v. Apfel, 113 F. Supp. 2d 181, 184, 71 Soc. Sec. Rep. Serv. 79 (D. Mass. 2000) (noting "heavy initial burden" of establishing disability through "credible evidence").

There are, however, some rules on medical evidence and allocating the burden of proof that help clarify what a claimant must show in order to prove eligibility for benefits. Some of these have been discussed earlier in other contexts, such as the "medical improvement" requirement for terminating benefits (Chapter 4) and the shifting of the burden of proof upon a showing that the claimant is unable to perform prior relevant work at Step 4 of the "sequential evaluation process" (Chapter 5). Another important set of rules on the weight and sufficiency of different types and sources of medical evidence are discussed later in this chapter.

Perhaps the most important point concerning proof of eligibility in difficult Social Security cases is that a court will uphold a final decision denying a claim for benefits if it is supported by "substantial evidence." As explained in Chapter 8, the substantial evidence rule applied on judicial review is defined as "more than a mere scintilla. It means such relevant evidence as a reasonable mind might accept as adequate to support a conclusion." Richardson v. Perales, 402 U.S. 389, 401 (1971) (quoting

Consolidated Edison Co. v. NLRB, 305 U.S. 197 (1938). SSA also uses the substantial evidence rule to review ALJ factual determinations at the Appeals Council. *See* 20 C.F.R. §§ 404.901, 416.1401 (defining substantial evidence as "such relevant evidence as a reasonable mind might accept as adequate to support a conclusion."). Therefore, in order to prevail on appeal, a claimant must present sufficient evidence at the administrative hearing level to impeach or contradict any evidence supporting a possible denial. The claimant's burden of proof becomes, in effect, more than an affirmative showing of disability; the claimant must also assure that there is an absence of substantial evidence of non-disability in the record—in case the claim is denied and relief will have to come on appeal.

Evidence supporting a claim for benefits must be, of course, both competent and legitimate. Moreover, SSA regulations advise that OASDI claimants "should also be aware that Section 208 of the Social Security Act provides criminal penalties for misrepresenting the facts or for making false statements to obtain social security benefits for [the individual] or someone else." 20 C.F.R. § 404.704. Although this regulation applies only to OASDI claims, the Social Security Act provides for criminal penalties in cases of false statement or representation of material facts in obtaining SSI benefits. *See* 42 U.S.C. § 1383a(a). The Act also provides for a redetermination of benefits if it appears that fraud or "similar fault" was involved in the claim. *See* 42 U.S.C. §§ 405(u)(1)(A), 1383(e)(7)(A). SSR 16–2p (2016) clarifies what "similar fault" means in this context: "A finding of similar fault can be made only if there is reason to believe that, based on a preponderance of the evidence, the person committing the fault knew that the evidence provided was false or incomplete. We cannot base a finding of similar fault on speculation or suspicion."

D. ADMINISTRATIVE HEARING AND THE ROLE OF THE ADMINISTRATIVE LAW JUDGE

As discussed in Chapter 8, the purpose of Social Security administrative hearings is to allow claimants the opportunity to present all relevant evidence concerning all relevant issues to an impartial decision-maker—an independent federal administrative law judge. In most cases, this is the only time that a claimant has the opportunity to present their case for entitlement to benefits to someone who can both receive live testimony and make an eligibility decision. The hearing is particularly important because, as discussed above and also in Chapter 8, the ALJ's factual findings will be set aside on Appeals Council or judicial review only if not supported by substantial evidence.

The ALJ conducts a *de novo* review of the claim based on all of the evidence already in the record and any supplemental evidence, including testimony, presented at the hearing. The hearing itself is informal and the rules of evidence do not apply; however, witnesses testify under oath and a transcript is made of the hearing. The informal nature of Social Security hearings was challenged unsuccessfully as unconstitutional in Richardson v. Perales, 402 U.S. 389, 91 S. Ct. 1420 (1971). The claimant in *Perales* objected to the introduction of several written medical reports on various grounds, including hearsay and the absence of an opportunity for cross-examination. Characterizing the disability adjudication system as one "which produces a mass of medical evidence in report form," the Court identified the central issues in the form of a question: "May material of that kind ever be 'substantial evidence' when it stands alone and is opposed by live medical evidence and the client's own contrary personal testimony?" 402 U.S. at 399. The Court then narrowed the constitutional question to "what procedural due process requires with respect to examining physicians' reports in a social security disability claim hearing" and concluded: "[A] written report by a licensed physician who has examined the claimant and who sets forth in his report his medical findings in his area of competence may be received as evidence in a disability hearing and, despite its hearsay character and an absence of cross-examination, and despite the presence of opposing direct medical testimony and testimony by the claimant himself, may constitute substantial evidence supportive of a finding by the hearing examiner adverse to the claimant, when the claimant has not exercised his right to subpoena the reporting physician and thereby provide himself with the opportunity for cross-examination of the physician." 402 U.S. at 402.

The right to subpoena evidence and testimony at the hearing stage, highlighted by the Court in *Perales*, is authorized in the Social Security Act and protected in 20 C.F.R. § 404.950(d) "when it is reasonably necessary for the full presentation of a case" and requested no later than ten days before a scheduled hearing. *See also Perales*, 402 U.S. at 397 ("It is to be noted at this point that § 205(d) of the Act, 42 U.S.C. § 405(d), provides that the Secretary has power to issue subpoenas requiring the attendance and testimony of witnesses and the production of evidence and that the Secretary's regulations authorized by § 205(a), 42 U.S.C. § 405(a), provide that a claimant may request the issuance of subpoenas, 20 C.F.R. § 404.926.") In *Perales*, the claimant was represented by counsel but did not request subpoenas at either of his two hearings. *See id* at 404–05 ("Although the claimant complains of the lack of opportunity to cross-examine the reporting physicians, he did not take advantage of the opportunity afforded him under 20 C.F.R. § 404.926 to request subpoenas for the physicians."); *id.* at 410 ("The matter comes down to the question of the procedure's integrity and fundamental fairness. We see nothing that works in derogation of that integrity and of that fairness in the admission of consultants' reports, subject as they are to being material and to the use of the subpoena and consequent cross-examination."). The circuit courts of appeals have differed on the extent of that subpoena right. *Compare* Lidy v. Sullivan, 911 F.2d 1075, 1076–77 (5th Cir. 1990) (holding that *Perales* conferred "an absolute right to subpoena a reporting physician") *with* Passmore v. Astrue, 533 F.3d 658, 663–65 (8th Cir. 2008) (finding only a qualified right to subpoena consulting physician consistent with SSA regulations, applying balancing approach of Mathews v. Eldridge, 424 U.S. 319, 335, 96 S. Ct. 893 (1976)).

1. NON-ADVERSARIAL HEARINGS

Social Security administrative hearings are non-adversarial. This means more than the fact that the Social Security Administration is not represented as such at a hearing; it means that SSA has no institutional position other than to award benefits to those persons entitled to benefits and to deny claims of those who are not. It also means that the ALJ has a greater role to play than the typical trial court judge. Social Security administrative law judges must participate actively both before and at the hearing in developing written evidence and obtaining relevant testimony from the claimant and other witnesses. The requirement that ALJs decide Social Security claims on the basis of a full and complete record means that they must be ready to participate in developing evidence and presenting witnesses whether a claimant is represented or not.

Although the claimant is responsible for providing proof of eligibility for benefits, the ALJ has the discretion to decide whether to seek out additional evidence in a particular case. Virtually all ALJs will question the claimant, at least with respect to the claimant's major impairments and past employment; most will also take an active part in questioning witnesses, together with the claimant or, if the claimant has one, the claimant's representative. The ALJ must also decide whether medical or vocational experts should testify at the hearing. Medical experts are rarely called but vocational experts are more commonly needed to testify in certain cases, especially those that are likely to be decided only at the fifth step of the sequential evaluation process. The role of vocational experts at the administrative hearing is discussed later in this chapter.

2. ROLE OF THE ADMINISTRATIVE LAW JUDGE AND DUTY TO DEVELOP THE RECORD

The non-adversarial nature of Social Security administrative hearings places the ALJ conducting those hearings in a difficult position. Their role has long been described as a "three hat" model. *See* Rausch v. Gardner, 267 F. Supp. 4, 6 (E.D. Wisc. 1967) ("It seems strange, but we use the terminology that we 'wear three hats.' We put on the first hat, and we represent the claimant, we present all the testimony on his behalf, and drag it out of him by questioning. We then represent the government, the Social Security Administration, and search the law—that's the second hat. We search our minds, and we search whatever other records are available, we search the evidence, and we present the best case that the government has. Then we turn around and put on the third hat, and we decide which evidence is most favorable, and in whose behalf.") Still, the model persists despite due process challenges. *See* Richardson v. Perales, 402 U.S. 389, 410, 91 S. Ct. 142 (1971) (challenge to the "advocate-judge-multiple-hat" adjudicative model "assumes too much and would bring down too many procedures designed, and working well, for a government structure of great and growing complexity."); *See generally* Carr v. Saul, 141 S. Ct. 1352 (2021) (describing non-adversarial and inquisitorial ALJ hearings and proceedings); Sims v. Apfel, 530 U.S. 103 (2000) (same).

This leaves ALJs with an affirmative duty to assist in developing a full and fair record upon which a decision on disability can be made, even where the claimant is represented. *See, e.g.*, Buccheri v. Astrue, 586 F. Supp. 2d 54, 60, 138 Soc. Sec. Rep. Serv. 855 (D. Conn. 2008) ("[b]ecause a hearing on disability benefits is a non-adversarial proceeding, it is well-settled that the ALJ has an affirmative obligation to develop the administrative record, even in cases in which the claimant is represented by counsel."); Tonapetyan v. Halter, 242 F.3d 1144, 72 Soc. Sec. Rep. Serv. 509 (9th Cir. 2001) (lay representative). Moreover, they must balance their responsibility to assure that they decide claims on the basis of a complete record following a full and fair hearing, with the potentially conflicting responsibilities of assuring not only that all evidence relevant to the position of an unrepresented Social Security Administration is included in the record but also assuring that the claimant's position, presented either by the claimant or a representative, is fully documented. This situation goes to the heart of the "three hats" dilemma of Social Security ALJs. *See* Battles v. Shalala, 36 F.3d 43, 45, 45 Soc. Sec. Rep. Serv. 604 (8th Cir. 1994) (case remanded where ALJ failed to develop record as to a mental impairment; "While the Secretary is correct that she is in under no duty to 'go to inordinate lengths to develop a claimant's case[,]' it is also true that she must 'make an investigation that is not wholly inadequate under the circumstances.' ") (citations omitted).

As the Supreme Court noted in Sims v. Apfel, 530 U.S. 103, 112 (2000), "a large portion of Social Security claimants either have no representation at all or are represented by non-attorneys." A Social Security ALJ's responsibility is far greater in cases where the claimant is unrepresented. As stated in an often-quoted passage from an early Second Circuit case where the claimant is not represented at a hearing (when appeals were heard by hearing examiners rather than administrative law judges), "a duty devolves on the hearing examiner to scrupulously and conscientiously probe into, inquire of, and explore for all of the relevant facts." Gold v. Secretary of Health & Human Services, 463 F.2d 38, 43 (2d Cir. 1972). Moreover, ALJs must be "especially diligent in ensuring that favorable as well as unfavorable facts and circumstances are elicited." Cox v. Califano, 587 F.2d 988, 991 (9th Cir. 1978) (quoting Rosa v. Weinberger, 381 F. Supp. 377, 381 (E.D.N.Y.1974)). This responsibility is taken seriously by reviewing courts. *See, e.g.*, Jozefick v. Shalala, 854 F. Supp. 342, 344, 44 Soc. Sec. Rep. Serv. 677 (M.D. Pa. 1994) ("Absence of counsel at the administrative hearing not only increases the responsibility of the ALJ, but also requires the court to undertake a searching review of the record to determine that the claimant has received a full and fair hearing."). For example, in cases with unrepresented claimants an ALJ shoulders a heightened duty to question vocational experts to clarify ambiguous, incomplete or undeveloped testimony or ensure that vocational expert testimony is methodologically sound and supported. *See, e.g.*, Rennaker v. Saul, 820 Fed. Appx. 474, 479 (7th Cir. 2020); Torres-Pagan v. Berryhill, 899 F.3d 54, 60 n.7, 258 Soc. Sec. Rep. Serv. 478 (1st Cir. 2018); Dobrowolsky v. Califano, 606 F. 403, 408–09 (3d Cir. 1979).

The ALJ's role when a claimant is unrepresented is still that of a judge, however, not the claimant's lawyer. *See* Thompson v. Sullivan, 933 F.2d 581, 586, 33 Soc. Sec. Rep. Serv. 407 (7th Cir. 1991) ("The ALJ does not act as counsel for claimant, but as an examiner who thoroughly develops the facts. The special duty assigned to the ALJ 'requires, essentially, a record which shows that the claimant was not prejudiced by lack of counsel.' ") (quoting Smith v. Schweiker, 677 F.2d 826, 829 (11th Cir. 1982)); Younger v. Shalala, 30 F.3d 1265, 1269, 45 Soc. Sec. Rep. Serv. 176 (10th Cir. 1994) ("Beyond the duty to develop the record as to issues, factual matters, and avenues raised by a claimant, an ALJ need not make out a claimant's case where, as here, claimants bear the burden of demonstrating entitlement to benefits.").

For other formulations of the ALJ's heightened duty to develop the record when a claimant is unrepresented, see Smith v. Harris, 644 F.2d 985, 989 (3d Cir. 1981) ("where the claimant is unrepresented by counsel, the ALJ has a duty to exercise 'a heightened level of care' and 'assume a more active role' "); Clark v. Harris, 638 F.2d 1347, 1351 (5th Cir. 1981) (The ALJ's " 'basic obligation to develop a full and fair record rises to a special duty when an unrepresented claimant unfamiliar with hearing procedures appears before him.' ") (quoting Barker v. Harris, 486 F. Supp. 846 (N.D. Ga. 1980)); D'Angelo v. Commissioner, 475 F. Supp. 2d 716, 720, 119 Soc. Sec. Rep. Serv. 453 (W.D. Mich. 2007) ("The ALJ has a 'special duty' to develop the administrative record and ensure a fair hearing for claimants that are unrepresented by counsel."). The ALJ also shoulders a heightened duty to develop the record when the claimant is represented by a non-attorney. *See* Smith v. Bowen, 687 F.Supp. 902, 906 (S.D.N.Y. 1988) ("The ALJ's duty to develop the comprehensive record requisite for an equitable determination of disability is greatest when claimant is unrepresented; but the duty still exists when plaintiff is represented and even more, as here, where plaintiff is represented by a paralegal."); *see also* Sears v. Bowen, 840 F.2d 394, 402 (7th Cir. 1988) ("[A]n ALJ can presume that a claimant represented by an attorney has presented his or her best case[;] the same is not true where the claimant is represented by a non-lawyer.").

The usual remedy when ALJs fails to meet their duty to develop the record fully is to remand the case to SSA for a supplemental hearing. *See, e.g.*, Smith v. Apfel, 231 F.3d 433, 337, 71 Soc. Sec. Rep. Serv. 627 (7th Cir. 2000) ("Although a claimant has the burden to prove disability, the ALJ has a duty to develop a full and fair record. Failure to fulfill this obligation is 'good cause' to remand for gathering of additional evidence.") (citations omitted); Fontanez ex rel. Fontanez v. Barnhart, 195 F. Supp. 2d 1333, 1338, 80 Soc. Sec. Rep. Serv. 388 (M.D. Fla. 2002) (claim turned on evidence of the claimant's functioning; "Contrary to his duty to fully develop the record, the ALJ failed to determine the significance of [the claimant]'s low scores. This requires remand."). Courts will not remand a case, however, if the evidence on file would support the denial of benefits notwithstanding the ALJ's failure to develop the record further. Thus, "[t]he ALJ's decision will be affirmed unless the claimant shows (1) that the ALJ failed to fulfill his duty to adequately develop the record and (2) that the claimant was prejudiced thereby." Wilson v. Barnhart, 129 F. App'x 912, 915, 104 Soc. Sec. Rep. Serv. 335 (5th Cir. 2005). *See also* Goodwater v. Barnhart, 579 F. Supp. 2d 746, 755, 137 Soc. Sec. Rep. Serv. 592 (D.S.C. 2007) ("An ALJ's failure to fulfill this duty to pro se claimants may result in remand where the absence of counsel results in prejudice to the claimant."). Whether the claimant was prejudiced depends on the court's expectations about the completeness of the evidentiary record at the hearing. *Compare* Luna v. Shalala, 22 F.3d 687, 692, 44 Soc. Sec. Rep. Serv. 348 (7th Cir. 1994) ("a significant omission is usually required before this court will find that the Secretary failed to assist pro se claimants in developing the record fully and fairly.") *with* Jozefick v. Shalala, 854 F. Supp. 342, 350 n. 2, 44 Soc. Sec. Rep. Serv. 677 (M.D. Pa 1994) ("A remand would not be warranted where it is clear that the claimant could not possibly establish entitlement to benefits or the "evidentiary gap" is not material to the disability determination."). Federal court remands are discussed more generally in Chapter 8.

E. WEIGHT AND SUFFICIENCY OF MEDICAL EVIDENCE

Medical evidence of disability is sufficient when it establishes that the applicable disability standard has been met. Some claims are supported by consistent, probative medical evidence that lead to relatively easy decisions. However, often the supporting evidence is inconclusive or inconsistent. When that happens, the state agency responsibility for determining disability or the administrative law judge may request additional evidence, possibly including one or more consultative examinations by a physician hired by SSA to evaluate the extent of the claimant's disability.

Problems concerning the weight and sufficiency of medical evidence arise most often when there is a conflict in medical opinions—often between the claimant's own doctor, referred to as a "treating physician," and an SSA-retained consulting physician. Moreover, staff medical consultants employed by the state agencies, who review the claim file without observing the claimant, may also have a conflicting opinion. As a result, the question whether there is sufficient medical evidence for a given claim depends to a large extent on the weight given to conflicting reports of two or three of these different types of medical sources.

1. GENERAL RULES ON WEIGHT AND SUFFICIENCY

As mentioned above, a claimant must present sufficient medical evidence to show that the applicable disability standard has been met. 20 C.F.R. §§ 404.1512(a), 416.912(a). The claimant may submit evidence that contains medical opinions, which includes statements from physicians and psychologists or other acceptable medical sources "about what [the claimant] can still do despite [their] impairments and whether [the claimant has] one or more impairment-related" physical, mental, sensory or environmental work-related restrictions or "judgments about the nature and severity of [the claimant's] impairment(s), [their] medical history, clinical findings, diagnosis, treatment prescribed with response, or prognosis." 20 C.F.R. §§ 404.1513(a)(2)–(3), 416.913(a)(2)–(3).

SSA assumes the responsibility for reviewing the medical evidence in order to determine whether the claim can be evaluated on the basis of that evidence alone, or whether it should request additional evidence, possibly including one or more consultative examinations. 20 C.F.R. §§ 404.1520b(b), 416.920b(b). SSA's findings will vary depending upon the consistency and completeness of the information in the claimant's file, resulting essentially in one of four scenarios set out in 20 C.F.R. §§ 404.1520b(a)–(b), 416.920b(a)–(b): (1) if all the evidence SSA receives is consistent and sufficient to decide whether the claimant is disabled, it will make its decision based on that evidence; (2) if any of the evidence is inconsistent, it will consider whether it can determine that the claimant is disabled based on that evidence; (3) if the evidence is consistent but insufficient to determine whether the claimant is disabled, SSA will take various steps to supplement the record with additional evidence and will then try to resolve any remaining inconsistency or insufficiency in the record in order to make a decision; (4) if there are inconsistencies that cannot be resolved or if the record remains incomplete despite SSA's efforts to obtain additional evidence, it will make a decision based on the evidence it has.

Social Security regulations draw a distinction between "acceptable medical sources," who can offer opinions on the existence of a medical impairment, and other sources who can provide evidence only of severity and functional limitations. *See generally* 20 C.F.R. §§ 404.1513, 404.1502, 416.913, 416.902. The list of "acceptable" sources includes licensed or certified physicians or psychologists, as well as licensed optometrists (only for purposes of establishing visual disorders), licensed podiatrists, and qualified speech-language pathologists (only for purposes of establishing certain disorders) and was expanded in 2017 to include, licensed advanced practice nurses, licensed physician assistants, and licensed audiologists (for audiological impairments). 20 C.F.R. §§ 404.1502(a), 416.902(a). Medical sources must be licensed or certified by a state and working within the scope of practice under state or federal law. *Id.*

Other sources include medical sources not listed as acceptable such as naturopaths, chiropractors, and licensed clinical social workers and other therapists, as well non-medical sources such as educational personnel, social workers, social welfare agency personnel, and spouses and other relatives, caregivers, friends, neighbors, and clergy. *See* 20 C.F.R. §§ 404.1502(e), 416.902(e). SSA has reiterated that while it considers some of the above professionals as "medical sources" and will consider "all relevant evidence we receive from all medical sources regardless of AMS [acceptable medical source] status," only an AMS can establish that an individual has a medically determinable impairment. 82 Fed. Reg. 5844, 5847 (January 18, 2017).

The most significant recent changes to the medical evidence regulations addressed the presumptive weight accorded assessments by claimants' treating physicians and the requirements for articulation of reasoning and for weighing and evaluating medical evidence. Thus, in 2017 SSA published regulations which provide that, for claims filed after March 27, 2107, SSA "will not defer or give any specific evidentiary weight, including controlling weight, to any medical opinion(s) or prior administrative medical finding(s), including those from your medical sources." 20 C.F.R. §§ 404.1520c(a), 416.920c(a). More specifically, the regulations provide that adjudicators will evaluate all medical opinions and findings using the factors delineated in the regulations; supportability and consistency are the most important factors and their application must be explained; other factors which "will be considered" and about which adjudicators "may, but are not required to explain" are the medical source's "treatment relationship" with the claimant, including the length, frequency, purpose and extent of the treating relationship, and whether the source has an examining (as opposed to a non-examining) relationship with the claimant; specialization; and "other factors" such as whether the source has familiarity with other evidence in the claim or understanding of the Social Security disability program's policies and evidentiary requirements. 20 C.F.R. §§ 404.1520c(b)–(c), 416.920c(b)–(c). The implication of these changes, both their historical context and current application, are discussed in detail below.

2. WEIGHING EVIDENCE FROM TREATING VS. CONSULTING VS. NON-EXAMINING PHYSICIANS

a. Relevance of Pre-2017 Caselaw and Rules

Because cases involving claims filed after March 2017 are just starting to trickle into the courts at the time of this writing, claims filed before that date, which are still evaluated under prior (pre-2017) regulations, are still common. In any event, the body of caselaw developed prior to the effective date of the new regulations may supply guidance or be integrated or incorporated in some form to interpretation of the present rules. *See* 20 C.F.R. §§ 404.1527, 416.927.

The state of the law applying the regulations applicable to claims filed prior to March 27, 2017 could be summarized as follows: "First, the ALJ must decide whether the opinion is entitled to controlling weight . . . so long as it 'is well-supported by medically acceptable clinical and laboratory diagnostic techniques and is not inconsistent with the other substantial evidence in [the] case record.'. . . Second, if the ALJ decides the opinion is not entitled to controlling weight, it must determine how much weight, if any, to give it. In doing so, it must 'explicitly consider' . . . '(1) the frequen[cy], length, nature, and extent of treatment; (2) the amount of medical evidence supporting the opinion; (3) the consistency of the opinion with the remaining medical evidence; and (4) whether the physician is a specialist.' " Estrella v. Berryhill, 925 F.3d 90, 95–96, 268 Soc. Sec. Rep. Serv. 343 (2d Cir. 2019) (citations omitted); *see also* Ghanim v. Colvin, 763 F.3d 1154, 1160–61, 207 Soc. Sec. Rep. Serv. 404 (9th Cir. 2014) (similar formulation, citing 20 C.F.R. § 404.1527); Krausner v. Astrue, 638 F.3d 1324, 1330, 116 Soc. Sec. Rep. Serv. 20 (10th Cir. 2011) (same). Moreover, when applying the regulations, "the ALJ must "give good reasons in [its] notice of determination or decision for the weight [it gives the] treating source's [medical] opinion." Estrella v. Berryhill, supra, 925 F.3d at 96.

Several circuit courts of appeals also expressly established a hierarchy of general evidentiary value and weight accorded the respective reports of treating physicians, consultant examining physicians (usually one-time examiners retained by the agency), and non-examining physicians (usually internal state agency physicians or medical advisors called to testify at a hearing). In this hierarchy, the position of the non-examining physician is at the bottom, with consulting examiners in the middle, and treating physicians at the top. *See, e.g.*, Garrison v. Colvin, 759 F.3d 995, 1012, 207 Soc. Sec. Rep. Serv. 14 (9th Cir. 2014) ("While the opinion of a treating physician is thus entitled to greater weight than that of an examining physician, the opinion of an examining physician is entitled to greater weight than that of a non-examining physician."); Gayheart v. Comm'r of Soc. Sec., 710 F.3d 365, 379, 188 Soc. Sec. Rep. Serv. 528 (6th Cir. 2013) ("As a general matter, an opinion from a medical source who has examined a claimant is given more weight than that from a source who has not performed an examination (a 'nonexamining source') and an opinion from a medical source who regularly treats the claimant (a 'treating source') is afforded more weight than that from a source who has examined the claimant but does not have an ongoing treatment relationship (a 'nontreating source').) (citations omitted), Robinson v. Barnhart, 366 F.3d 1078, 1084 (10th Cir. 2004) ("The opinion of an examining physician is generally entitled to less weight than that of a treating physician, and the opinion of an agency physician who has never seen the claimant is entitled to the least weight of all.") (citations omitted).

b. Interaction of Case Law and Regulations on Medical Evidence

Before the Social Security Administration adopted any regulations on the weight to be accorded to and the manner of evaluating medical evidence, several circuit courts of appeals interpreted the Social Security Act as extending great weight to treating physician assessments. *See, e.g.*, Gold v. Sec. H.E.W., 463 F.2d 38, 43 (2d Cir. 1972) ("The expert opinions of plaintiff's treating physicians as to plaintiff's disability . . . are binding upon the referee if not controverted by substantial evidence to the contrary."); Branham v. Gardner, 383 F.2d 614, 630 (6th Cir. 1967) (same). Those caselaw principles concerning the proper weight accorded opinions of treating physicians remained controversial until the early 1990s, when the SSA issued its first regulations establishing standards for evaluating medical opinions. Nevertheless, several circuit courts of appeals interpreted the agency's 1991 medical evidence regulations as consistent with or codifying pre-existing circuit caselaw interpreting the Act and extending greater deference to treating physician assessments. *See, e.g.*, Nelson v. Sullivan, 966 F.2d 363, 367–68, 37 Soc. Sec. Rep. Serv. 489 (8th Cir. 1992) (1991 medical evidence regulation "merely codifies this circuit's law regarding the opinions of treating physicians."). Only the Second Circuit expressly ruled that the regulations accorded less deference to the opinions of treating physicians than required by its pre-1991 decisions. *See* Schisler v. Sullivan, 3 F.3d 563, 567, 42 Soc. Sec. Rep. Serv. 184 (2d Cir. 1993)("by granting the treating physician's opinion 'controlling weight' only if it is 'well-supported by medically acceptable clinical and laboratory diagnostic techniques and is not inconsistent with the other substantial evidence,' the regulations accord less deference to unsupported treating physician's opinions than do our decisions."). *Cf.* Castellano v. Sec. of Health & Human Services, 26 F.3d 1027, 1029, 44 Soc. Sec. Rep. Serv. 561 (10th Cir. 1994) ("In contrast to the situation in the Second Circuit, . . . in this circuit the regulations have merely codified existing law.").

It is not clear at present whether the courts' evaluation of treating physician and other medical evidence based on current medical evidence regulations will vary materially from their analysis under the 1991 regulations or pre-existing caselaw interpreting the Social Security Act. As largely occurred after 1991, many courts may attempt to harmonize present regulations with pre-existing case law interpreting the Act, rather than attempt to discern which body of law controls. Courts may also seek to reconcile provisions in the current regulations with those in prior regulations. *See, e.g.*, Cuevas v. Comm'r of Soc. Sec., No. 20-CV-0502 (AJN) (KHP), 2021 WL 363682, at *9 (S.D.N.Y. 2021) (collecting and surveying Second Circuit district court cases considering current regulations; concluding they show that "the essence" of the treating physician's rule remains the same and "the factors to be considered in weighing the various medical opinions in a given claimant's medical history are substantially similar," noting that this "is not surprising considering that, under the old rule, an

ALJ had to determine whether a treating physician's opinion was supported by well-accepted medical evidence and not inconsistent with the rest of the record before controlling weight could be assigned.") (cases omitted).

c. Current Limited Statutory and Regulatory Preference for Treating Physician Evidence

As part of a broad-reaching set of policy directives aimed at regularizing the Social Security disability determination process, Congress amended the Social Security Act in 1984 to require that the Social Security Administration "make every reasonable effort" to utilize reports from treating physicians in making disability determinations before relying on reports from outside consultants. 42 U.S.C. § 423(d)(5)(B). *See generally* Social Security Disability Benefits Reform Act of 1984, Pub. L. No. 98–460, 98 Stat. 1794. Current SSA regulations still designate the claimant's treating physician as the preferred source for the needed consultative evaluations. *See* 20 C.F.R. §§ 404.1519h, 416.919h. Notwithstanding these statutory and regulatory directives, the agency rarely obtains the needed consultative evaluations from other than non-treating sources who have no knowledge or familiarity with the claimants or their treatment history.

3. OTHER RULES FOR EVALUATING MEDICAL EVIDENCE

The circuit courts of appeals have adopted a variety of rules for weighing and evaluating certain common categories of medical evidence. A sampling of the most common such judge-made rules is provided below.

a. "Cherry Picking"

ALJs may not "cherry pick," selectively rely on, or pick-and-choose among only the damaging parts of medical reports or testimony and disregard or reject parts of the same evidence which are supportive of disability, without adequate explanation. *See, e.g.*, Chapo v. Astrue, 682 F.3d 1285, 1292 (10th Cir. 2012) ("We have repeatedly held that '[a]n ALJ is not entitled to pick and choose through an uncontradicted medical opinion, taking only the parts that are favorable to a finding of nondisability.' ") (citations omitted); Ghanim v. Colvin, 763 F.3d 1154, 1164 (9th Cir. 2014) ("[T]he ALJ improperly cherry-picked some of Dr. Dees's characterizations of Ghanim's rapport and demeanor instead of considering these factors in the context of Dr. Dees's diagnoses and observations of impairment."); Scott v. Astrue, 647 F.3d 734, 740 (7th Cir. 2011) ("Those notes show that although Scott had improved with treatment, she nevertheless continued to frequently experience bouts of crying and feelings of paranoia. The ALJ was not permitted to 'cherry-pick' from those mixed results to support a denial of benefits.").

b. ALJ "Playing Doctor"

ALJs are also prohibited from relying on speculation or what amount to personal medical opinions beyond their competence. *See, e.g.*, Liskowitz v. Astrue, 559 F.3d 736, 741 (7th Cir. 2009) ("[A]n ALJ cannot play the role of doctor and interpret medical evidence [or] . . . disregard medical evidence simply because it is at odds with the ALJ's own unqualified opinion."); Morales v. Apfel, 225 F.3d 310, 317–18 (3d Cir. 2000) ("An ALJ may not make speculative inferences from medical reports and may reject a treating physician's opinion outright only on the basis of contrary medical evidence and not due to his own credibility judgments, speculation or lay opinion."); Irizarry-Sanchez v. Commissioner of Social Sec., 253 F. Supp. 2d 216, 219 (D.P.R. 2003) ("the ALJ is a lay fact finder who lacks the expertise to make a medical conclusion. As such, he cannot interpret raw, technical medical data.").

c. Inferences from Omission or Silence in Medical Evidence

ALJs may not construe omissions or silence in medical reports and other medical evidence as affirmative evidence of the omitted proposition. *See, e.g.*, Rosa v. Callahan, 168 F.3d 72, 81 (2d Cir. 1999) (consulting physician report that did not identify any serious impairment cited to support finding the claimant had RFC for sedentary work; "Those reports were consistent with this conclusion, however, only to the extent that they were silent on the issue.

Indeed, there was no indication in the reports that the consultants intended anything by their silence or that they set out to 'express [an] opinion on [the] subject' of Rosa's sedentary work capacity.") (citation omitted); Allen v. Bowen, 881 F.2d 37, 42 (3d Cir. 1989) (consulting physician report "absolutely silent" as to claimant's physical limitations; "We decline to interpret this silence as affirmative evidence that the . . . consulting physician considered Allen to have no weight restrictions. Rather, we believe that the proper inference from the report's silence is that the physician simply did not consider the issue.").

d. "Retrospective" Medical Opinions

"Retrospective" medical opinions are those opinions and medical assessments by physicians reflecting that evaluation of a claimant's conditions during periods of time prior to the inception of the physician-patient relationship. In general, courts accept retrospective diagnoses made by treating physicians, so long as the physician can supply reasoned and legitimate reasons for those diagnoses. As noted in Chapter 2, retrospective evidence is often essential in OASDI disability claims where the claimants apply for benefits long after they were last insured for disability purposes. Courts generally require consideration and evaluation of such evidence in those cases. *See* Bird v. Commissioner of Social Sec. Admin., 699 F.3d 337, 341 (4th Cir. 2012) (noting that earlier evidence can establish progressive degeneration, "[t]he possibility of such a linkage, and thus the appropriateness of retrospective consideration of medical evidence, may be enhanced further by lay observations of a claimant's condition during the relevant time period."); Boyd v. Heckler, 704 F.2d 1207, 1211 (11th Cir. 1983) ("a treating physician's opinion is still entitled to significant weight notwithstanding that he did not treat the claimant until after the relevant determination date.").

F. VOCATIONAL EXPERTS AND VOCATIONAL EVIDENCE

Vocational experts can play an important role in Social Security disability cases because a claimant's ability to engage in substantial gainful activity—the measure of severity set out in the statutory disability standard—must be evaluated by taking into account, in addition to any physical or mental impairments, the claimant's age, education, and prior work experience. Because vocational evidence is considered at only three steps of the five-step sequential evaluation process and the vocational issues involved at two of those steps are quite narrow (Step 1, limited to current employment; Step 4, limited to past relevant work), the use of vocational experts is concentrated at Step 5 adjudications. The sequential evaluation process is covered in detail in Chapter 5.

ALJs often call vocational experts to testify at hearings, particularly where SSA denied the claim before reaching Step 5 and vocational evidence was not well developed at the state agency responsible for making disability determinations. Also, by the time a claim gets to the administrative hearing level a significant percentage involve the more difficult vocational issues. Yet even at Step 5, vocational expertise is not needed for every claim. While a vocational expert may be used to provide evidence as to where a claimant falls within a particular "grid" in SSA's Medical-Vocational Guidelines, vocational expertise is most useful for claims where the grid rules are not conclusive and specific evidence is required as to whether the claimant—given their age, education, and prior work experience—can perform and adjust to a significant number of jobs in the national economy. Those types of Step 5 determinations typically require proof of a claimant's ability to perform specified jobs, and vocational experts are deemed qualified to provide that proof. Claimants can also try to retain and use a vocational expert to support their case, either with a written report before or after the hearing or through live testimony at a hearing. *See generally* Allen v. Barnhart, 417 F.3d 396, 407–08 (3d Cir. 2005) (recognizing need for providing notice and opportunity for "calling claimant's own [vocational] expert.").

There are no readily available published standards for VE certification, selection, or training. The Social Security Administration's internal Vocational Expert's Handbook, provided to vocational experts but not to the public at large, provides some guidance on qualifications by describing selection criteria as follows: "[U]p-to-date knowledge of, and experience with, industrial and occupational trends and local labor market conditions; an understanding of how we determine whether a claimant is disabled, especially at steps 4 and 5 of the sequential evaluation process. . .; involvement in or knowledge of counseling and the job placement of adult, handicapped workers into jobs; [and] knowledge of and experience using vocational reference sources of which the agency has taken administrative notice [including the Dictionary of Occupational Titles]." Social Security Administration, Vocational Expert's Handbook 8–9 (June 2020). *But see* Donahue v. Barnhart, 279 F.3d 441, 446 (7th Cir. 2002) ("We asked the parties at oral argument what makes a vocational expert an 'expert' (and where the information in the [Dictionary of Occupational Titles] came from). They did not know. Maybe both the authors of the [DOT] and the vocational expert in this case are talking out of a hat."); Liskowitz v. Astrue, 559 F.3d 736, 743 n.6 (7th Cir. 2009) ("In the past, we have expressed confusion over how a person becomes a 'vocational expert.' ") (quoting *Donahue*).

1. VOCATIONAL EXPERTS AND HYPOTHETICAL QUESTIONS

Typically, vocational expert testimony is solicited by means of hypothetical questions. The hypothetical must include all limitations supported by the record, including the side effects of medication. Osenbrock v. Apfel, 240 F.3d 1157, 1167, 72 Soc. Sec. Rep. Serv. 433 (9th Cir. 2001) (hypothetical omitted mention of side effects of medication; "When the ALJ relies on the testimony of a vocational expert, the judge must propound a hypothetical that incorporates all of the medical and vocational limitations of the claimant set forth in the record."). Hypothetical questions must present the claimant's limitations accurately, including the full extent of any limitations. *See, e.g.*, Charbonneau v. Apfel, 76 F. Supp. 2d 98, 103, 66 Soc. Sec. Rep. Serv. 74 (D. Mass. 1999) (record indicated that the claimant's "limited education and limited ability to read and write" were "more profound" than assumed in the hypothetical presented to the vocational expert; failure to mention that the claimant "can do no arithmetic at all" considered "especially significant" since the types of jobs the expert suggested that claimant could do required certain math skills); Gamret v. Colvin, 994 F. Supp. 2d 695, 700 (W.D. Pa. 2014) (ALJ's hypothetical question narrowed claimant's reaching limitation to overhead movement; "it is possible, even likely, that a broader reaching limitation would have affected the VE's conclusions"). Most importantly, hypothetical questions must reflect the medical evidence in the record accurately and fairly so that vocational experts' answers are helpful to the decisionmaking process. *See* Carey v. Apfel, 230 F.3d 131, 148, 71 Soc. Sec. Rep. Serv. 393 (5th Cir. 2000) (vocational expert's opinion cannot be relied on when based on an inaccurate summary of the medical report); Embrey v. Bowen, 849 F.2d 418, 423, 22 Soc. Sec. Rep. Serv. 124 (9th Cir. 1988) ("Because the hypothetical posed by the ALJ to the vocational expert did not reflect all of [the claimant's] limitations, the expert's opinion has no evidentiary value").

Claims involving mental limitations such as with concentration, persistence or pace pose difficulties because adjudicators often oversimplify these types of mental limitations as only restricting capacity for jobs at certain work-skill or task-complexity levels, rather than acknowledging that limitations on concentration, persistence or pace can undermine competitive work production-output or performance-speed at any skill level and even for jobs characterized as unskilled, "simple" and "routine. As explained in SSR 85–15 (1985): *"[T]he skill level of a position is not necessarily related to the difficulty an individual will have in meeting the demands of the job*. A claimant's condition may make performance of an unskilled job as difficult as an objectively more demanding job, for example, a busboy need only clear dishes from tables. But an individual with a severe mental disorder may find unmanageable the demand of making sure that he removes all the dishes, does not drop them, and gets the table *cleared promptly* for the waiter or waitress." (emphasis added). Nevertheless, the circuit courts of appeals are divided on addressing this issue in the context of hypothetical questions to vocational experts. *Compare* Thomas v. Berryhill, 916 F.3d 307, 312–13 and n.5 (4th Cir. 2019) (RFC findings in a hypothetical question to the VE that included restrictions to "simple, short routine tasks," with several additional interpersonal contact restrictions and limitations relevant to work not requiring "production rate" or "demand pace," was still insufficient in accounting for the claimant's moderate restrictions in concentration, persistence and pace because the ALJ "will need to establish how long and under what conditions, [the claimant] can focus on [her] work activities and stay on task at a sustained rate") *with* McIntyre v. Colvin, 758 F.3d 146, 152, 206 Soc. Sec. Rep. Serv. 355 (2d Cir. 2014) (failure to include documented moderate limitations on concentration, persistence and pace in the VE hypothetical can be harmless error if: "(1) medical evidence demonstrates that a claimant can engage in simple, routine tasks or unskilled work despite limitations in concentration, persistence, and pace,' and the challenged hypothetical is limited 'to include only unskilled work'; or (2) the hypothetical 'otherwise implicitly account[ed] for a claimant's limitations in concentration, persistence, and pace[.]' ") (citation omitted).

It is also important that the role of a vocational expert not be confused with that of a medical expert. A vocational expert's conclusion, even though it may encompass both medical and vocational judgments, must be based on competent underlying medical evidence. *See, e.g.*, Nalley v. Apfel, 100 F. Supp. 2d 947, 953, 70 Soc. Sec. Rep. Serv. 77 (S.D. Iowa 2000) ("It is error for an ALJ to ask a vocational expert to interpret the medical evidence or to base testimony on the expert's own observations.).

2. USE OF THE DICTIONARY OF OCCUPATIONAL TITLES (DOT)

The principal source of documentary evidence utilized by vocational experts and SSA to identify, classify, and define jobs is the United States Department of Labor's Dictionary of Occupational Titles (DOT). The DOT has been called "the Bible of vocational experts." McClesky v. Astrue, 606 F.3d

351, 354, 154 Soc. Sec. Rep. Serv. 33 (7th Cir. 2010). The DOT is an occupational classification system which provides detailed descriptions of almost all occupations in the United States economy. It provides scales and ratings systems for the skills which each occupation requires and a narrative with comprehensive descriptions of the tasks involved in each occupational category. Each occupation is then assigned a DOT occupational code. VEs typically utilize these codes at Steps Four and Five of SSA's sequential evaluation process when determining the requirements of a claimant's past work and of other work to which a claimant can make a work adjustment. The DOT creates a rebuttable presumption as to the classification of a job with a DOT occupational code and SSA has taken "administrative notice" of the Dictionary of Occupational Titles by regulation. *See* 20 C.F.R. §§ 404.1566(d)(1), 416.966(d)(1).

As discussed in more detail below, courts have adopted different approaches when a vocational expert's opinion conflicted with the DOT. The problem stems in large part from the fact that the DOT has not been updated in many years and is no longer current. Indeed, the courts, the U.S. Department of Labor (DOL), and the U.S. General Accounting Office (GAO) have each found that the DOT is "obsolete" as it has not been updated in over thirty years and is based largely on data from a fundamentally different 1960's labor market and American economy. *See generally* JON C. DUBIN, SOCIAL SECURITY DISABILITY LAW AND THE AMERICAN LABOR MARKET (2021); *see also*, Browning v. Colvin,

766 F.3d 702, 709 (7th Cir. 2014) ("A further problem is that the job descriptions used by the Social Security Administration come from a 23-year-old edition of the Dictionary of Occupational Titles, which is no longer published, and mainly moreover from information from 1977–37 years ago. No doubt many of the jobs have changed and some have disappeared. We have no idea how vocational experts and administrative law judges deal with this problem."). As recognized at 20 C.F.R. §§ 404.1565(a), 416.965(a): "[a] gradual change occurs in most jobs so that after 15 years it is no longer realistic to expect that skills and abilities acquired in a job done then continue to apply." SSA is working with the U.S. Department of Labor through the Occupational Information System Project, to create a new job classification taxonomy for both SSA disability adjudication and DOL labor market purposes with completion anticipated by 2024.

3. CONFLICTS BETWEEN VOCATIONAL EXPERT TESTIMONY AND THE DOT

Because of the DOT's continued centrality to vocational expert occupational and job classifications and descriptions and to past work and work adjustment assessments at Steps 4 and 5 of the sequential evaluation process, caselaw emerged about how to address potential conflicts between VE testimony and the DOT. Some courts have held that when there is a conflict between the testimony of a vocational expert and the DOT, the DOT controls. Others have held that the expert's testimony "trumps" the DOT. Some followed a middle ground position allowing adjudicators to rely on a vocational expert's testimony in conflict with the DOT if the record reflects a substantial reason for deviating from the DOT. *See, e.g.*, Carey v. Apfel, 230 F.3d 131, 146, 71 Soc. Sec. Rep. Serv. 393 (5th Cir. 2000) ("To the extent that there is any implied or indirect conflict between the vocational expert's testimony and the DOT in this case, we agree with the majority of the circuits that the ALJ may rely upon the vocational expert's testimony provided that the record reflects an adequate basis for doing so.").

Eventually SSA issued a Social Security Ruling on this issue in late 2000. The Ruling provides that "[w]hen there is an apparent unresolved conflict between [vocational expert or vocational specialist] evidence and the DOT, the adjudicator must elicit a reasonable explanation for the conflict before relying on the [vocational expert or vocational specialist] evidence to support a determination or decision about whether the claimant is disabled." SSR 00–4p (2000). The Ruling also states explicitly that "[n]either the DOT nor the [vocational expert or vocational specialist] evidence automatically 'trumps' when there is a conflict. The adjudicator must resolve the conflict by determining if the explanation given by the [vocational expert or vocational specialist] is reasonable and provides a basis for relying on the [vocational expert or vocational specialist] testimony rather than on the DOT information." *Id.*

The circuit courts of appeal have grappled with the nature of ALJs' duty to resolve VE-DOT conflicts, how "apparent" a conflict must be to trigger ALJs' affirmative obligation to inquire further, and steps required to reconcile such a conflict. For example, the Ninth Circuit has suggested that job "tasks that aren't essential, integral, or expected parts of a job are less likely to qualify as apparent conflicts that the ALJ must ask about[ ] [or] where the job itself is a familiar one—like cashiering—less scrutiny by the ALJ is required." Gutierrez v. Colvin, 844 F.3d 804, 808 (9th Cir. 2016). On the other hand, the Fourth Circuit suggested that less obvious conflicts can be "apparent" requiring the ALJ to resolve them pursuant to SSR 00–4p. *See* Thomas v. Berryhill, 916 F.3d 307, 313 (4th Cir. 2019) ("the ALJ must ask the VE whether his or her testimony conflicts with the DOT. If the answer is 'yes,' the ALJ 'must elicit a reasonable explanation for the conflict before relying on' the testimony. But even if the VE answers 'no,' the ALJ has an affirmative 'duty to make an independent identification of apparent conflicts.' This means that the ALJ must recognize and resolve ways in which a VE's testimony '*seems to, but does not necessarily,' conflict with the 'express language' of the DOT—even if the conflict is not 'obvious.'* ") (citation omitted; emphasis added).

The Eleventh Circuit has explained how the ALJ's duty to identify and reconcile VE-DOT conflicts extends beyond merely asking the VE if the testimony is consistent with the DOT. *See* Washington v. Comm'r of Soc. Sec., 906 F.3d 1353, 1363, 261 Soc. Sec. Rep. Serv. 19 (11th Cir. 2018) (noting that SSR 00–4p provides that the ALJ "must explain the resolution of the conflict irrespective of how the conflict was identified" and "anticipates the ALJ will satisfy the duty to identify in many ways."; "if that were not the case, the ALJ could ignore explaining and resolving any apparent conflict simply by asking one question of the VE and relying on his erroneous answer."). The court also explained how SSA's inquisitorial adjudicative scheme supports the ALJ's affirmative duties to investigate and resolve potential conflicts between the DOT and VE testimony as set out in SSR 00–4p: "ALJs do not simply act as umpires calling balls and strikes. They are by law investigators of the facts, and are tasked not only with the obligation to consider the reasons offered by both sides, but also with actively developing the record in the case. Accordingly, although independently identifying and resolving the points of apparent conflict between expert testimony and other evidence would be out of character for most judges, for a Social Security ALJ it can be fairly said to come with the territory." 906 F.3d at 1356.

Perhaps signaling its position on the issue, the Supreme Court granted *certiorari* and vacated and remanded an earlier Eleventh Circuit decision "for further consideration in light of [the Eleventh Circuit's] opinion in Washington." Baker v. Berryhill, 139 S. Ct. 1257, 1257–1258 (2019.) *Baker* was decided before *Washington* and had relied on pre-SSR 00–4p Eleventh Circuit caselaw holding that "the VE's testimony 'trumps' the DOT 'whenever the two conflict.' " *See* Baker v. Comm'r of Soc. Sec., 729 Fed. Appx. 870, 872 (11th Cir. 2018) (quoting Jones v. Apfel, 190 F.3d 1224, 1229–30 (11th Cir. 1999)). In *Washington,* the Eleventh Circuit found that its earlier, pre-SSR 00–4p caselaw had merely "set a floor on SSA procedures" and "[t]hereafter, the SSA stepped in, explained and clarified the governing rules and exercised its prerogative to strengthen its own procedural requirements, and established an enhanced duty on the part of the ALJ to discern and resolve conflicts" through the enactment of SSR 00–4p. Washington v. Commissioner, *supra*, 906 F.3d at 1363.

A commonly litigated issue which has divided the circuit courts of appeals is whether potential conflicts between certain DOT occupational reasoning levels and VE testimony about jobs limited to "simple, short, routine, and/or repetitive" tasks should be deemed a sufficiently apparent conflict to be identified and reconciled by the ALJ pursuant to SSR 00–4p. For example, the court in Thomas v. Berryhill, 916 F.3d 307, 313 (4th Cir. 2019) held that "the ALJ should have identified and resolved a conflict between the DOT and the testimony of the VE" because there is an " 'apparent conflict' between a limitation to 'short, simple instructions' (as found in the claimant's RFC) and a need to carry out 'detailed but uninvolved . . . instructions' (as found in jobs requiring [DOT] Level 2 reasoning)." (citations omitted). *See also* Stanton v. Comm'r of Soc. Sec., 899 F.3d 555, 558–59, 258 Soc. Sec. Rep. Serv. 485 (8th Cir. 2018) (VE testimony identifying jobs limited to "simple, one to two step tasks" is in "apparent conflict" with DOT reasoning level 2 in the jobs identified by the VE, and should have been identified and reconciled by the ALJ pursuant to SSR 00–4p). On the other hand, the court in Terry v. Astrue, 580

F.3d 471, 478 (7th Cir. 2009) reasoned that because the claimant "did not identify any conflict at the hearing, she would have to show that the conflict was 'obvious enough that the ALJ should have picked up on [it] without any assistance,'" and because the plaintiff's "educational background and cognitive abilities appear to match the requirements of GED reasoning level three, . . . any conflict is not so obvious that the ALJ should have pursued the question." *See also* Zirnsak v. Colvin, 777 F.3d 607, 618 (3d Cir. 2014) (VE's identification of jobs for claimant "limited to simple and repetitive tasks involving routine work processes and settings" did not create an apparent conflict with DOT reasoning level 3 jobs identified by the VE, where the claimant's attorney did not raise the issue at the hearing to alert the ALJ); *cf.* Hackett v. Barnhart, 365 F.3d 1168, 1176 102 Soc. Sec. Rep. Serv. 252 (10th Cir. 2005) (finding claimant's limitation to "simple, routine work tasks" creates apparent conflict with VE-identified DOT reasoning level 3 jobs, but appears "more consistent" with DOT reasoning level 2 jobs; conflict issue need not have been raised by claimant's counsel during the administrative proceedings as per the Supreme Court's rejection of issue exhaustion to SSA proceedings in Sims v. Apfel, 530 U.S. 103 (2000)).

4. METHODOLOGICAL PROBLEMS WITH VOCATIONAL EXPERT TESTIMONY

While the DOT is the usual basis relied upon by vocational experts and SSA to identify and classify jobs, this source has its limits for disability adjudication purposes. As described in Chapter 5, at Step 5 of the sequential evaluation process SSA shoulders a burden of producing evidence of significant work which exists in the economy to which a claimant can adjust, taking into account the claimant's residual functional capacity (RFC), age, education, and past work experience. The DOT provides no information at all about the number or location of jobs or occupations in the economy, or the characteristics of jobs not properly classified in the now-dated DOT.

However, an ALJ's reliance on the testimony of a vocational expert "is permissible only if the testimony is reliable" and a lack of reliable methodology undermines substantial evidence support for the ALJ's vocational findings. *See* Chavez v. Berryhill, 895 F.3d 962, 967, 259 Soc. Sec. Rep. Serv. 559 (7th Cir. 2018); *see also id.* 895 F.3d at 969 (" '[a] finding based on unreliable VE testimony is equivalent to a finding that is not supported by substantial evidence and must be vacated.' ") (citation omitted). Referencing the requirements for laying the foundation for the admissibility of expert testimony under Rule 702 of the Federal Rules of Evidence and the Supreme Court's decision in Daubert v. Merrell Dow Pharmaceuticals, Inc., 509 U.S. 579 (1993), the court explained in Donohue v. Barnhart, 279 F.3d 441, 446, 78 Soc. Sec. Rep. Serv. 144 (7th Cir. 2002) that "the idea that experts should use reliable methods does not depend on Rule 702 alone, and it plays a role in the administrative process because every decision must be supported by substantial evidence. Evidence is not "substantial" if vital testimony has been conjured out of whole cloth."

Taking the above considerations into account, an increasing number of circuit courts of appeals decisions have found VE testimony methodologically inadequate to supply substantial evidence to support a determination of non-disability based on a claimant's ability to perform and adjust to a significant number of jobs in the economy. These identified methodological deficiencies include unfounded or unsupported extrapolation, reliance on the DOT for job incidence data (as opposed to job characteristic information) and DOT obsolescence even as to job characteristic information, and reliance on unspecified or inapposite allegations of VE "knowledge" or "experience." As the Seventh Circuit explained in Alaura v. Colvin, 797 F.3d 503, 507–08 (7th Cir. 2015): "The problem appears to be that the only reliable statistics are census data for broad categories of jobs, rather than for jobs in the narrower categories that the applicant for benefits is capable of doing. Typically, it appears, the vocational expert simply divides the number of jobs in the broad category that includes the narrow category of jobs that the applicant can perform by the number of narrow categories in the broad category, thus assuming that each narrow category has the same number of jobs as each other narrow category—which is preposterous. A vocational expert's stated number of jobs in a narrow category seems likely, therefore, to be a fabrication." (citations omitted)

Further potential obstacles to the evaluation of vocational testimonial reliability and evidentiary sufficiency are limits on claimants' (and their representatives') access to VE data and source materials at ALJ hearings in order to confront and effectively question VE methodology. VE's rarely supply the bases of their job incidence and work adjustment testimony and are typically not questioned on or requested to disclose such source materials by the ALJs. In cases where claimants are represented by attorneys, claimants' counsel may request VE supporting materials in order to question or cross-examine the bases of the VE testimony. However, in such circumstances ALJs rarely order disclosure of VE source materials or grant requests for administrative subpoenas seeking such materials. Most often the VE's bottom line job incidence numbers conclusion provides the basis for an ALJ's denial decision and the VE's methodology and data supporting that job incidence testimony remain undisclosed.

The circuit courts of appeal were divided on the question of what to do in these circumstances. In Donahue v. Barnhart, supra, 279 F.3d at 446, the Seventh Circuit held that claimants who question the VE's bases are entitled to have the ALJ "make an inquiry (similar though not necessarily identical to that of Rule 702 [of the Federal Rules of Evidence]) to find out whether the purported expert's conclusions are reliable." More specifically, the court has held that while a VE "is free to give a bottom line . . . the data and reasoning underlying that bottom line must be available on demand." McKinnie v.

Barnhart, 368 F.3d 907, 911 (7th Cir. 2003) (citation and quotations omitted). Other circuits expressly rejected the Seventh Circuit's broader approach to VE testimony as going too far and accepted contested VE testimony despite the VE's failure to supply, or the ALJ's refusal to compel, the VE's supporting evidence or methodology. *See, e.g.*, Bayliss v. Barnhart, 427 F.3d 1211, 1217–18 (9th Cir. 2005); Brault v. Social Sec. Admin., Comm'r, 683 F.3d 443, 449–50 (2d Cir. 2012). Those courts have reasoned that because admissibility of expert testimony and evidence in administrative hearings is not governed by the formal rules of evidence and related caselaw applicable to expert testimony, "no additional foundation is required" for the VE's testimony other than the VE's "recognized expertise." Bayliss, 427 F.3d at 1218; Brault, 683 F.3d at 449 (citing Bayliss).

The Supreme Court addressed this circuit conflict in Biestek v. Berryhill, 139 S. Ct. 1148, 266 Soc. Sec. Rep. Serv. 23 (2019). The Court rejected the Seventh Circuit's position that there is or should be a "categorical rule" that the data upon which the vocational expert has based her opinion must be available upon demand, without charge to the claimant, if the claimant challenges the expert's opinion. Instead, the Court adopted a "case-by-case" approach to determining the substantiality of vocational expert evidence, hypothesizing a situation when vocational testimony should properly be deemed as meeting the substantial evidence standard despite the vocational expert's refusal or failure to supply underlying supporting data. 139 S. Ct. at 1155–57. While the Court declined to decide whether the VE testimony met the substantial evidence standard under the particular circumstances of Biestek's case, it provided some guidance for the "case-by-case" evaluation of evidentiary sufficiency in future cases. First, "[o]f course, the [vocational expert] testimony would be even better—more reliable and probative—if she had produced supporting data, a point with which the Court noted "the SSA itself appears to agree" since its Vocational Expert Handbook states: "You should have available, at the hearing, any vocational resource materials that you are likely to rely upon" because "the ALJ may ask you to provide relevant portions of [those] materials." 139 S. Ct. at 1155. Second, providing such supporting data therefore "would be a best practice for the SSA and its experts . . . [a]nd of course, a different (maybe less qualified) expert failing to produce such data might offer testimony that is so feeble, or contradicted, that it would fail to clear the substantial-evidence bar." 139 S. Ct. at 1155 and n.2. Third, "[s]ometimes an expert's withholding of such data, when combined with other aspects of the record, will prevent her testimony from qualifying as substantial evidence [such as] if the expert has no good reason to keep the data private and her testimony lacks other markers of reliability." 139 S. Ct. at 1155–56. Fourth, both the reviewing court and ALJ, may, on a case-by-case basis, "properly consider obstacles to such questioning when deciding how much to credit an expert's opinion." 139 S. Ct. at 1157. Finally, "even without specific data, an applicant may probe the strength of testimony by asking an expert about (for example) her sources and methods—where she got the information at issue and how she analyzed it and derived her conclusions." 139 S. Ct. at 1156.

In the first two major circuit court of appeals decisions to explore *Biestek*'s implications in evaluating VE methodology to resolve an individual case on the merits, the Eleventh and Seventh Circuits appeared to interpret the *Biestek* guidelines as justifying heighted scrutiny of VE methodology. *See* Goode v. Commissioner of Social Security, 966 F.3d 1277, 1281–83 (11th Cir. 2020) (VE must have a reliable methodology and, in particular, must address the "matching problem" from "using one system to supply the job titles [the DOT] and another [the Standard Occupational Classification (SOC)] for the number of the jobs"); *id.* at 1283 ([based on the SOC]; *id.* at 1281 (citing Chavez, 895 F.3d at 965). This means that after figuring out the total number of jobs in a broad SOC occupational group, the VE must take "an additional step to approximate how many of those are the specific job or jobs that the claimant could perform." *Id.* at 1283); Brace v. Saul, 970 F.2d 818, 822 (7th Cir. 2020) (VE's job incidence estimate "must be supported with evidence sufficient to provide some modicum of confidence in its reliability" and "the ALJ 'must require the VE to offer a reasoned and principled explanation of the method [the VE] used to produce it' "; VE "job-number testimony will survive review under the substantial-evidence standard as long as it rests on a well-accepted methodology and the expert describes the methodology 'cogently and thoroughly.' ") (citations omitted).

Two other post-*Biestek* circuit court of appeals decisions suggest that the courts may be more receptive to challenges to VE methodology as in *Goode* and *Brace*, as opposed to the ALJ's failure to compel disclosure of VE data and source material when requested at hearings. In Krell v. Saul, 931 F.3d 582, 586–87, 277 Soc. Sec. Rep. Serv. 422 (7th Cir. 2019), the Seventh Circuit, in reliance on *Biestek*, held that there is no categorical or "automatic" right to a pre-hearing subpoena for the vocational expert's supporting source material or data, reasoning that "it is within an ALJ's discretion to issue a prehearing subpoena . . . when the subpoena is 'reasonably necessary for the full presentation of a case' and when certain 'facts could not be proven without issuing a subpoena.' " (citations omitted) In Ford v. Saul, 950 F.3d 1141 (9th Cir. 2020), the Ninth Circuit suggested that *Biestek* together with the regulatory 5-day (now 10-day) rule for subpoena requests, support further limits on claimants' post-hearing efforts to subpoena or otherwise obtain and challenge the sources, data and methodology supporting VE jobs testimony after such testimony is supplied for the first time at the hearing. The court has since reaffirmed the right of claimants to challenge VE testimony and methodology through post-hearing submissions and has remanded ALJ decisions where those post-hearing submissions undermined the sufficiency or reliability of the VE's testimony. *See, e.g.*, Erickson v. Saul, 840 Fed. Appx. 167, 168 (9th Cir. 2021) (decision remanded where post-hearing submission to the ALJ showed only 19,000 jobs in the entire ophthalmic goods SOC occupational group, raising questions, unresolved by the ALJ, of the validity of VE testimony that a single DOT lens inserter occupation in that entire SOC group alone comprised 25,000 national jobs); Jaquez v. Saul, 840 Fed. Appx. 246, 247 (9th Cir. 2021) (remand where post-hearing evidence submitted to Appeals Council and considered, but not reconciled, undermined reliability of VE testimony of 90,200 usher jobs since the post-hearing evidence showed that 90% of usher jobs are only part-time positions).

G. CREDIBILITY OF CLAIMANTS AND LAY WITNESSES

Information from claimants and lay witnesses can be important at any stage in the administrative process. As discussed earlier, statements by claimants and their witnesses are among the types of evidence of disability specifically recognized by federal regulations. *See* 20 C.F.R. §§ 404.1513, 416.913 (defining "evidence" as "anything you or anyone else submits to us or that we obtain that relates to your claim."). Claimants and their witnesses must, of course, be credible and claimants'—and their witnesses'—credibility is particularly important at the administrative hearing because it is the only point in the administrative process, except for reconsideration disability hearings when benefits are terminated on the basis of nondisability, that the decision maker meets face-to-face with claimants and witnesses. An ALJ's assessment of claimant and witness credibility can be a critical factor in determining disability and other factual matter relevant to a claim for Social Security benefits.

Claimants and lay witnesses can testify about a claimant's pain and other subjective symptoms, as well as more generally about how impairments affect a claimant's ability to work, and about a wide range of other non-expert matters. The credibility of any witness is important; however in SSR 16–3p (2016) SSA specifically repudiated the use of the term "credibility" in SSA witness assessments in the sense of suggesting evaluation of witness character or general believability, as opposed to more specific testimonial supportability: "In doing so, we clarify that subjective symptom evaluation is not an examination of an individual's character. Instead, we will more closely follow our regulatory language regarding symptom evaluation." *See also id.*: "In evaluating an individual's symptoms, our adjudicators will not assess an individual's overall character or truthfulness in the manner typically used during an adversarial court litigation. The focus of the evaluation of an individual's symptoms should not be to determine whether he or she is a truthful person." More specifically, the Ruling continues: "Rather, our adjudicators will focus on whether the evidence establishes a medically determinable impairment that could reasonably be expected to produce the individual's symptoms and given the adjudicator's evaluation of the individual's symptoms, whether the intensity and persistence of the symptoms limit the individual's ability to perform work-related activities or, for a child with a title XVI disability claim, limit the child's ability to function independently, appropriately, and effectively in an age-appropriate manner."

ALJs must also provide adequate reasoning for their findings with respect to lay witness and claimant testimony. *See, e.g.*, Lewis v. Apfel, 236 F.3d 503, 511, 72 Soc. Sec. Rep. Serv. 263 (9th Cir. 2001) ("Lay testimony as to a claimant's symptoms is competent evidence that an ALJ must take into account, unless he or she expressly determines to disregard such testimony and gives reasons germane to each witness for doing so. One reason for which an ALJ may discount lay testimony is that it conflicts with medical evidence. The ALJ's decision in this case met these standards.") (citations omitted). *Cf.* Stout v. Commissioner, 454 F.3d 1050, 1053, 112 Soc. Sec. Rep. Serv. 496 (9th Cir. 2006) ("Numerous regulations command the ALJ to consider, throughout the sequential process, lay testimony as to how claimants' impairments affect their ability to work. And, as we have held on many occasions, if the ALJ wishes to discount such testimony in accord with this obligation, 'he must give reasons that are germane to each witness.' ") (citations omitted). Moreover, for judicial review to function properly, the ALJ "must let the parties and the reviewing courts know, in some intelligible fashion, where they stand on the pivotal issues of fact posed by the applications they adjudicate." Chiappa v. Secretary, 497 F. Supp. 356, 358 (S.D.N.Y. 1980). *See also* SSR 16–3p (2016) ("The determination or decision must contain specific reasons for the weight given to the individual's symptoms, be consistent with and supported by the evidence, and be clearly articulated so the individual and any subsequent reviewer can assess how the adjudicator evaluated the individual's symptoms.").

Courts have increasingly criticized and often remanded ALJ decisions utilizing cut and pasted "boilerplate" credibility findings from SSA's internal templates for ALJ decisions. *See, e.g.*, Bjornson v. Astrue, 671 F.3d 640, 644–46 (7th Cir. 2012) (suggesting that SSA "had better take a close look at the utility and intelligibility of its 'templates'," described to the court by SSA as "a passage drafted by the Social Security Administration for insertion into any administrative law judge's opinion to which it pertains."). *See also* Mascio v. Colvin, 780 F.3d 632, 639 (4th Cir. 2015) ("We agree with the Seventh Circuit that this boilerplate 'gets things backwards' by implying 'that ability to work is determined first and is then used to determine the claimant's credibility.' ") (citations omitted); Treichler v. Commissioner of Social Security Administration, 775 F.3d 1090, 1103 (9th Cir. 2014) ("Credibility findings must have support in the record, and hackneyed language seen universally in ALJ decisions adds nothing.").

Testimony of friends and family members sometimes is viewed with suspicion, especially when there is little or no corroborating evidence. *See e.g.*, Rautio v. Bowen, 862 F.2d 176, 180, 24 Soc. Sec. Rep. Serv. 7 (8th Cir. 1988) (testimony of claimant's fiancé discounted "as she lives with [the claimant] and has a financial interest in the case"); Tremblay v. Secretary, 676 F.2d 11, 13 (1st Cir. 1982) (testimony of family members "hardly neutral"). However, the mere fact that a witness is a member of the claimant's family is not a basis for rejecting their testimony. *See* Smolen v. Chater, 80 F.3d 1273, 1289, 50 Soc. Sec. Rep. Serv. 500 (9th Cir. 1996) (ALJ rejected testimony from "family witnesses" as "understandably" the claimant's advocates and "biased"; "This amounted to a wholesale dismissal of the testimony of all the witnesses as a group and therefore does not qualify as a reason germane to each individual who testified. . . . The fact that a lay witness is a family member cannot be a ground for rejecting his or her testimony.").

INDEX

References are to Pages
